# GlobaLinks: Resources for World Studies, Grades K–8

Peggy Beck

Published by Linworth Publishing, Inc.
480 East Wilson Bridge Road, Suite L
Worthington, Ohio 43085

Copyright © 2002 by Linworth Publishing, Inc.

All rights reserved. Reproduction of this book in whole or in part is prohibited without written permission of the publisher.

ISBN 1-58683-040-6

5 4 3 2 1

# Table of Contents

**Acknowledgements/About the Author** .................................................................v
**Introduction** ...........................................................................................vii
    Why Is This Book Needed? ................................................................vii
    How Did This Book Evolve? ...............................................................ix
    Who Can Use This Book? : Teachers, Librarians, Parents,
        and the Young Researcher ..........................................................ix
    What's Inside? .................................................................................x
    How Were the Print and Nonprint Resources Selected? ...........................x
    A Note on Video and CD-ROM Selections ...........................................xi
    How Were the Web Sites Selected? .....................................................xi
    Caveats for Internet Sites .................................................................xi

**Part I**     **General World References: Print and Nonprint**
    Ancient Civilizations and History ..........................................................1
    Ancient Civilizations and History: Videos and CDs ..................................7
    The Arts ..........................................................................................9
    Biographies .....................................................................................11
    Biographies: CDs ............................................................................15
    Country Resources ..........................................................................17
    Country Resources: Videos and CDs ..................................................23
    Festivals, Foods, Holidays, Customs, and Games ................................25
    Flags, Anthems, and Foreign Languages ............................................35
    Folktales, Fairy Tales, Myths, and Legends .........................................36
    Folktales, Fairy Tales, Myths, and Legends: Videos ..............................51
    Geography and Maps .....................................................................52
    Geography and Maps: CDs ..............................................................58
    Human Rights, Racism, and Social Issues .........................................58
    The Immigrant Experience ...............................................................64
    Religion and Philosophy ..................................................................65
    Religion and Holiday: Videos ...........................................................69
    Science and Nature .........................................................................70
    Science and Nature: Videos and CDs ................................................77

**Part II**     **General World Resources: Web Sites**
    The Arts .........................................................................................79
    Biographies ....................................................................................82
    Country Resources ..........................................................................83
    Current Events and News .................................................................94
    Dates in History ..............................................................................95
    Encyclopedias and Dictionaries .........................................................96
    Festivals and Foods ........................................................................98
    Flags and Anthems .........................................................................99
    Foreign Languages ........................................................................101

|  |  |  |
|---|---|---|
| | Geography and Maps | 101 |
| | Human Rights | 104 |
| | Religion and Philosophy | 104 |
| | Science and Nature | 108 |
| **Part III** | **Keypal/Pen Pal Projects and Resources** | 109 |
| **Appendix A** | **Web Site Title Index** | 115 |
| **Appendix B** | **Short Story/Folktale Title Index** | 118 |
| **Indexes** | | |
| | Author/Illustrator Index | 121 |
| | Title Index | 125 |
| | Subject Index | 130 |

# Acknowledgements

Many people have assisted me over the years with gathering and evaluating books and Web sites. Special thanks to my respected colleague and friend, Judy Freeman, "Book Talk" columnist for *Instructor Magazine* and author of *Books Kids Will Sit Still For*, *More Books Kids Will Sit Still For*, and *Hi, Ho Librario! Songs, Chants, and Stories to Keep Kids Humming: A Book and CD*. She encouraged me and shared many passionate discussions and workshops. Thanks to Dr. Lesley Solomon for sparking my interest; to Keith Haines and Nina Kemps for their support and shared resources; to Bonnie Herman and Kim Laskey and the children who worked during the summers to free me up for research; and to Joyce Kasman Valenza, "tech.k12" columnist for *The Philadelphia Inquirer* and author of *Power Tools*, for her weekly Web site guides. I would be remiss if I did not acknowledge my mother, my family (the Becks, Kellys, and Parkers), Gerald Kerrigan, Simon Aslanian, Betty Hill, and my other colleagues and friends who stoically accepted my "captivity," especially during these past two years of writing. Finally, my heartfelt thanks to my editor, Betty J. Morris, and to Carol Simpson, Wendy Medvetz, Amy Murch, and the editors and staff of Linworth Publishing for their belief in this book and in me.

## About the Author

Peggy Beck is Media Facilitator at Cherry Hill High School East in Cherry Hill, New Jersey. She taught English for 19 years, was Media Department Chairperson for five years, and was an elementary school library media specialist in Cherry Hill for six years. Peggy has a Master's Degree in School and Public Librarianship from Rowan University and a Master's Degree in English Education from the College of New Jersey. She is the author of *GlobaLinks: Resources for Asian Studies, K-8*; reviews for *Library Talk*, *The Book Report*, and *ForeWord*; and writes the K-12 "Booktalk" column for the NJEA Review. She is past editor of the *New Jersey English Journal* and *Signal Tab*, the newsletter of the Educational Media Association of New Jersey (EMAnj).

Ms. Beck is the recipient of the 1997 EMAnj/Winnebago Progressive School Library Media Award. Other honors include recognition in *Who's Who in American Education* and *Who's Who Among American Women*. Peggy is a storyteller and presents workshops on children's and young adult literature, library skills, and Internet resources. Peggy Beck has been an adjunct professor at Rowan University and the College of New Jersey, is a member of ALA, AASL, and ALSC, and is active in her state and local media associations.

In addition to reading, Peggy enjoys spending time with her mother, two sisters, brother, and their families (including nine nephews and nieces and two great-nephews). She lives in Maple Shade, New Jersey, with her Bichon Frise Desdemona.

*In memory of my father, Raymond S. Beck, Jr.,
mentor and friend (1919–1995)*

# Introduction

## Why Is This Book Needed?

The majesty and mystery of the ancient world, fascinating cultures, enthralling tales and legends, and global arts await you. Open the door to new worlds with these exceptional print, nonprint, and Internet global links and keypal/pen pal projects and resources.

The growing accessibility of the Internet in schools and homes has removed borders and barriers to learning. Countries that were once exotic are now within the click of a mouse. With these changes, it is increasingly important for children to develop awareness of cultural differences and respect for people of all cultures. For years, criticism of education in the United States has focused on the nation as ethnocentric. The focus of classroom curricula had been Western civilization. Educators today try to address the clamor for recognition of non-Western cultures, history, and contributions to mankind.

Schools can maximize the students' multicultural experiences by developing curricula that heighten global consciousness and responsibility. The purpose of this book is to offer current resources available for purchase or through school and public libraries that help fulfill national standards for social studies, geography, language arts, information literacy, science, technology, life skills, and character education.

Librarians can use these resources to help students meet the American Association of School Librarians' standards for

- Information literacy ("accesses information efficiently and effectively," "evaluates information critically and competently," and "uses information accurately and creatively"),
- Independent learning ("pursues information related to personal interests," "appreciates literature and other creative expressions of information," and "strives for excellence in information seeking and knowledge generation"), and
- Social responsibility ("recognizes the importance of information to a democratic society," "practices ethical behavior in regard to information and information technology," and "participates effectively in groups to pursue and generate information") (http://www.ala.org/aasl/ip_nine.html).

Teachers and librarians can offer integration of subject matters and holistic views of culture through addressing the cross-curricular "Ten Thematic Strands in Social Studies" approved by the National Council for the Social Studies:

- Culture and cultural diversity;
- Time, continuity, and change;
- People, places, and environments;
- Individual development and identity;
- Individuals, groups, and institutions;
- Power, authority, and governance;
- Production, distribution, and consumption;
- Science, technology, and society;
- Global connections; and
- Civic ideals and practices

and the Geographic Education National Implementation Project's "Five Central Themes in Geography":

- Location,
- Place,
- Human-Environmental Relations,
- Movement, and
- Regions.

This book offers teachers and librarians the opportunity to integrate the multicultural/global awareness concept through science and technology strands, as well as environmental relations.

## Resources

*Expectations for Excellence: Curriculum Standards for Social Studies, 1994.* National Council for the Social Studies, 3501 Newark Street, NW, Washington, DC 20016, (202) 966-7840, fax (202) 966-2061

Or search online:
National Council for the Social Studies
http://www.ncss.org/standards/toc.html

"Information Literacy Standards for Student Learning," of *Information Power: Building Partnerships for Learning*, 1998. American Library Association and Association for Educational Communications and Technology. ISBN 0-8389-3470-6.

The following print materials are available from the National Council for Geographic Education, Indiana University of Pennsylvania, 16A Leonard Hall, Indiana, PA 15705 1087, (724) 357-6290, fax (724) 357-7708:
*7–12 Geography: Themes, Key Ideas, and Learning Opportunities*
*Geography for Life: National Geography Standards 1994 (Geography Education Standards Project)*
*Guidelines for Geographic Education: Elementary and Secondary Schools National Council for Geographic Education*
*K–6 Geography: Themes, Key Ideas, and Learning Opportunities*
*Key to the National Geography Standards*

Or search online:
*Geography for Life—The National Geography Standards Online Tutorial* presented by The National Council for Geographic Education, 1998–2000. http://www.ncge.org/publications/tutorial/
*The Eighteen National Geography Standards* presented by the National Council for Geographic Education, 1998–2000.
http://www.ncge.org/publications/tutorial/standards/

## How Did This Book Evolve?

In 1997, I participated in an Asian Studies Focus Grant for Educators program sponsored by the National Endowment for Humanities to further teachers' understanding of specialized areas. Dr. Lesley Solomon, of the Cherry Hill Public Schools in Cherry Hill, New Jersey, wrote and coordinated "Traditions and Change in East Asia: An Interdisciplinary Approach." For a year and a half, we met with visiting literature, art, and history professors, shared their lectures, and discussed guided readings. Every new discovery increased my desire to create a resource book for teachers and librarians with quality materials appropriate for kindergarten through eighth grades.

I have been actively gathering favorite books and Web sites for three years for this book. The original scope was the non-Western world. I had planned to include Asia, Africa, the Middle East, Antarctica, Australia and Oceania, Central/Middle America, and South America. My wise editor, Betty J. Morris, saw that this original book is really a series of books. *GlobaLinks: Resources for Asian Studies, K–8* offers print, nonprint, and Web sites for the diverse countries of Asia. Future planned volumes will focus on other areas of the non-Western world.

## Who Can Use This Book?: Teachers, Librarians, Parents, and the Young Researcher

This book is intended as a guide for unlocking the treasures of the world. Teachers, librarians, parents, and students may use this book to explore recent resources about the different countries of the world to foster global awareness and multicultural experiences. Web sites offer valuable resources to supplement and update recommended print and nonprint materials. Readers can draw upon the keypal/pen pal projects and resources to add another dimension to their global studies.

Elementary and middle school teachers and children's librarians can use this book as a quick reference for locating appropriate titles and Web sites to include for individual class activities or to help shape unit lessons or research assignments. They might also use the book to find collaborative readings to extend titles they plan to use with classes. Teachers can use these recommendations to work alone or in teams for problem solving and collaboration. These resources make it possible to tell folktales from around the world, listen to national anthems and songs, examine artworks of the world, participate in archaeological digs, discover secrets of the scientific world, explore the wonders of the world, learn about the people who have molded history, unearth mysteries of the past, and debate social issues.

With this book, parents can encourage their children to satisfy their research needs, pursue hobbies, and cultivate new interests. Some of the resources are homework helpers and research centers to assist children with learning. There are also many games, both entertaining and educational.

With these annotated resources, students can readily locate materials relevant to their research. They can pursue special interests and explore unknown fields. Children from novice to expert at navigating the Internet can benefit from independent searching of approved sites in the classroom or at home.

## What's Inside?

Part I is an annotated bibliography of print and nonprint resources for study of the world, with emphasis on the non-Western world. The books, CDs, and videos are arranged alphabetically by the last name of the author within subject areas. Each entry includes full bibliographic data, a recommended age level, and a detailed annotation. Topics include ancient civilizations and history, the arts; biographies; country resources; festivals, foods, holidays, customs, and games; folktales, fairy tales, myths, and legends; flags and anthems, foreign languages; geography and maps; human rights, racism, and social issues; the immigrant experience; religion and philosophy; and science and nature.

Part II is an annotated Webography of the world. Entries are arranged alphabetically by the name of the Web site within subject areas, followed by the Uniform Resource Locator (URL). Each entry has a summary of the Internet site contents at the time of the writing of the book and a recommended grade level. Web site topics include the arts; biographies; country resources; current events and news; dates in history; encyclopedias and dictionaries; festivals and foods; flags and anthems; foreign languages; geography and maps; human rights; religion and philosophy; and science and nature.

Part III is an annotated Webography of keypal/pen pal projects and resources available for classroom collaborations or individual pursuit. These will enable classes to establish communication with other children and teachers in other countries of the world.

Appendix A is an alphabetical listing of each Web site by title. Appendix B is an alphabetical listing of short story and folktale titles specifically mentioned in annotations. There is an author/illustrator, a title, and a subject index to facilitate location of resources.

## How Were the Print and Nonprint Resources Selected?

There is a wealth of resources available to learn about Asia. This is by no means a definitive collection. It represents books I have loved, admired, or found valuable for classroom use and research. The selections were affected by personal choice and availability. Your favorite resources may not be included; I encourage you to share those with your colleagues, as well as to examine those highlighted here.

My guidelines required that
1. I personally examine each source I recommend here,
2. The materials support and enrich K–8 curricula,
3. I test resources with children in kindergarten through eighth grade, and
4. Materials fall within copyright limits.

Let me expand upon these criteria.
1. I have read all of the biography, fiction, folktales and fairy tales annotated here and all or a significant sampling of each of the nonfiction and reference books. Some are materials I selected from among the thousands of books and nonprint materials I have reviewed for *NJEA Review*, *Library Talk*, and *Book Report* magazines. There were many other titles I read and rejected. This selection does not include every publisher since some chose not to send review materials and are thus not represented.

2. I have researched curriculum requirements for many states to determine the relevance of world culture studies. Although grade levels for the specific country studies varied, all of the schools in each state included mandatory study of continents, world countries, and global awareness.
3. Some of these recommended resources are materials I have presented at national workshops on Asian Studies and workshops on Best Books K–12. Many of the fiction and folktales have been successfully tested with elementary school, middle school, and high school students or with adults in storytelling programs. Other titles are discoveries that colleagues have shared with me over the years.
4. I have tried to include fiction, folktales, fairy tales, myths, and legends published between 1990 and 2000. In most cases, nonfiction and reference titles fall within my guidelines of 1995 to 2000. The exceptions to this limit are country cookbooks that are still relevant, historical works that describe the end of the Union of Soviet Socialist Republics and establishment of the commonwealth of Independent States, and country studies awaiting revisions. Since online encyclopedias, databases, and sites are updated on a regular basis, the Internet offers an essential means to update print resources. Whenever the latest statistics are needed, teachers and students are encouraged to search the Internet for the most current information available.

## *A Note on Video and CD-ROM Selections*

The original intent of this study was to include only books and Web sites. I have also included some videos and CD-ROMs. I do not presume to recommend them as the best of the best. I haven't even begun to scratch the surface of what is available in those media. So view these titles as serendipitous, titles I have reviewed, chanced upon, or purchased for my district. They are supplementary titles only.

## *How Were the Web Sites Selected?*

At the time of publication, all of the sites were viable. Resources were selected based on the following criteria: Web sites
- Support and supplement K–8 global studies curricula; provide resources for educators, librarians, and parents; and offer enrichment resources for students.
- Provide free, current, and updated resources.
- Name the Webmasters, state the authority and background of the creator, and cite sources of information.
- Are easy to navigate.

## *Caveats for Internet Sites*

The nature of the Internet requires the following caveats:
- Web site addresses (URLs) may alter. If you get an error message, try to remove fields one at a time from the right of the address to see if the site still exists. A fascinating approach to this can be found at a University of Bristol online tutorial for Web evaluation called *Internet*

*Detective*, http://sosig.ac.uk/desire/internet detective.html. After you register, search under Practical Steps, then URLs, for clues for interpreting and locating Web sites.
- Students created some sites. Although there may be errors in spelling or grammar and the content may be limited, it is important for children to see the work of other children. Inclusion of these sites is not intended to minimize the importance of correctness. The emphasis is on content and design. Just as teachers do not correct every spelling and usage error in an essay or story, some teachers have not corrected every detail of student work.
- Since some of these sites originate in non-English speaking countries, the Webmasters who are producing the sites may have limited knowledge of English and thus, some spelling and grammar may be unconventional.
- Some sites are personal Web sites and may no longer be available. They have been included here because of their perspective and diversity. Web sites may disappear from the Internet as students graduate, people change jobs, or interests in Web site topics wane. Some Web sites also disappear because Webmasters discover they have infringed upon copyright laws.
- Although I have personally visited and explored all of the Web sites included, I cannot guarantee the content of each. Content may change daily. Menus, features, and files change daily. Always personally examine Web sites before recommending them to children.
- I have suggested ages for Web sites. These are only guidelines. You are the only one who knows the ability levels and maturity of your students. I have also recommended some sophisticated resources that serve as Teacher Reference. Middle school students may also do well with searching the sites with guidance. If your students are strong readers in the lower grades, they may be comfortable accessing some of the sites recommended for grades three and four.
- Some sites are commercial that offer valuable introductory information about a country or the people of the country. Caution children not to click into advertisements.
- Some sites prevent you from moving back to the prior page. For PC users, click on the BACK button in the upper left and hold your left side of the mouse to bring up a list of past sites surfed. Drag the mouse down to the one you want to access and click. It will take you to a previous site. For Macintosh users, in Netscape Communicator select the "go" menu, pull down, and release.
- Some sites represent the best of what I have seen. Share your personal finds with colleagues. I would love to hear from you (pbeck@recom.com) about other sites not to be missed.
- Most of the Web sites are free, although a few have a fee or have only a portion of the site available without subscription. I have tried to indicate these.

My hope is that schools will more actively incorporate research activities and projects that explore the non-Western world and beyond. May this book help colleagues and students create and implement collaborative research projects that enhance understanding of the richness of world cultures and history, celebrate and respect commonalties and differences, and accept responsibility for the earth and her resources.

# Part I

# General World References: Print and Nonprint

## Ancient Civilizations and History

***Ancient Civilizations.*** **Danbury, CT: Grolier Educational, 2000. ISBN 0-7172-9471-4 set. 80 pages. Grade 5+**
With its appealing color photography and illustrations, scholarly text, color-blocked insets of fascinating facts, time lines and glossary, this 10-volume encyclopedia is a valuable resource for study of countries and peoples of the past. Interesting features are the use of "see-also" notes that refer the reader to other topics of interest and overviews of the major civilizations under topics like astronomy, food and drink, legal codes, tombs and burial rites, social organizations, tools and technology, and transportation.

**Austrian, Guy I.** ***Ancient Times: A Watts Guide for Children.*** **New York: Franklin Watts, 2000. ISBN 0-531-11731-6. 112 pages. Grades 4–8**
Austrian shows how past civilizations helped shape the language, literature, customs, and ideas of the modern world. Explore the people, places, and accomplishments of the ancient world from Abraham and the Aeneid to Virgil and Women in this accessible and valuable resource for children.

**Avi-Yonah, Michael.** ***Piece by Piece! Mosaics of the Ancient World.*** **Buried worlds series. Minneapolis: Runestone Press, 1993. ISBN 0-8225-3204-2. 64 pages. Grade 5+**
The art of mosaics can be traced back 5,000 years. Because of the durability of the materials used, archaeologists have discovered amazing examples of floor and ceiling mosaics that help us understand ancient cultures. Examine examples of mosaic art from Greece, Rome, and the Middle East through color photos and historical illustrations.

**Collard, Sneed B.** *1,000 Years Ago on Planet Earth.* Boston: Houghton Mifflin, 1999. ISBN 0-395-90866-3. Grades 3–6

Collard underscores the major accomplishments of different areas of the world at the turn of the last millennium. His statistical comparison of 1,000 years ago and today will provoke thought and discussion.

**Corrick, James A.** *The Byzantine Empire.* World history series. San Diego: Lucent Books, 1997. ISBN 1-56006-307-6. 112 pages. Grades 6+

"Important Dates in the History of the Byzantine Empire" leads students into a comprehensive overview of this influential civilization from the founding of Constantinople in 330 AD to the end of the Byzantine Empire in 1453. The author includes b&w maps and photos and illustrations of artifacts that help archaeologists chronicle the time. He examines the legacy of the empire, the society, religion, culture, rule and conquest. He weighs the effects of barbarian attacks by the Slavs, Avars, Persians, Muslims, and Bulgars. The primary and secondary sources help to establish the seeds of discontent and conflict in this same area in the 21st century. The sidebars, maps, diagrams, b&w pictures, and bibliographies for student research and of works consulted are helpful.

*Dazzling! Jewelry of the Ancient World.* Prepared by Geography Department, Runestone Press. Buried worlds series. Minneapolis: Runestone Press, 1995. ISBN 0-8225-3203-4. 64 pages. Grade 5+

Archaeologists have discovered jewelry was far more than ornamentation. The type of design, metal, and stone can reveal a great deal about the status, background, religion, and technology of the ancient people. Examine some of the treasures of the Middle East, Asia, Europe, and the Americas through color and b&w photography and illustrations.

**Dineen, Jacqueline.** *100 Greatest Archaeological Discoveries.* 100 Greatest series. Danbury, CT: Grolier, 1997. ISBN 0-7172-7690-2. 111 pages. Grade 3+

This volume of the series includes one-page summaries and color photography and illustrations of discoveries that have offered insights into the peoples and world of the past. Dineen presents the archaeological finds in chronological order. She includes dinosaurs, *Homo Erectus* and Cro-Magnon from First Humans, Tomb of Tutankhamen and Sumers of Urak from Early Civilizations, Assurbanipal's Library from 1000 BC to 500 BC, Rosetta Stone from 500 BC to 1 AD, Dead Sea Scrolls from AD 1 to 500, Sutton Hoo Boat Burial from AD 500 to 1000, and Caves of the Thousand Buddhas from 1000 to 1750.

**Garfield, Gary M., and Suzanne McDonough.** *Dig That Site: Exploring Archaeology, History, and Civilization on the Internet.* Englewood, CO: Libraries Unlimited, 1997. ISBN 1-56308-534-8. 135 pages. Teacher Reference for grades 3–8

This is one of my favorite books for teachers. Garfield and McDonough created challenging and exciting lesson plans for each continent of the world centered around sites on the Internet. They include objectives, time required, materials, and procedure for each plan. Take children to the market in Beirut, to Masada, to Israel and the Dead Sea Scrolls, to see the terra cotta warriors of China, to Young Tut's Tomb, to Antarctica, and beyond.

**Gilchrist, Cherry.** *Sun-Day, Moon-Day: How the Week Was Made.* **Illustrated by Amanda Hall. New York: Barefoot Books, 1998. ISBN 1-901223-63-9. 80 pages. Grades 3–7**
In the introduction, Gilchrist credits the Babylonians with inventing the concept of the week with a name and character for each day. She shows how the Vikings, Romans, Greeks, and Egyptians also shaped our present week. For each day of the week, Hall creates a spectacular double-page spread of images in motion. Gilchrist retells the legend that gave each day its name. Don't miss "Did You Know That…?" for fascinating facts and folk beliefs. The final page graphs the names of the days of the week in different languages and the deities of the week by planet and deity names for the major contributing nations.

**Gonen, Rivka.** *Charge! Weapons and Warfare in Ancient Times.* **Buried worlds series. Minneapolis: Runestone Press, 1993. ISBN 0-8225-3201-8. 72 pages. Grade 5+**
From the earliest times, man has fashioned weapons for hunting, protection, and survival. Children will be fascinated with Gonen's overview of different kinds of weapons (hand-to-hand combat, medium-range, distance), armor, and artillery. Illustrations and photos share archaeologists' findings to document the data.

**Gonen, Rivka.** *Fired Up! Making Pottery in Ancient Times.* **Buried worlds series. Minneapolis: Runestone Press, 1993. ISBN 0-8225-3202-6. 72 pages. Grade 5+**
What can archaeologists learn about ancient peoples through pottery artifacts? In this beautifully illustrated volume, see how men and women crafted daily ware and utensils through the ages and how some created great works of art.

*Grolier Student Library of Explorers and Exploration.* **Danbury, CT: Grolier Educational, 1997. ISBN 0-7172-9135-9 set. 80 pages per volume. Grade 5+.**
B&w illustrations and historical photos, color sketches and photos, and sidebars with fascinating points of interest accompany the articulate text of this 10-volume encyclopedia of the discoveries of the world. The set includes volumes on the Earliest Explorers; the Golden Age of Exploration: 1450 to 1600; Europe's Imperial Adventures: 1600 to 1800; Scientists and Explorers: 1800 to 1850; Latin America; North America; Asia and Australasia; Africa and Arabia; Polar Explorers; and Space and Underwater Exploration.

*The Kingfisher Facts and Records Book.* **New York: Kingfisher, 2000. ISBN 0-7534-5270-7. 96 pages. Grade 3+**
Did you know 240,000 people died in China in the 1976 earthquake, there is a 4,200-year-old cake preserved from an Egyptian tomb, and Bahrain and Qatar have a zero percent income tax rate? Explore the world of the earth, nature, man, the human body, sports, science, the material world, money, art and culture, and the future in this provocative text. Each double-page layout is crammed full of fascinating text and illustrations. Facts and Figures boxes and Databank insets are sure to engage even the most reluctant readers.

**Knight, Judson.** *Ancient Civilizations Almanac.* **Edited by Stacy A. McConnell and Lawrence W. Baker. Detroit: Gale, 1999. ISBN 0-7876-3982-6. 419 pages. Grade 5+**
Many resources are valuable for their overviews of ancient civilizations, but this almanac transcends the others. Its key strengths are its cohesive and deft text and the comparisons among cultures that existed at the same time in other parts of the world. Sidebar boxes,

maps, b&w photos and illustrations, and cross-reference points enhance the text. Chapters are arranged by geographic regions, each concluding with a bibliography and Web sites. The supplementary features are exceptional. Knight includes a Reader's Guide, Glossary, Pronunciation Guide, extensive Time line and Research and Activity Ideas.

**Madgwick, Wendy.** *Ancient Civilizations.* **Questions and answers series. New York: Kingfisher, 2000. ISBN 0-7534-5310-X. 40 pages. Grades 4–7.**
Madgwick spans early nomads (25,000 BC to 2000 BC) to the Roman and Mayan empires (AD 1 to AD 800) in this visually appealing, fact-filled text. She concisely introduces different civilizations and asks and answers questions to reveal their customs and lifestyles. The bold question headings and color illustrations of ancient people, artifacts, and architecture pepper the double-page spreads. Children can pick and choose what interests them.

**Maestro, Betsy and Giulio.** *The Story of Clocks and Calendars: Marking a Millennium.* **New York: Lothrop, Lee and Shepard, 1999. ISBN 0-688-14548-5. All ages.**
The Maestros explain the Gregorian, Hebrew, Muslim, and Chinese calendars and why there is confusion about the dates for the millennium.

**Mason, Antony.** *The Children's Atlas of Civilizations: Trace the Rise and Fall of the World's Great Civilizations.* **Brookfield, CT: Benchmark Books, 1994. ISBN 1-56294-490. 96 pages. Grade 5+**
Bordered double-page spreads combine text, sidebars, color maps, and photos of the countries and artifacts of the cultures. Mason overviews the evolution of man and early civilizations of the Sumerians and Akkadians, Ancient Egypt, the Indus Valley, and Ancient China. From this point, he presents the civilizations by continent and region and considers West Asia, Europe, South Asia, East Asia, the Americas, Africa, and Australasia and Oceania. This book is a valuable addition to the middle school library.

**Millard, Anne.** *The Atlas of Ancient Worlds.* **Illustrated by Russell Barnett. New York: Dorling Kindersley, 1994. ISBN 1-56458-471-2. 64 pages. Grade 3+**
Plan to dig into this stunning atlas. The text is well-organized, lively, and meticulous. Each lavish double-page spread treats a topic of the ancient world with photos of artifacts and ancient buildings; wonderful illustrations of cultural, historical, and geographical interest; and maps illustrated with key trade routes, people, crops, objects, and monuments of the region.

***Reader's Digest Book of Amazing Facts: A Children's Guide to the World.* Pleasantville, NY: Reader's Digest, 2000. ISBN 0-276-42434-4. 400 pages. Grades 4–8.**
If children want to learn about earth, science, the human body, or the history of the world, here's an appealing and inviting volume. Each topic has an introduction, a series of bold-heading questions and answers, fact boxes, and wonderful cross-references. Each double-page spread features color illustrations and photos, and diagrams. The last third of the book is a ready-reference Fact File with key events in history, famous people, endangered species, major diseases, geological time scale, space exploration time line, living zones, biggest-smallest figures for plants and animals, and much more.

**Nardo, Don.** *The Assyrian Empire.* **World history series. San Diego: Lucent Books, 1998. ISBN 1-56006-313-0. 96 pages. Grade 6+**

"Important Dates in the History of the Assyrian Empire" leads students into a comprehensive overview of this influential civilization from the settlement in the Tigris and Euphrates river valleys in 5500 BC to the defeat of the Assyrians by the Babylonians in 610 AD. The author includes b&w maps and photos and illustrations of artifacts that help archaeologists chronicle the time. Sidebars offer fascinating commentary on topics like "Royal Sibling Squabbles," "Dealing with Omens and Demons," and "A Message in Stone." Nardo profiles a people "who lived and died by the sword." He uses primary and secondary source materials to examine the early peoples of Mesopotamia, the rise of the Assyrian Empire, the power of Sargon and his heirs, Assyrian life and culture, the collapse of the empire, and the lasting legacy.

**Rice, Chris, and Melanie Rice.** *How Children Lived: A First Book of History.* **New York: Dorling Kindersley, 1995. ISBN 1-56458-876-9. 45 pages. Grade 3+**

Children from around the world beckon us to travel to other worlds and other times. This engaging history of children has an appealing format with bold and large text, sidebars, colorful illustrations and photos of artifacts. Learn what life was like for children in Ancient Egypt, Greece, and China; the Roman Empire; the Mali Empire; a Spanish castle; Renaissance Italy; Aztec Mexico; Moghul India; Tokugawa Japan; an Australian desert; France before the French Revolution; industrial Britain; on the American plains; and in 1920s America.

**Rice, Earle.** *Life During the Crusades.* **The way people live series. San Diego: Lucent Books, 1998. ISBN 1-56006-379-3. 96 pages. Grade 6+**

Although I did not actively research the Crusades, I have included this text because of the objective treatment of the subject and the emphasis on the legacy of the non-Western world. The series succeeds in its goal to "flesh out the traditional, two-dimensional views of people in various cultures and historical circumstances." Rice weaves in primary and secondary materials and includes b&w maps, photos, and illustrations to create an unbiased chronicle of the Crusades. He shows both sides as committed, religious, and honorable in their mission. The chronology, glossary, and bibliographies encourage further research.

*Scrawl! Writing in Ancient Times.* **Prepared by Geography Department, Runestone Press. Buried worlds series. Minneapolis: Runestone Press, 1994. ISBN 0-8225-3209-3. 72 pages. Grade 5+**

Cave drawings, carvings, and stone tablets help unlock the secrets of man's early communication. This fascinating book traces the early writing systems of the Middle East, Mediterranean, China, and the Americas with illustrations and photos of artifacts.

**Skurzynski, Gloria.** *On Time: From Seasons to Split Seconds.* **Washington, DC: National Geographic Society, 2000. ISBN 0-7922-7503-9. 48 pages. Grade 4+**

In this engaging book, Gloria Skurzynski chronicles the history of the measurement of time. The fluid text and color photos and illustrations take us on a journey from Stonehenge and the recognition of seasons to Egypt to measure years, month, and weeks with sundials. Trace the creation of calendars by the Aztecs and Romans; heavenly bodies by Chinese astronomers; and mechanical clocks from Italy and Holland. Finally, see how man has calculated time to split seconds with modern-day atomic clocks and what the space clock means for the future.

***Sold! The Origins of Money and Trade.*** **Prepared by Geography Department, Runestone Press. Buried worlds series. Minneapolis: Runestone Press, 1994. ISBN 0-8225-3206-9. 64 pages. Grade 5+**

Around the world, archaeologists have retrieved pebbles, shells, feathers, beads, oddly shaped ingots of silver, bronze, and gold, all believed to be man's early forms of money. Learn about the standards of value, the first minting of coins, the interchange of monies, and hidden treasures with skillful narrative and historical illustrations and photos.

***Street Smart! Cities of the Ancient World.*** **Prepared by Geography Department, Runestone Press. Buried worlds series. Minneapolis: Runestone Press, 1994. ISBN 0-8225-3208-5. 80 pages. Grade 5+**

Archaeologists marvel at the level of sophistication of some ancient cities. In addition to the more familiar cities of the Mediterranean, read about Middle East wonders like the ziggurats of the Sumerians, Babylon, the Egyptian city of Tell al-Amarna, and Africa's Great Zimbabwe. See Mohenjo-Daro and Harappa in India and Pakistan and ruins of Changan, Zhengzhou, and An-yang in China. Examine the worlds of the Aztecs, Olmec, and Maya in the Americas.

**Wood, Tim.** ***Ancient Wonders.*** **New York: Viking, 1997. ISBN 0-670-87468-X. 48 pages. Grade 4+**

Wood takes you on a tour (complete with overlays) of the Seven Wonders of the World and other spectacular sites reconstructed through archaeology. Explore the Mesopotamian ziggurats, pyramids and Sphinx, Gardens of Babylon, Alexandria, Easter Island, and Chichen Itza with a combination of photography and color illustrations. Children will love the overlays for the Egyptian tombs, the Palace of Knossos, the city of Petra, and Hagia Sophia. Key dates and glossary follow.

**Woods, Michael, and Mary B. Woods.** ***Ancient Agriculture: From Foraging to Farming.*** **Ancient technology series. Minneapolis: Runestone Press, 2000. ISBN 0-8225-2995-5. 96 pages. Grade 5+**

In this fascinating volume, the authors discuss what we know about the hunting and farming habits of early man through archaeological findings and examine the technologies of Rome and Greece. They also show the accomplishments of the Middle East (domestication of wheat and many animals; methods for making bread, olive oil, wine, beer, and cheese; the first cookbook in 1700 BC; creation of fabrics); the Egyptians (first beekeepers); the Chinese (technologies for irrigation and biological pest control, domestication of silkworms, invention of ice cream); and the Americas (experimentation with crops of corn, beans, potatoes, tomatoes, and chocolate; slash-and-burn agriculture; reservoirs).

**Woods, Michael and Mary B.** ***Ancient Machines: From Wedges to Waterwheels.*** **Ancient technology series. Minneapolis: Runestone Press, 2000. ISBN 0-8225-2994-7. 88 pages. Grade 5+**

The authors show how all machines come from six simple machines (lever, wheel and axle, inclined plane, pulley, wedge, and screw), all devised during ancient times. They trace the development of each and chronicle the accomplishments of the ancient civilizations of the Middle East, Egypt, China, Greece, and Rome from 3000 B.C. to 476 AD. The text is interesting and well-written with wonderful photos, maps, and illustrations.

**Woods, Michael and Mary B.** *Ancient Medicine: From Sorcery to Surgery.* Ancient technology series. Minneapolis: Runestone Press, 2000. ISBN 0-8225-2992-0. 88 pages. Grade 5+

Learn how ant sutures, pus pullers, and grease salves helped heal ancient man. This volume promises plenty of blood in its history of medicine. It also delivers a fascinating look at early doctors and philosophies of healing from the Stone Age through the ancient worlds of Egypt, India, China, Greece, and Rome.

**Woods, Michael and Mary B.** *Ancient Transportation: From Camels to Canals.* Ancient technology series. Minneapolis: Runestone Press, 2000. ISBN 0-8225-2993-9. 96 pages. Grade 5+

What a wealth of information the authors unveil in this volume as they trace transportation techniques from the Stone Age through the ancient worlds of the Middle East, Egypt, India and China, Mesoamerica, Greece and Rome. See how man devised ways of crossing water, snow, and ice, creating roads, towing, and harnessing animals.

# *Ancient Civilizations and History: Videos and CDs*

*Chronicle Encyclopedia of History* [interactive multimedia]. New York: DK Multimedia, 1997. ISBN 0-7894-1734-0. Grade 5+

The breadth of this CD-ROM encyclopedia is staggering. DK offers more than 15,000 news articles, sound files, animations, and graphics to explore the history of the world. The "Biographies of 100 of the most influential men and women" is especially helpful for research.

*Chronicle of the 20th Century* [interactive multimedia]. New York: DK Multimedia, 1996. ISBN 0-7894-1222-5. Grade 6+

This CD-ROM program offers an overview of the 20th century around the world. It highlights famous people and events of the 20th century from politics to cinema to sports.

*The Complete National Geographic: 108 years of* National Geographic Magazine *on CD-ROM* [interactive multimedia]. Washington, DC: National Geographic Society, 1997. ISBN 0-7911-2671-4 (set). Grade 4+

This 10-volume CD-ROM program, although sometimes cumbersome to access, allows children to access the wealth of full-text articles with color graphics upon which *National Geographic* has built its reputation. CDs are arranged by decades.

*The Explorers: A Century of Discovery* [videorecording]. Produced by National Geographic Society and WQED/Pittsburgh; written and produced by Nicholas Noxon; narrated by E.G. Marshall; edited by Barry Nye; music by Lee Holdridge. Washington, DC: National Geographic Video, 1993. ISBN 0-8001-2662-9. 90 minutes. Grade 5+

Give students an appreciation of the magnitude of the risks, dangers, and contributions of the world's explorers. With stunning photography and visuals, National Geographic chronicles 100 years of expeditions to discover unknown corners of the world and to challenge the extremes of endurance.

*Eyewitness Children's Encyclopedia* **[interactive multimedia]. New York: Dorling Kindersley, 1997. ISBN 0-7894-2234-4. Grades 2–6**
This visually appealing, easy-to-navigate CD-ROM encyclopedia is perfect for children. They will spend hours exploring the wonders of the world with pop-up screens, sidebars, animations, and video.

*Eyewitness History of the World* **[interactive multimedia]. New York: Dorling Kindersley, 1995. ISBN 0-7894-2947-0. Grade 3+**
This two-CD-ROM encyclopedia is filled with articulate text, wonderful photos and graphics, and well-indexed articles to make the world of the past come alive for students.

*Kids Culture: The Great Explorers* **[interactive multimedia]. MAC/WIN. Portland, OR: Pierian Spring Software, 1998. Grades 4–6**
Join narrator Terry the Tern in this CD-ROM stand-alone that reinforces problem-solving skills while examining world and space exploration. Kids Culture explores Ancient Greece, Polynesia, Ancient China, Mali, the Incas, Singapore, People of the Totem, and Medieval Europe, including architecture, foods, customs, people, transportation, animals, arts, music, recipes, celebrations, and games. Video-clips enhance the program. Topics can be studied independently or as a class. One of the strengths is a multicultural approach with emphasis on women (including Amelia Earhart) and non-western explorers (including Aborigines and Islamic traders). Topics are well organized. "Bright Ideas" sections of each topic offer stimulating questions and extended activities for each time period.

*ResourceLink* is an ABC-CLIO series of quality CD-ROMs that examine the world by centuries. Each is specially designed to accommodate Social Studies and Geography National Standards and Core Curricula. For each, the search possibilities are endless. Search by topic (culture, economy, environment, government, law, population, society) or by type (biography, documents, events, glossary, maps, organizations, photos, quotes, tables). Type the keyword in the query box. Browse the alphabetical list of people, places, and events. Students can even print, export, and create multimedia presentations. Here are the bibliographic details for each title in the series:

*ResourceLink: 17th-Century World History* **[interactive multimedia]. Santa Barbara, CA: ABC-CLIO, 2000. ISBN 1-57607-141-3. Grade 5+**
The world of Akbar, Bacon's Rebellion, Basho, Descartes, El Greco, Galileo, Moliere, Qing Dynasty, the Reformation, Rembrandt, Salem witch trials, and Shakespeare comes alive through this thrilling series. Primary resources, secondary source essays, and pithy historical perspective combine with multimedia to create this exceptional 17th century resource of more than 800 articles. The browse list also allows students to search 17th-century East Asia, India, Islam, Middle East, Russia, and South America.

*ResourceLink: 18th-Century World History* **[interactive multimedia]. Santa Barbara, CA: ABC-CLIO, 2000. ISBN 1-57607-140-5. Grade 5+**
Explore the world of Abigail and John Adams, Anna Ivanova, Bach, Blake, Buddhism,

Diderot, Kabuki, Native Americans, Seven Years' War, and Taoism through the more than 900 entries.

***ResourceLink: 19th-Century World History*** **[interactive multimedia]. Santa Barbara, CA: ABC-CLIO, 2000. ISBN 1-57607-138-3. Grade 5+**
Meet key world figures like Simón Bolívar, Cezanne, Dickens, Japanese samurai, Louis Pasteur, and Sitting Bull. Relive moments in history like the Anglo-Burmese War, California Gold Rush, the potato famine, opening of Suez Canal, Trail of Tears, and the Zulu Wars. This remarkable CD-ROM historical overview features more than 1,200 entries.

***ResourceLink: 20th-Century World History*** **[interactive multimedia]. Santa Barbara, CA: ABC-CLIO, 2000. ISBN 1-57607-138-3. Grade 5+**
Examine key issues like population, apartheid, suffrage, acid rain, and abortion. Experience African democracy, the end of the Berlin Wall, the Great Depression, the bombing of Hiroshima, and the Korean and Vietnam wars. Learn more about fascinating movers and shakers like Madeleine Albright, Deng Xiaoping, Amelia Earhart, Bill Gates, and Pol Pot through these more than 1,600 entries.

***Twentieth (20th) Century Video Almanac*** **[interactive multimedia]. Novato, CA: Mindscape, 1994. Grade 4+**
Share in some of the key moments of the 20th century with this CD-ROM program. Photos and videos will bring immediacy to the study of history.

# *The Arts*

***Art: A World History.*** **A millennium classic limited edition collection. New York: Dorling Kindersley, 1998. ISBN 0-7894-2382-0. 720 pages. Grade 7+ and Teacher Reference.**
Imagine all the treasures of the world within your grasp. Imagine a private tour guide to answer all your questions. *Art: A World History* offers it all. Stunning color photography and meticulous, articulate text make this comprehensive guide to world art an essential resource. The authors chose to combine European, Asian, and art of developing worlds by time period in a narrative format. This is an extensive and insightful survey of 20th century art. The interspersed time lines are also an asset.

**Frank, Vivien, and Deborah Jaffe.** ***Make a Book: Six Different Books to Make, Write, and Illustrate.*** **New York: Dutton, 2000. ISBN 0-525-46446-8. 32 pages. Grade 3+**
The authors give a brief overview of the history of making books and provide six lush book projects with details and actual pull-out pages. Create a Thai folding book, a Japanese scroll, a medieval Book of Hours, a flip book, a newspaper, or a movable book.

**Gaylord, Susan Kapuscinski.** ***Multicultural Books To Make and Share: Easy-to-Make, Authentic, Cross-Curricular.*** **New York: Scholastic Professional Books, 1994. ISBN 0-590-48921-6. 136 pages. Grades 2–5**
Gaylord guides children through book projects from Africa, Central America, North America, Europe, and Asia.

**Kohl, Mary Ann F., and Jean Potter.** *Global Art: Activities, Projects, and Inventions from Around the World.* **Illustrated by Rebecca Van Slyke. Beltsville, MD: Gryphon House, 1998. ISBN 0-87659-190-X. 189 pages. Grades K–6**

Develop cultural awareness through more than 130 art activities. Arranged by continent with maps and sidebar information, these exciting projects include experience level, art techniques, planning and preparation, materials, and process.

**Lakin, Patricia.** *Creativity: Around the World.* **We all share series. Woodbridge, CT: Blackbirch, 1995. ISBN 1-156711-142-4. 32 pages. Grades 2–4**

All people share a creative instinct. Lakin offers an overview of the world to show creativity through art, music, dance and handicraft. She includes ballet in Russia, weaving in Iran, cloth-making in Mexico, bossa nova and samba dances in Brazil, calligraphy in China, inlay art in India, carving in Kenya, and music in Israel.

**Nye, Naomi Shihab.** *This Same Sky: A Collection of Poems from Around the World.* **Compiled by Naomi Shihab Nye. New York: Simon and Schuster, 1992. ISBN 0-02768-440-7. 212 pages. Grade 4+**

Nye is a respected poet and anthologist. In this collection, Nye features more than 129 poets from 68 countries. The poems help children applaud different traditions and cultures while they marvel at the universality of dreams, fears, and relationships. The translations effectively capture the rhythm and power of the poems.

**Philip, Neil, ed.** *It's a Woman's World: A Century of Women's Voices in Poetry.* **New York: Dutton, 2000. ISBN 0-525-46328-3. Grade 6+**

Philip's selections span a wide range and depth of experiences as women from diverse cultures "speak for themselves about love and war, work and play, marriage and family, power, and ambition." The b&w photos are as expressive as the poems by Korean, Japanese, Chinese, Indian, American, Native American, African-American, and Nigerian women.

**Philip, Neil, ed.** *War and the Pity of War.* **Illustrated by Michael McCurdy. New York: Clarion, 1998. ISBN 0-395-84982-9. 96 pages. Grade 7+**

Michael McCurdy's b&w scratchboard illustrations and bold black print reinforce the anti-war message and starkness of the loss, pain, and gore of war, in these translated selections from ancient China to Bosnia.

**Roche, Denis.** *Art Around the World: Loo-Loo, Boo, and More Art You Can Do.* **Boston: Houghton Mifflin, 1998. ISBN 0-395-85597-7. Grades 2–6**

Use your "pawsport" to explore the "Table of Continents" in this clever world tour of arts and crafts. Try projects from Bali, China, Egypt, France, India, Italy, Java, Mexico, Norway, Peru, and Togo.

**Rohmer, Harriet.** *Honoring Our Ancestors: Stories and Pictures by Fourteen Artists.* **San Francisco: Children's Book Press, 1999. ISBN 0892391588. All ages**

Harriet Rohmer asked a diverse group of artists (including Hung Liu, Judith Lowry, and George Crespo) to summarize the influences on their art. This uplifting tribute to the sources of artists' inspiration assaults the senses with bold, colorful, and memorable illustrations and moving text.

**Rosenberg, Liz, ed.** *Light-Gathering Poems.* **New York: Henry Holt, 2000. ISBN 0-8050-6223-8. 146 pages. Grade 7+**

In another stunning collection from Rosenberg, poets from around the world, past and present, voice their pain and joy. Some of these poems move from darkness to light, but all are about finding the light and healing. Rosenberg includes translations of world poets, spanning the psalms of David, to Persia's mid-11th century Omar Khayyam and 13th century Rumi, to late 15th century Shinto priest Arakida Moritake, late-18th century Japanese haiku master Issa, late 19th century Mexican poet Amada Nervo and Indian poet Rabindranath Tagore, to 20th century Russian poet Marina Tsvetaeva.

*Voices: Poetry and Art from Around the World.* **Selected by Barbara Brenner. Washington, DC: National Geographic Society, 2000. ISBN 0-7922-7071-1. 96 pages. Grade 5+**

Stunning double-page color photo spreads introduce a cross-section of each continent's artistic and poetic expression. Brenner collects contemporary and traditional poetry and art from eminent "voices" (Botticelli, Chagall, Lorca, Langston Hughes, Pablo Neruda, Frida Kahlo) and lesser-known ones. The words and images barrage the senses with oral poetry, lyrics, haiku, chants, folk art, and much more. The themes are universal and transcend time. This spectacular sampling will whet the appetite for more.

**Yolen, Jane, ed.** *Sleep Rhymes Around the World.* **Illustrated by 17 International Artists. Honesdale, PA: Boyds Mills, 2000. ISBN 1-56397-923-3. 40 pages. Grades K–2**

Cherished babies sleep in trees, lotus blossoms, rocking chairs, arms, and rocking horses. The universality of bedtime emerges in this melodic collection as mothers soothe their babies to sleep. Sample songs from around the world, including Uganda, Korea, Ukraine, Thailand, Iran, Afghanistan, and Nigeria. Yolen has gathered English versions, translations, and transliterations of lullabies that capture the rhythms and rhymes of the world. The lulling words are accompanied by unique illustrations by artists from the country of the song's origin. Accompanying notes profile each illustrator.

**Yolen, Jane, ed.** *Street Rhymes Around the World.* **Illustrated by 17 International Artists. Honesdale, PA: Boyds Mills, 2000. ISBN 1-56397-894-6. 39 pages. Grades K–2**

Children chant magical verses as they bounce balls, play hopscotch, jump rope, and play other street games around the world. Children will recognize common elements in these rhymes, translations, and transliterations from many countries including Brazil, Armenia, Russia, Israel, Japan, and India. Artists from the country of the song's origin offer an array of styles and media in their accompanying illustrations for the buoyant songs. Profiles of each illustrator follow.

# *Biographies*

*1000 Makers of the Millennium.* **New York: Dorling Kindersley, 1999. ISBN 0-7894-4709-6. 256 pages. Grade 3+**

If you had to choose the most influential people of the millennium, whom would you feature? This selection offers brief profiles of key figures in history, arranged chronologically by the date of birth. The entries include the last name, first name, birth and death dates, nationality, and achievements. As the book moves to the later centuries, the number of entries increases. Here is a sample of some of those highlighted: 11th century—Omar Khayyam; 12th century—Saladin and Genghis Khan; 13th century—Marco Polo and Mansa Musa; 14th century—playwright Kiyotsugu and Ibn Battuta; 15th century—Songhai and Suleiman I; 16th century—Ivan the Terrible and Ieyasu Tokugawa; 17th century—Basho and Gobind Singh; 18th century—Catherine the Great and Shaka; 19th century—authors Leo Tolstoy and Fyodor Dostoevsky; and 20th century—Ayatollah Khomeini, Achmed Sukarno, and Hirohito.

**Avakian, Monique.** *Reformers: Activists, Educators, Religious Leaders.* **Remarkable Women: Past and Present, Women of Achievement series. Austin, TX: Raintree Steck-Vaughn, 2000. ISBN 0-8172-5733-0. 80 pages. Grades 4–8**
From Hortensia in the 1st century BCE to modern-day activist Patricia Ireland, women have had the courage to speak out and take action to improve the quality of life. These profiles span all cultures and all times. Each brief entry, arranged alphabetically, gives biographical highlights, including the woman's contributions as a reformer. Some entries include b&w photos and illustrations. A time line and index are included. Avakian encourages students to research further and use these brief biographies as introductions to these admirable women.

**Benedict, Kitty, and Karen Covington.** *The Literary Crowd: Writers, Critics, Scholars, Wits.* **Remarkable Women: Past and Present, Women of Achievement series. Austin, TX: Raintree Steck-Vaughn, 2000. ISBN 0-8172-5732-2. 80 pages. Grades 4–8**
The authors chose 150 women whose writings represent different styles, times, and countries. Some, like Laura Ingalls Wilder, Anne Frank, Emily Dickinson, and Maya Angelou, will be familiar to students. Others, like Ding Ling from China, Anita Desai from India, and Uno Chiyo from Japan, will be refreshing discoveries. Encourage students to find examples of their work to read. Each brief entry, arranged alphabetically, gives biographical highlights, including the person's contributions as a reformer. Some entries include b&w photos and illustrations. A time line and index are included.

**Covington, Karen.** *Creators: Artists, Designers, Craftswomen.* **Remarkable Women: Past and Present, Women of Achievement series. Austin, TX: Raintree Steck-Vaughn, 2000. ISBN 0-8172-5725-X. 80 pages. Grades 4–8**
Women have always expressed their creativity through art. Since the art world was a man's domain, we have few records of early work by women. Covington's research took her back to the 1st century BCE, but most of the 150 women she profiles here are from the past century. Students may recognize names like Beatrix Potter, Faith Ringgold, Margaret Bourke-White, and Frida Kahlo. Introduce them to other creators like photographer Dorothea Lange, sculptor Properzia de' Rossi, and painter Kuan Tao-sheng. Each brief entry, arranged alphabetically, gives biographical highlights, including the contributions as a reformer. Some entries include b&w photos and illustrations. A time line and index are included.

**Felder, Deborah G.** *The 100 Most Influential Women of All Time.* **New York: Citadel, 1995. ISBN 0-8065-1726-3. 374 pages. Grade 4+**
The author explains her criteria for selection of these 100 remarkable women. She includes women from the past and present who have left an indelible mark on history.

The entries have b&w illustrations and average three and one half pages in length. The text is deft and engaging. Many of the women Felder selected are from politics and the arts, including Indira Gandhi, Cleopatra, Catherine the Great, Frida Kahlo, Golda Meir, and Murasaki Shikibu.

**Green, Robert.** *Dictators.* **History makers series. San Diego: Lucent Books, 2000. ISBN 1-56006-594-X. 128 pages. Grade 6+**

The word "dictator" summons images of persecution and suffering. Green characterizes the six leaders as "ambitious men" who "sacrificed their people's political and personal freedoms for what they decreed was the greater good of the nation." The in-depth profiles of Francisco Franco, Adolf Hitler, Joseph Stalin, Mao Zedong, Fidel Castro, and Saddam Hussein reveal similarities in philosophy, methodology, and hubris. Students will find this collection stimulates discussion of the difference between conquerors and dictators. Green reinforces the ambiguous nature of dictators as heroic to some and demonic to others. The b&w photos, illustrations, maps, and primary and secondary source material encourage additional study. The comprehensive index, student bibliography, and works consulted are helpful.

**Krull, Kathleen.** *Lives of Extraordinary Women: Rulers, Rebels (and What the Neighbors Thought).* **Illustrated by Kathryn Hewitt. San Diego, CA: Harcourt, 2000. ISBN 0-15-20087-1. 95 pages. Grades 3–7**

Krull and Hewitt collaborate on another of their phenomenal biographies of the famous and infamous. Krull manages to dig up the most unusual and startling details about these women to add to the standard facts that have made them famous. Readers of all ages will delight in Hewitt's caricatures and in interpreting the items she chooses to portray. Krull poses these questions in the introduction: "Whose secret to success was the library?" "Who took only two baths in her entire life?" "Whose lips turned green after she nibbled her macaroni necklace?" Answer these after reading captivating biographies of Cleopatra, Isabella I, Nzingha, Golda Meir, Indira Gandhi, Eva Peron, Aung San Suu Kyi, and more.

**Langley, Andrew.** *100 Greatest Tyrants.* **100 Greatest series. Danbury, CT: Grolier, 1997. ISBN 0-7172-7688-0. 111 pages. Grade 3+**

This volume of the series includes one-page biographies and color photography and illustrations. Langley profiles the infamous from those born between 700 BC and AD 500 (Herod and Nero) to those born after 1920 (Idi Amin, Saddam Hussein, and Eva Peron). Other tyrants include Genghis Khan, Vlad Dracula, Ivan the Terrible, Ieyasu Tokugawa, Shaka, Syngman Rhee, Adolf Hitler, Kim Il-Sung, and Augusto Pinochet.

**Lewin, Ted.** *Touch and Go: Travels of a Children's Book Illustrator.* **New York: Lothrop, Lee and Shepard, 1999. ISBN 0-688-14109-9. 96 pages. Grade 4+**

If you think illustrating children's books is a sedentary profession, think again. Award-winning illustrator and author Lewin freezes moments in time in this memoir. He includes color photos and illustrations of the memorable people and experiences from his world travels. Relive the graphic gutting of a wildebeest in the Kalahari Desert of Botswana; Ted wading across a crocodile-infested river; his encounters with caribou, grizzlies, and polar bears; and Ted wearing an eight-foot boa constrictor around his neck in Brazil.

McClure, Judy. *Healers and Researchers: Physicians, Biologists, Social Scientists.* Remarkable Women: Past and Present, Women of Achievement series. Austin, TX: Raintree Steck-Vaughn, 2000. ISBN 0-8172-5734-9. 80 pages. Grades 4–8

From oceans and jungles of the world to laboratories, classrooms, and space, these women challenged themselves to uncover secrets of science. The authors chose 150 women from different branches of science and different countries throughout the ages. Some, like Mae Jemison, Elizabeth Blackwell, and Margaret Mead, may be familiar to students. Others, like Sylvia Alice Earle, Elisabeth Kubler-Ross, and Mamphela Ramphele, may open doors for new discoveries. Each brief entry, arranged alphabetically, gives biographical highlights, including the woman's contributions as a reformer. Some entries include b&w photos and illustrations. A time line and index are included.

Nardo, Don. *Women Leaders of Nations.* History makers series. San Diego: Lucent Books, 1999. ISBN 1-56006-397-1. 112 pages. Grade 6+

From the warriors of the Amazon to the present, women have played key roles in the development of the world. Most of the figures Nardo selected to profile are obvious choices, but his documentation is persuasive. The legacy of Cleopatra, Elizabeth I, Catherine the Great, Victoria, Golda Meir, Margaret Thatcher, and Benazir Bhutto cannot be argued. Nardo offers in-depth coverage of their lives, careers, and accomplishments. The most interesting choice is Queen Isabella of Spain, for Nardo recognizes the global impact of her support of Columbus and exploration. Maps, b&w illustrations and photos, and primary and secondary sources place the leaders in historical perspective. The comprehensive index, student bibliography, and works consulted are helpful.

Pear, Nancy, and Daniel B. Baker. *Explorers and Discoverers: From Alexander the Great to Sally Ride.* Edited by Jane Hoehner. Detroit: UXL, 1999. ISBN 0-7876-3681-9. 225 pages. Grade 5+

Pear and Baker profile men, women, and objects (such as the National Air and Space Museum and the S.S. Manhattan) in this skillful and valuable biographical seven-volume set. Many of the biographies are familiar (Neil Armstrong, Vasco Nunez de Balboa, Linda Finch and Thor Heyerdahl). But this is also a valuable resource because it introduces students to some lesser-known non-Western and women explorers. Each in-depth biography discusses the explorer or discoverer in the context of his or her time; describes the subject's expeditions, failures, and successes; and assesses his or her contributions to mankind. Each also includes a pen-and-ink drawing or b&w illustration and sources. Each volume includes a Chronology of Exploration, arranged alphabetically by country, and a cumulative index to all seven volumes. An extensive collection of route maps can be found at the beginning of each volume.

Pollard, Michael. *100 Greatest Explorers.* 100 Greatest series. Danbury, CT: Grolier, 1997. ISBN 0-7172-7682-1. 111 pages. Grade 3+

This volume of the series includes one-page biographies and color photography and illustrations of famous and lesser-known explorers. Among the well-known are Ferdinand Magellan, David Livingstone, Roald Amundsen, and Erik the Red. Non-western explorers include Suleyman the Merchant, Ibn Battuta, and Yuri Gagarin. Explorers like Mary Kingsley, Naomi Uemura, Zhang Qian, and Xuan Zang may be unfamiliar to students.

**Pollard, Michael.** *100 Greatest Men.* Danbury, CT: Grolier, 1997. ISBN 0-7172-7679-1. 111 pages. Grade 3+

> This volume of the series includes one-page biographies and color photography and illustrations. Among the top 100 men who have had the most impact on life throughout the world and time are Chiune Sugihara, Desmond Tutu, The Dalai Lama, Confucius, Hammurabi, Kublai Khan, Mahatma Gandhi, Nelson Mandela, and Mikhail Gorbachev.

**Price-Groff, Claire.** *Great Conquerors.* History makers series. San Diego: Lucent Books, 2000. ISBN 1-56006-612-X. 128 pages. Grade 6+

> If you could select only six conquerors from history, whom would you choose? Price-Groff offers in-depth biographies of the lives, careers, and accomplishments of Alexander the Great, Augustus the Great, Attila, Charlemagne, Genghis Khan, and Napoleon Bonaparte with b&w photos, illustrations, and maps. She places the leaders in historical perspective with the use of primary source materials and establishes credibility with her secondary source citations. The comprehensive index, student bibliography, and works consulted are helpful.

**Royston, Angela.** *100 Greatest Women.* 100 Greatest series. Danbury, CT: Grolier, 1997. ISBN 0-7172-7680-5. 111 pages. Grade 3+

> This volume of the series includes one-page biographies and color photography and illustrations. Royston profiles famous women throughout history from around the world. Featured are Mother Teresa, Cleopatra, Indira Gandhi, and Benazir Bhutto, among others. Lesser-known women include Sirimavo Bandaranaike, the first female Indonesian prime minister; Qiu Jin, an early Chinese revolutionary and advocate of women's rights; and Murasaki Shikibu, author of *The Tale of Genji.*

**Sommerville, Donald.** *100 Greatest Sports Champions.* 100 Greatest series. Danbury, CT: Grolier, 1997. ISBN 0-7172-7686-4. 111 pages. Grade 3+

> This volume of the series includes one-page biographies and color photography. Sommerville profiles famous world athletes in baseball, basketball, cycling, football, golf, gymnastics, ice hockey, skiing, soccer, sumo wrestling, swimming, tennis, triathlon, and track and field.

## *Biographies: CDs*

***Current Leaders: Rulers of Nations in the 1990s*** [interactive multimedia]. Santa Barbara, CA: ABC-CLIO, 1998. ISBN 1-57607-015-8. Grade 6+

> This extraordinary CD-ROM is designed to meet social studies curriculum and standards needs and is guaranteed to be a favorite of teachers and students. More than 500 in-depth biographies of current world leaders give their background, worldview, and politics. Time lines help place the leader in world and time perspective. It is user-friendly; entries are indexed by both ruler name and country. Profiles include illustrations or photos, bibliographies, hyperlinks to related topics, glossary definitions, and maps. Users can search by name, subject, attribute (time period, title or occupation, place of origin, ethnicity, and gender), or text. Of special help for research is CLIOview, which enables users to browse search result summaries and sort by title, occupation, or birth date. Data

can be printed, exported, or bookmarked for continuing study. Biographies represent all corners and cultures of the world: Emperor Akihito, Corazon Aquino, Yasir Arafat, King Hussein, Slobodan Milosevic, Nelson Mandela, Shimon Peres, Margaret Thatcher, and Boris Yeltsin, and others.

***Founding Leaders: Shapers of Modern Nations*** **[interactive multimedia]. Santa Barbara, CA: ABC-CLIO, 1998. ISBN 1-57607-014-4. Grade 5+**

The lives of familiar military, political, and intellectual leaders—Aung San, David Ben-Gurion, Chou En-lai, Indira Gandhi, Mikhail Gorbachev, Saddam Hussein, and Nelson Mandela—and those of lesser-known men and women who shaped world history are all within the click of a mouse. Research couldn't be easier or more enticing. The design of these programs guarantees success and the content meets social studies curriculum and standards needs. This CD-ROM features more than 300 in-depth biographies of founders of nations from the 12th century to the present. Essays, maps, photos, illustrations, glossary, and hyperlinks flesh out the portraits with personal facts and social factors relevant to decision-making. A separate reference section gives data on individual nations, a subject index, and a country index. Users can search by name, subject, attribute (time period, title or occupation, place of origin, ethnicity, and gender), or text. Research aids include CLIOview, which enables users to browse search result summaries and sort by title, occupation, or birth date. Data can be printed or exported. Students can use the note-taking or bookmark features.

***Women Leaders: Rulers Throughout History*** **[interactive multimedia]. Santa Barbara, CA: ABC-CLIO, 1998. ISBN 1-57607-116-6. Grade 5+**

Although ancient civilizations had women warriors and queens like Nzingha and Cleopatra, it has been a struggle for women to gain acceptance in key political roles. This superior CD-ROM recognizes the essential role of women throughout history. The 350 biographies highlight the lives, careers, and accomplishments of female leaders, de facto rulers, and constitutional monarchs of the countries, kingdoms, and civilizations of the world. The chronology by century helps place the women in historical and geographic perspective. Articles, photos, and hyperlinks offer insights into the lives of powerful and influential women such as Corazon Aquino, Benazir Bhutto, Catherine the Great, Catherine de Medici, Hatshepsut, Isabella, Queen Liliuokalani, Golda Meir, Margaret Thatcher, and Queen Victoria. Users can search by name, subject, attribute (time period, title or occupation, place of origin, ethnicity, and gender), or text. CLIOview enables users to browse search result summaries and sort by title, occupation, or birth date. Data can be printed or exported. Students can use the note-taking or bookmark features.

***World Military Leaders*** **[interactive multimedia]. Santa Barbara, CA: ABC-CLIO, 1999. ISBN 1-57607-166-9. Grade 5+**

Meet more than 300 admired and abhorred leaders from the 19th and 20th centuries through this intriguing, easy-to-use CD-ROM designed to meet curriculum and standards needs. In addition to dictators and generals, the interactive program features a diverse cross-section of heroes and heroines who affected the course of history and impacted mankind: Idi Amin, Clara Barton, Daniel Boone, Che Guevara, Cochise, Dorothea Dix, Francisco Franco, Mata Hari, Adolf Hitler, T.E. Lawrence, Jean Moreau, Napoleon, Ho Chi Minh, Osceola, Florence Nightingale, Yitzak Rabin, and King Shaka.

Users can search by name, subject, attribute (time period, title or occupation, place of origin, ethnicity, and gender), or text. CLIOview enables users to browse search result summaries and sort by title, occupation, or birth date. Students can print or export data, use note-taking or bookmark features.

*World Political Leaders* [interactive multimedia]. Santa Barbara, CA: ABC-CLIO, 1999. ISBN 1-57607-164-2. Grade 5+

*World Political Leaders* contains more than 600 biographies of those who held office or were instrumental in creating and implementing world policy in the 19th and 20th centuries: Simón Bolívar, Winston Churchill, John Foster Dulles, Friedrich Engels, Haile Selassie, Mao Zedong, Karl Marx, Benito Mussolini, Margaret Thatcher, Queen Victoria, Otto von Bismarck, and many others. Searches are easy and bring students to concise articles, photos, and hyperlinks to extend research. The CD-ROM is designed to meet curriculum and standards needs. Users can search by name, subject, attribute (time period, title or occupation, place of origin, ethnicity, and gender), or text. CLIOview enables users to browse search result summaries and sort by title, occupation, or birth date. Students can print or export data, use the note-taking or bookmark features.

*World Social Leaders* [interactive multimedia]. Santa Barbara, CA: ABC-CLIO, 1999. ISBN 1-57607-169-3. Grade 5+

If you had to select the men and women who have improved society by their brilliant minds, irrepressible spirits, courage, perseverance, and cunning, whom would you choose? This valuable easy-to-use CD-ROM profiles 600 abolitionists, artists, authors, economists, environmentalists, health reformers, human rights activists, humanitarians, political philosophers, religious leaders, scientists, teachers, and women's rights activists of the 19th and 20th centuries. Among this diverse group are Chinua Achebe, Simone de Beauvoir, Mary McLeod Bethune, Rachel Carson, Cesar Chavez, the Dalai Lama, Princess Diana, Carl Jung, Martin Luther King, Jr., Charles Lindbergh, Rigoberta Menchu, Eleanor Roosevelt, Rabindranath Tagore, and Brigham Young. This CD-ROM is designed to meet curriculum and standards needs. Users can search by name, subject, attribute (time period, title or occupation, place of origin, ethnicity, and gender), or text. CLIOview enables users to browse search result summaries and sort by title, occupation, or birth date. Students can print or export data, use the note-taking or bookmark features. The abundant articles, photos, and hyperlinks will encourage additional research.

# *Country Resources*

Ajmera, Maya, and Anna Rhesa Versola. *Children from Australia to Zimbabwe: A Photographic Journey Around the World.* Foreword by Marian Wright Edelman. Watertown, MA: Charlesbridge, 1997. Originally published by SHAKTI for Children. ISBN 0-88106-999-X. Grades 3–5

Edelman, President of the Children's Defense League, emphasizes the commonality of children of the world: "They all play, need their families, have basic needs, deserve protection, can contribute to society, and are a mighty force." Aimera and Versola take us on a journey around the world from Australia to Zimbabwe with expressive color photos that capture the charm and essence of the world's children.

**Bernhard, Emery.** *A Ride on Mother's Back: A Day of Baby Carrying Around the World.* **Illustrated by Durga Bernhard. San Diego, CA: Harcourt Brace, 1996. ISBN 0-15-200870-5. 32 pages. Grades K–3**

The Bernhards take us on a loving journey around the world, capturing moments shared between mother and child. Children will see ways that babies can be carried—in a sling around the shoulder (Bali), in mother's parka hood (Canada), in a woolen shawl (South America), or in a net bag hanging from mother's head (Papua New Guinea). Be prepared for giggles at sights like Guatamalan mother nursing her baby.

**Bieniek, Denise.** *Explore the World: Social Studies Projects and Activities.* **Illustrated by Ellen Sasaki. Mahwah, NJ: Troll Creative Teacher Ideas, 1996. ISBN 0-8167-3878-5. 96 pages. Teacher Reference**

Bieniek offers project ideas and extended activities for elementary school classes centered on social studies standards, cultural awareness, thinking skills, and creative writing. Topics include the Seven Wonders of the World, Chinese Dynasties, Wars of the World, African Latitude and Longitude, Worldwide Charts, Our Communities, Population Explosion, Languages of the World, Foreign Foods, and Money of the World. Reproducible unit pages will be helpful to teachers. Units can be adapted for older students.

**Blackaby, Susan.** *One World: Multicultural Projects and Activities.* **Mahwah, NJ: Troll Associates, 1992. ISBN 0-8167-2598-5. 96 pages. Teacher Reference for Grades K–6**

Blackaby suggests multicultural activities to complement classic works of literature from African American, Native American, Hispanic American, and Asian American authors. Project Pages suggest tracing roots, taking an Asian river trip, oral histories, and art forms.

**Bonk, Mary Rose, ed.** *Worldmark Yearbook 2000.* **Detroit: Gale, 2000. ISBN 0-7876-4931-7. 3 volume set. 3694 pages. Grade 7+ and Teacher Reference**

The benchmark *Worldmark Encyclopedia of the Nations* offers in-depth studies of the world's nations and territories. This yearly reference complements it with the most up-to-date information on the countries compiled for easy reference. The introduction offers an overview of the year, putting nations in global perspective. The encyclopedic entries for each of the 220 nations and territories include a fast facts box, introductory survey (recent history, government, defense, economic affairs, social welfare, and education); year's key events time line by month; analysis of events of the year (business and the economy, government and politics, culture and society); directory (central government, political organizations, diplomatic representation, judicial system, and further reading); and statistical data for the country (geography, human factors, education, government and law, labor force, production sector, manufacturing sector, finance, economics, and trade). Gale maximizes the use of this reference tool by providing a free online subscription to "Worldmark Yearbook Online" for the year of the purchase of the yearbook. It offers an updated searchable full-text database of the print set, as well as additional search options for countries, organizations, essays, maps, and more.

**Chiarelli, A. B. and Anna Lisa Bebi.** *The Atlas of World Cultures.* **Illustrated by Paola Ravaglia. New York: Peter Bedrick Books, 1997. ISBN 0-87226-499-8. 62 pages. Grades 3–6**

This is one of the best one-volume resources to help children understand the vastness of the world. Chiarelli and Bebi highlight people of the world with appealing color illustrations and fascinating facts on double-page spreads, by areas of the world. There are also valuable features on language and writing; religions; food and costume; art, dance, and song; and cultures in conflict.

***Circling the Globe: A Guide to Countries and Cultures of the World.*** **Austin, TX: Raintree Steck-Vaughn, 1995. ISBN 0-8114-4085-3. Grades 3–7**
This easy-to-use 10-volume set has an overview of the people, history, geography, and politics of the regions of the world. The photos and illustrations are clear and colorful. The maps are concise. Regions are arranged by Northern and Northeastern Europe; Southern and Eastern Europe; Northern and Western Africa; Southern and Eastern Africa; North America, Central America, and the West Indies; South America; Russia, Western Asia, and the Middle East; Southern and Eastern Asia; Australia, the Pacific Islands, and Earth in space.

***Culturgrams: The Nations Around Us.*** **Chicago: Ferguson Publishing Co., 2000. ISBN 0-89434-262-2. Grade 5+**
Every middle school and high school library should have *Culturgrams*, the definitive text for study about the countries of the world. It is updated annually with overviews of 160 countries. Volume One includes the Americas and Europe; Volume Two includes Asia, Africa, and Oceania. Each concise, articulate four-page profile features the country's background, people, lifestyle, and society. The "Customs and courtesies" section should be required reading since it explains the countries' greetings, gestures, visiting, and eating customs. "For the traveler" provides embassy addresses and phone numbers, travel advice, and warnings.

**DeRolf, Shane.** ***The Crayon Box That Talked.*** **Illustrated by Michael Letzig. New York: Random House, 1997. ISBN 0-679-88611-7. All ages**
This seemingly simple poem from the 1997 National Anti-Discrimination Campaign for Children emphasizes the uniqueness of each color and shows how wondrously they combine. DeRolf celebrates diversity and establishes the commonality of mankind.

**George, Lindsay Barrett.** ***Around the World: Who's Been Here?*** **New York: Greenwillow, 1999. ISBN 0-688-15268-6. Grades 1–3**
Miss Lewis, a teacher, travels around the world and sends letters to her class describing all the animals she sees in their natural habitats. The illustrations are sometimes amusing, and the two-page spreads of the animals are breathtaking. Factual notes on the animals follow.

**Glaser, Linda.** ***Our Big Home: An Earth Poem.*** **Illustrated by Elisa Kleven. Brookfield, CT: Millbrook Press, 2000. ISBN 0-7613-1650-7. 32 pages. Grades K–3**
In Glaser's poetic images, children from all around the world share the earth. Kleven's illustrations burst with life and are filled with delightful details of children from many countries enjoying earth's bounty. The final note shares the hope that "their vision of Earth as the shared home of all peoples and animals and plants will offer children a deeper understanding of humankind's responsibility to care for our planet."

**Hamanaka, Sheila.** *All the Colors of the Earth.* **Illustrated by the author. New York: Morrow, 1994. ISBN 0-688-11131-9. 32 pages. Grades K–2**
In this wonderful introduction to multiculturalism, Hamanaka celebrates people's differences, assaulting us with the children's colors and with rhythmic language and exquisite oils, from "the roaring browns of bears and soaring eagles" to "the tinkling pinks of tiny seashells by the rumbling sea." Hamanaka explains even hair can be different, but love comes in all colors.

**Hollyer, Beatrice.** *Wake Up, World! A Day in the Life of Children Around the World.* **With an introduction by Tony Robinson. New York: Henry Holt, in association with Oxfax, 1999. ISBN 0-8050-6293-9. 40 pages. Grades K–4**
Many books interview children from other countries and offer insights into their cultures. What makes this book unique is the format. By examining each time of the day and providing charming color photos of the children in action and simple narrative text from the representative countries side by side, Hollyer creates a valuable resource for comparative cultural studies. Meet Paide from the United Kingdom, Natali from the United States, Cidinha from Brazil, Anusibuno from Ghana, Sasha from Russia, Linh from Vietnam, Alexis from Australia, and Shakeel from India. The back endpapers profile the children and their cultures.

**Judd, Naomi.** *Love Can Build a Bridge.* **Illustrated by Suzanne Duranceau, with an audiotape of the story/song performed by the Judds. New York: HarperCollins, 1999. ISBN 0-06-027206-6. Grades pre-K+**
Radiant illustrations accompany the words of this simple song, showing children of all races sharing, caring, and making the world better.

*Junior Worldmark Encyclopedia of Cities,* **4 volumes. Edited by Jill Copolla and Susan Bevan Gall. Detroit: UXL, 2000. ISBN 0-7876-4869-8. 800 pages. Grade 6+**
Travel to Bangkok, Beijing, Bombay, Cairo, Johannesburg, Nairobi, Sydney, Tokyo, and other major cities with this impressive research tool. The in-depth articles include maps, charts, tables, color photos, and fun facts, providing information on key aspects of the geographical, historical, and cultural life. The editors also include essays about Africa, Asia, Europe, the Middle East, the Pacific, and the United States, placing the areas in perspective and fostering comparison and contrast.

*Junior Worldmark Encyclopedia of World Cultures,* **9 volumes. Edited by Timothy L. Gall and Susan Bevan Gall. Detroit: UXL, 1999. ISBN 0-7876-1756-X. 2,090 pages. Grade 6+**
The Gale resources are acclaimed for their impeccable research, attention to detail, and thoughtful design. This is a definitive resource for world studies for middle school and high school students. More than 290 culture groups are explored in this phenomenal nine-volume set, arranged alphabetically by country. Twenty topics are explored for each country, including introduction, location, language, folklore, religion, major holidays, rites of passage, relationships, living conditions, family life, clothing, food, education, cultural heritage, employment, sports, recreation, crafts and hobbies, social problems, and bibliography. If a country has more than one cultural group, each group is presented with the same 20 topics. For example, Tanzania includes Tanzanians, Chagga, Maasia, Nyamwez, Shambaa, and Swahili. Each culture also includes a b&w map, photograph,

and recipe. The subheadings, glossary, cumulative index, annotated maps, textual pronunciations and definitions, and at-a-glance statistics enhance the ease of searching.

**Junior Worldmark Encyclopedia of World Holidays,** 4 volumes. Edited by Robert H. Griffin and Ann H. Shurgin. Detroit: UXL, 2000. ISBN 0-7876-3927-3. 820 pages. Grade 6+
This valuable resource offers in-depth profiles of religious and civil holidays around the world. Learn about the customs, rituals, traditions, food, music, dance, costumes, arts, and folklore of countries as you celebrate holidays like Buddha's birthday, Ramadan, Day of the Dead, and independence days. The abundant color photos, the country-by-country descriptions, and cumulative indexes make the volumes appealing, informational, and easy-to-use.

**Kindersley, Barnabas and Anabel.** *Children Just Like Me.* **New York: Dorling Kindersley, 1996. ISBN: 0-7894-0201-7. 80 pages. Grades 2–5**
This celebration of children around the world, produced in association with UNICEF to mark its 50th anniversary, captures children's families, homes, and customs in vivid color photos. Depicting their friends, lives, and favorite games makes children recognize all children are alike. Gain insights into our different-but-same world through visits with Oscar from Bolivia, Omar from Mexico, Olia from Russia, Mohammed from Egypt, Houda from Morocco, Guo Shuang from China, Ngawaiata from New Zealand, and many others.

**Lakin, Patricia.** *Family: Around the World.* **We all share series. Woodbridge, CT: Blackbirch, 1995. ISBN 1-56711-143-2. 32 pages. Grades 2–4**
Lakin features a two-page spread per country with a color photo of family members and a brief summary of family life in Israel, Brazil, India, China, Russia, Panama, Nigeria, Iraq, and Egypt.

**Lakin, Patricia.** *Growing Up: Around the World.* **We all share series. Woodbridge, CT: Blackbirch, 1995. ISBN 1-56711144-0. 32 pages. Grades 2–4**
Lakin features a two-page spread per country with a color photograph of family members and a brief summary of the way of life in Russia, Brazil, Israel, Iraq, Saudi Arabia, China, India, New Guinea, Cameroon, and Nepal.

**Levinson, David.** *Ethnic Groups Worldwide: A Ready Reference Handbook.* **Phoenix, AZ: Oryx Press, 1998. ISBN 1-57356-019-7. 436 pages. Teacher Reference**
Dr. Levinson stresses the importance of ethnic identity, relations, conflict, and immigration in the contemporary world. In this comprehensive up-to-date volume, he surveys the ethnic groups of the world alphabetically within geographic area, including Europe, Africa, Asia and the Pacific, and the Americas. Each section begins with an introduction, analysis of the types of ethnic groups and the ethnic relations of the area, and a bibliography. Each country profile includes ethnic composition and ethnic relations.

**Macdonald, Fiona and Gerald Wood.** *Exploring the World.* **Voyages of discovery series. New York: Peter Bedrick, 1996. ISBN 0-8722-6487-4. 48 pages. Grade 3+**
Journey with the first explorers as they discover new worlds. The color illustrations and maps bring the explorations into perspective for young readers.

**Morris, Ann.** *Families.* **New York: HarperCollins, 2000. ISBN 0-688-17198-2. 32 pages. Grades K–3**

This visual feast shows different family make-ups (no children, one child, stepfamilies, foster families). The glorious color photos from other countries celebrate what all families of the world have in common—loving, caring, and sharing. Morris selected photos from Ethiopia, Vietnam, Canada, the United States, Saudi Arabia, Brazil, Russia, India, Japan, South Korea, and the United Kingdom.

**Perry, Phyllis J.** *Keeping the Traditions: A Multicultural Resource.* **Illustrated by Joe Pancake. Golden, CO: Fulcrum, 2000. 262 pages. Teacher Reference for Grades 4–8**

Perry acknowledges the ways the United States has benefited from the cultures of her immigrants. This ambitious resource gathers legends from 20 countries to help children understand and feel pride in the richness of these heritages. After each retelling, Perry presents background information, history, government, religion, education, immigrants, language, the arts and sciences, food, recreation, and customs and traditions for each country. Her suggested activities (writing, reading, vocabulary, math, social studies, geography, music, art, drama/movement, dress) and culminating activity foster cross-curricular connections. She also includes suggested reading for each country.

**Sechi-Johnson, Patricia.** *100 Greatest Manmade Wonders.* **100 Greatest series. Danbury, CT: Grolier, 1997. ISBN 0-7172-7689-0. 111 pages. Grade 3+**

This series includes one-page features and color photography and illustrations. Sechi-Johnson organized her 100 greatest within time periods. Choices include the Seven Wonders of the World (2500 BC–0 AD), Petra in Jordan (0–100), Angkor Wat in Kampuchea (1000–1500), Statues of Easter Island (1500–1900), Mount Rushmore (1900–1960), the Opera House in Sydney (1960–1980), and the MIR Space Station (1981–1995).

**Simon, Norma.** *All Kinds of Children.* **Illustrated by Diane Paterson. Morton Grove, IL: Albert Whitman, 1999. ISBN 0-8075-0281-2. 32 pages. Grades K–2**

Simon fosters acceptance of others by showing what all children have in common. Paterson's watercolors joyously capture children of different ages and ethnic backgrounds.

**Sis, Peter.** *Madlenka.* **New York: Farrar Straus Giroux, 2000. ISBN 0-374-39969-7. 32 pages. Grades K–2**

Madlenka has a loose tooth and wants to share the news. Her exuberance takes her on a tour of her neighborhood in New York that seems more like a United Nations tour. She visits the French baker, the Indian news vendor, the Italian ice cream man, the Latin American grocer, a retired opera singer from Germany, an African-American school friend, and an Asian shopkeeper. Die-cuts alternate between Madlenka and her neighbors' memories from their homelands in this clever adventure.

**Smith, Miranda.** *Eyewitness Living Earth.* **New York: Dorling Kindersley, 1996. ISBN 0-7894-0644-6. 192 pages. Grades 3–7**

Lush color photos, skillful text, sidebars with fascinating facts, maps, and graphics chronicle the world around us in this wonderful resource.

**Steele, Philip.** *Being Human: The Human Race,* **Volume 8. Danbury, CT: Grolier Educational, 1999. ISBN 0-7172-9427-7. 48 pages. Grade 4+**

In this compact volume, Steele explores the world of the human race from evolution to social units (like tribes, clans, colonies) to political systems (like democracy). He considers how people live and how we are all one world. Issues affecting all mankind include labor, economics, acid rain, global warming, pollution, population, and racism.

**Swain, Gwenyth.** *Smiling.* **Small world series. Minneapolis: Carolrhoda Books, 1999. ISBN 1-57505-371-3. 24 pages. Grades K–1**

Smiles are universal and contagious. Nowhere is this more evident than in Swain's book. Children will smile as they read the rhymed text. In vivid color photos, Swain features smiling faces of a girl from Sudan, a family from China, Aborigine boys from Australia, a Mexican girl, and other people from around the world.

**Weiss, Nicki.** *The World Turns Round and Round.* **Illustrated by the author. New York: Greenwillow, 2000. ISBN 0-688-17213-X. 32 pages. Grades K–2**

Join children from Mexico, the United States, Kenya, Japan, Russia, India, Egypt, Vietnam, and Haiti in this joyful celebration of cultures of the world. Each page includes the country's word for the relative and the present as the children describe their gifts. The final pages include the multicultural class with a list of where their families came from with the story's key: "But it's really not so far, Not so far from there to here. Kaffiyeh, sari, dep in pairs—Dashiki, shapka, mittens to wear. We're part of here and part of there, And the world turns round and round."

## *Country Resources: Videos and CDs*

*Going to Grandma's Around the World* **[videorecording]. A Sing, Color 'n Say World of Languages Fun Video. Directed by Phillip Siadi. Troy, MI: Worldkids Press, 1998. ISBN 1-880449-21-8. 20 minutes. Grades K–2**

In this charming animated film, children sing the popular title song and travel to 10 countries. Fun Facts sections introduce them to each country's culture, customs, and traits. They'll learn to say "I love you, Grandma" in Arabic, Hebrew, Japanese, French, Spanish, Polish, Hungarian, Russian, and Italian.

*EXEGY: Current Country Profiles* **[interactive multimedia]. Santa Barbara, CA: ABC-CLIO, 2000. ISSN 1076-8653. Grade 4+**

*EXEGY* (now *World Geography Online* ISSN: 1531-1244) is phenomenal. The quality of the content is superior, and the format is both visually appealing and easy to navigate. Search by countries (A to Z) or subject index (names, places, topics). CLIOview adds a new dimension to research: It allows students to view data from different countries simultaneously and to compare and contrast the information for a better grasp of world dynamics. "Internet" brings students to the Web links. "Trail" allows students to view their search path. For each country, EXEGY includes maps and flags and summarizes the geography, recent history, economic status, and facts. "History" traces from the ancient world to today. "Government" presents the form, officials, and election data. "Facts and Figures" chronicles geography, military, world population, currency, and other statistics. "Events" highlights news in reverse chronological order with current events first. "Biographies" profiles leading figures of the country. "Organizations" lists political parties and government agencies. "Documents" offers abstracts or full texts of treaties, resolutions, speeches, and constitutions. The Calendar of World Holidays, Teacher Resources (with tips, lesson plans, ideas, and grade-level-appropriate activities), and Student Resources (activities, games, research projects) are spectacular. (Note: A product that includes the Culture and Environment modules is also available that adds 1,000 more entries on cultural diversity and environmental concerns.)

***My First Amazing World Explorer*** **[interactive multimedia]. New York: Dorling Kindersley Multimedia, 1996. ISBN 0-7894-0922-4. Grades K–4**
Children of all ages will enjoy traveling around the world with this CD-ROM program. They can visit cities, learn about landmarks, and solve mysteries along the way. It's fun for the children to get their photos taken, passports stamped, and stickers stored in their journals. Even younger children don't seem to mind that some of the quiz questions are difficult.

***Sesame Street Celebrates Around the World*** **[videorecording]. A Children's Television Workshop production. Executive Producer: Nina Elias Bamberger; Director: Chuck Vinson; Writer: Lou Berger; with special guest appearance by Lily Tomlin; Starring Alison Bartlett, Savion Glover, and Sesame Street Muppet Performers Carol Spinney, Frank Oz, Martin P. Roninson, Kevin Clash, Jerry Nelson, and Fran Brill. New York: Sony Wonder, 1996. ISBN 1-57330-556-1. 60 minutes. Grades K–2**
This video is a perfect way to introduce children to multiculturalism. The Monster News Network takes us to New Year's celebrations around the world. Join Big Bird, Cookie Monster, Bert, Ernie and the Sesame Street cast on location in Japan, Israel, Mexico, Portugal, Germany, and Norway as each sees in the New Year. Songs include "We're Gonna Stay Up Late and Party," "Mexican Folk Song," "Oshogatsu," "Bashanah Hanaah," "Rummel Pot Song," "It's New Year's Eve," "New Year Chorale for Six Grouches," and "Faces That I Love."

***Travel the World with Timmy*** **Deluxe [interactive multimedia]. Redmond, WA: Edmark, 1999. Grades K-2**
In this delightful animated program, children can travel to Argentina, France, Japan, Kenya, and Russia to learn about the countries' people, places, and cultures. They can learn songs, hear stories, try arts and crafts, play games, and practice word activities. This edition also features a talking picture dictionary. The CD-ROM is easy to navigate. Teachers can print materials for use in the classroom. A school version is also available with a teacher's manual.

***Where in the World is Carmen Sandiego?*** **[interactive multimedia]. Novato, CA: Broderbund Software, Inc., 1992. Grade 3+**
Geography is fun with this popular program available in both video and CD-ROM formats. Follow Carmen Sandiego and her gang as they travel the world stealing famous treasures and landmarks. Become a detective with the Acme Detective Agency and decipher clues from the *World Almanac and Book of Facts* to stop this crime spree. Kids enjoy mastering progressive levels of difficulty.

***Where on Earth is Carmen Sandiego?*** [videorecording]. **Produced by Michael Maliani; directed by Joe Barruso. Beverly Hills, CA: Fox Kids Video, 1995. ISBN 0-7939-8742-3. 43 minutes. Grade 3+**

Join Zack and Ivy as they follow Carmen Sandiego's clues. With the help of Acme's Detective Armando, they track Carmen as she steals the Mona Lisa's smile, the eyes of a van Gogh painting, and a note from Picasso. Although the video is no longer produced, children will enjoy the adventure if the school or public library has a copy available.

***Year 2000 Grolier Multimedia Encyclopedia School Edition*** [interactive multimedia]. **Danbury, CT: Grolier Interactive, 2000. Grade 4+**

Look for yearly updates of this quality multimedia encyclopedia that combines the worlds of CD-ROM and the Internet. The 37,000 entry articles, dictionary, research starters, and *New York Times* Science Questions and Answers are user-friendly. Children will love the ease of use and the interactive multimedia features that take them into the world of graphics, audio clips, and 3D cutaways. The one-CD school edition features a valuable 125-page teacher's guide.

# *Festivals, Foods, Holidays, Customs, and Games*

**Ajmera, Maya, and Michael Regan.** *Let the Games Begin!* **Developed by Shakti for Children. Foreword by Bill Bradley. Watertown, MA: Charlesbridge, 2000. ISBN 0-88106-067-4. 32 pages. Grades 3–6**

In the foreword, former senator and New York Knicks star Bill Bradley sets the stage by talking about the importance of sports in his life. The book encourages children to find joy and values of confidence, teamwork, and perseverance through sports. The format is visually appealing; each two-page spread is devoted to an aspect of sports with five color illustrations of children of various nations involved in the sport. The children's quotes offer valuable advice to children about participating in the sport.

**Angell, Carole S.** *Celebrations Around the World: A Multicultural Handbook.* **Golden, CO: Fulcrum, 1996. ISBN 1-55591-945-6. 256 pages. All ages**

Angell introduces more than 300 fixed and non-fixed holidays by month with background and context in this invaluable resource. The appendices are especially pleasing: trade books, recipes, and music of each country, followed by a bibliography and index.

**Baker, Beth A., ed.** *Holidays and Anniversaries of the World: A Comprehensive Catalogue Containing Detailed Information on Every Month and Day of the Year,* **3rd ed. Detroit: Gale, 1998. ISBN 0-8103-5477-2. 1,184 pages. Grade 6+**

Want to know what happened on your birthday throughout history? Need to see when a certain holiday will be in 2004? This valuable resource has more than 26,000 brief entries for regional, national, and international holidays; birth dates of noted people in all fields; and historical events that have affected the world—each arranged chronologically within selections for holidays, religious calendar, birth dates, and historical events. Baker explains how the modern calendar came to be, presents movable holidays and a perpetual calendar, time words, and an extensive glossary. Information is readily accessible through the index of names, terms, and events.

**Campbell, Louise.** *A World of Holidays!* Family ties series. Illustrated by Michael Bryant. New York: Silver Moon Press, 1993. ISBN 1-881889-08-4. 61 pages. Grades 3–5

Campbell introduces different types of holidays and explains how they are celebrated around the world. She follows each with a story showing how a particular culture celebrates the day. Midori understands her mistakes are forgiven in "The Beautiful Birds," a New Year's story from Japan. In "The New Moon," a sensitive Ramadan and Eid-ul-Fitr story from Pakistan, Mahmood learns responsibility for his brother and Khalid learns responsibility for the poor. In "The Great Day," Paandu learns why Independence Day is so special in Namibia. Winona appreciates the gifts of nature in "The Three Sisters" from Canada. Rosa and Lourdes discover the unselfish way to celebrate Las Posadas in Mexico in "The Marvelous Time."

**Cappelloni, Nancy.** *Ethnic Cooking the Microwave Way.* Easy menu ethnic cookbooks series. Photos by Robert L. and Diane Wolf. Minneapolis: Lerner, 1994. ISBN 0-8225-0929-6. 47 pages. Grade 3+

This volume of the popular series addresses the merits and methods of microwave cooking. Cappelloni includes recipes from around the world for beverages, appetizers, soups, side dishes, main dishes, and desserts. Try recipes like beaten egg soup from Japan, pearl meatballs from China, and red lentil curry from Sri Lanka.

**Cole, Trish.** *Why Do We Wear That?* Why do we series. New York: Franklin Watts, 1996. ISBN 0-531-14396-1. 32 pages. Grades 4–7

Cole surveys the history of clothing and accessories in this fascinating book. Double-page spreads with color illustrations (some cartoons) answer why we wear clothes and who wears the pants. Cole looks at footwear, lingerie, skirts, saris, sport clothes, jackets, shirts, waistcoats, suits, uniforms, hats, wigs, jewelry, make-up, hairdos, and tattoos through the ages. There are so many interesting and fun facts to share that the pages are overcrowded and the text is small.

*Desserts Around the World.* Easy menu ethnic cookbooks series. Photos by Robert L. and Diane Wolf. Minneapolis: Lerner, 1991. ISBN 0-8225-0926-1. 55 pages. Grade 3+

What could be more tempting than an international array of desserts? Directions are easy to follow for recipes, including sweet balls from Ghana, stuffed pancakes from Lebanon, mango with cinnamon from Mexico, and milk pudding from Brazil.

**Doney, Meryl.** *Games.* World crafts series. New York: Franklin Watts, 1996. ISBN 0-531-14405-4. 32 pages. Grade 2+

This illustrated history of games features maps highlighted to show the origins of the games. It shows games that are similar in different countries and includes projects for creating games.

**Doney, Meryl.** *Festivals.* World crafts series. New York: Franklin Watts, 1997. ISBN 0-531-14431-3. 32 pages. Grade 2+

Follow the easy instructions to create crafts for holidays from around the world, including projects for Chinese New Year and honoring ancestors, Burmese and Indian Founder's Day, Pakistani Eid festivals, Russian Easter and everyday celebrations, and India's Festival of Lights, Christmas, and Spring Festival.

**Doney, Meryl.** *Papercraft.* **World crafts series. New York: Franklin Watts, 1997. ISBN 0-531-14446-1. 32 pages. Grade 3+**

Trace the history of paper throughout the world. Learn how to make paper and how to create objects from paper with folding and cutting techniques.

**Dooley, Norah.** *Everybody Bakes Bread.* **Illustrated by Peter J. Thornton. Minneapolis: Carolrhoda, 1996. ISBN 0-87614-864-X. 48 pages. Grades K–3**

In this sequel to *Everybody Cooks Rice* (see below), Carrie and Anthony are restless when their mother is baking great-grandmother's Italian bread. Mother sends Carrie off to the multi-ethnic neighborhood to find a three-handled rolling pin. As Carrie goes on her impossible quest, she discovers everybody is baking bread. After she samples coconut bread from Barbados, chapattis from India, pocket bread from the Middle East, challah from Israel, and pupusa from El Salvador, she returns home full. Mother has finished her baking, too. Recipes follow.

**Dooley, Norah.** *Everybody Cooks Rice.* **Illustrated by Peter J. Thornton. Minneapolis: Carolrhoda, 1991. ISBN 0-87614-412-X. 48 pages. Grades K–3**

It's dinnertime, and Anthony is missing. His sister Carrie searches the neighborhood and receives a tour of the world as she samples rice dishes everyone is cooking for dinner. Dooley and Thornton create a multi-ethnic neighborhood filled with friendly people and weave in a lesson about some of their foods. Carrie samples various rice dishes (with black-eyed peas from Barbados, with pigeon peas from Puerto Rico, with nuoc cham sauce from Vietnam, with tofu and vegetables from China, with hot peppers and red beans from Haiti, and biryani from India) and arrives home to find Anthony safe and sound as her mother serves visie bisi (rice with green peas). Recipes follow.

**Dooley, Norah.** *Everybody Serves Soup.* **Illustrated by Peter J. Thornton. Minneapolis: Carolrhoda, 2000. ISBN 0-87614-422-1. 48 pages. Grades K–3**

In this now familiar pattern, Dooley and Thornton show the riches of a multi-ethnic neighborhood. During a snowstorm, Carrie tries to earn money for her mother's Christmas gift. After shoveling snow and warming up with soup at the neighbors' homes, Carrie discovers the perfect gift: a soup cookbook. "It's not just soup. It comes from the heart," she says. Recipes for Puerto Rican chuleton, Greek avgolemono, Japanese miso, and other soups follow.

**Dunn, Opal.** *Acka Backa Boo! Playground Games from Around the World.* **Illustrated by Susan Winter. New York: Henry Holt, 2000. ISBN 0-8050-6424-9. 46 pages. Grades K–3**

In this joyful international collection, Dunn emphasizes the benefits of play and the globalization of traditional games. Children learn language, values, and socialization by playing games. She divides games by similar techniques and goals, including Easy-Peasy, You're It, Hands and Feet, catching, ball, hide-and-seek, singing, and clap, skip, and jump games. Left side borders list the names, descriptions, and countries of origin of the games. The remainder of the double-page spread features charming watercolors of multicultural groups of children and rhymes to accompany the games.

**Erlbach, Arlene.** *Sidewalk Games Around the World.* **Illustrated by Sharon Lane Holm. Brookfield, CT: Millbrook Press, 1997. ISBN 0-7613-0008-2. 64 pages. Grades 3–5**
Erlbach introduces the history, description, and rules of children's "sidewalk" games from 26 countries around the world. Holms decorates the pages with items appropriate to the country and provides maps showing the origins of the games.

**Feldman, Eve B.** *Birthdays! Celebrating Life Around the World.* **Children's art provided by Paintbrush Diplomacy Exchange Program. Mahwah, NJ: BridgeWater, 1996. ISBN 0-8167-3494-1. 32 pages. Grades K–3**
Birthdays are special in every country of the world. Feldman's simple text and joyful, ingenuous paintings by children share some of the ways birthday celebrations are alike and different in other countries.

**Gilchrist, Cherry.** *A Calendar of Festivals.* **Illustrated by Helen Cann. New York: Barefoot Books, 2000. ISBN 1-84148-244-7. 80 pages. Grades 3–7**
This is a joyful collection of introductions to eight multicultural holidays, including Purim, Holi, Vesak, Tanabata, Halloween, Christmas, Kwanzaa, and New Year. Cann's glowing borders and fluent characters grace Gilchrist's accompanying stories that provide insight into Jewish, Hindu, Buddhist, Japanese, Celtic, Christian, Caribbean, and Russian traditions.

**Gulevich, Tanya.** *Encyclopedia of Christmas.* **Illustrated by Mary Ann Stavros-Lanning. Detroit: Omnigraphics, 1999. ISBN 0-7808-0387-6. 450 pages. Teacher Reference**
Learn about Christmas and the season from Advent to Zagmuk. The subtitle of this ambitious volume says it all: "Nearly 200 alphabetically arranged entries covering all aspects of Christmas, including folk customs, religious observances, history, legends, symbols, and related days from Europe, America, and around the world. Supplemented by a bibliography and lists of Christmas Web sites and associations, as well as an index." There are some b&w illustrations, but the scope and depth of the text are the strength of this volume.

**Gulevich, Tanya, ed.** *World Holiday, Festival, and Calendar Books.* **Detroit: Omnigraphics, 1998. ISBN 0-7808-0073-7. 477 pages. Teacher Reference**
This valuable annotated bibliography of more than 1,000 books about celebrations is organized by World Holidays, Religious Holidays, Ethnic and National Holidays, and Calendar and Time-Reckoning Systems. Get more information from the periodicals, associations, and Web sites found in the appendices.

**Gust, John, and J. Meghan McChesney.** *Learning About Cultures: Literature, Celebrations, Games and Art Activities.* **Illustrated by Marilynn G. Barr. Carthage, IL: Teaching and Learning Company, 1995. ISBN 1-57310-012-9. 138 pages. Grades 3–6**
Gust and McChesney provide an overview of African-American, Arabic, Chinese, Japanese, Jewish, Korean, Mexican, and Native American cultures through literature, games, and crafts.

**Haven, Kendall.** *New Year's to Kwanzaa: Original Stories of Celebration.* **Golden, CO: Fulcrum, 1999. ISBN 1-55591-962-6. 226 pages. Grades 3–8**
Storyteller Kendall Haven created 36 original stories to capture the customs and rites of

holidays from diverse cultures and religions that are celebrated in the United States. Share stories about Vietnamese, Chinese, and Nigerian New Year's, Japanese Tanabata Matsuri, Mexican Day of the Dead, Nigerian harvest festival, and India's Holi. Haven introduces each story and offers follow-up questions to explore and suggested activities for each in this valuable multicultural resource.

**Henderson, Helene and Sue Ellen Thompson, eds.** *Holidays, Festivals, and Celebrations of the World Dictionary.* **Detroit: Omnigraphics, 1997. ISBN 0-7808-0012-5. 885 pages. Teacher Reference**
This is one of the most extensive references available, indexing more than 2,000 events by ethnic and geographic, religious, chronological, folkloric, and historic, as well as by state, country, subject, and alphabetical order. The second edition also has Web sites, contacts, sources, and a special section on the millennium.

**Kindersley, Barnabas and Anabel.** *Children Just Like Me: Celebrations!* **New York: Dorling Kindersley, 1997. ISBN 0-7894-2027-9. 64 pages. Grades 2–5**
Photographer-and-writer team Barnabas and Anabel Kindersley traveled around the world, interviewing children about their festivals, carnivals, and feast days. Learn about Chinese New Year in Hong Kong, Carnival in Brazil, N'cwala in Zambia, Hina Matsuri in Japan, Holi in India, Fassika (Easter) in Ethiopia, Cocuk Bayrami in Turkey, Kodomono-hi in Japan, Esala Perahera in Sri Lanka, Raksha Bandhan in India, Eid ul-Fitr in Jordan, Trung Thu in Vietnam, Day of the Dead in Mexico, and Diwali in India.

**Kirtland, Mark.** *Why Do We Do That?* **Why do we series. New York: Franklin Watts, 1996. ISBN 0-531-14394-5. 32 pages. Grades 4–7**
Kirtland offers an illuminating history of manners and customs. Double-page spreads with color illustrations (some cartoons) address greeting and saying good-bye to people, talking and writing, courting, meeting people, serving food, royalty, behavior at school and work, entertainment, sports, fighting, artistic expressions, and showing power and wealth. There are so many interesting and fun facts to share that the pages are overcrowded and the text is small.

**Lakin, Patricia.** *Play: Around the World.* **We all share series. Woodbridge, CT: Blackbirch, 1995. ISBN 1-156711-141-6. 32 pages. Grades 2–4**
Enjoy games and diversions of the children of the world with this joyful book. Learn how children play in Brazil, China, Russia, Mexico, Kenya, Israel, Egypt, and Pakistan.

**Lankford, Mary D.** *Dominoes Around the World.* **Illustrated by Karen Dugan. New York: Morrow, 1998. ISBN 0-688-14052-1. 40 pages. Grades 3–5**
Lankford explains variations of dominoes from other countries, including Malta, Ukraine, and Vietnam. She provides background on the game, rules for playing, and the game origins for each of the eight countries featured. Dugan's cheerful illustrations show children in action enjoying the game.

**Lankford, Mary D.** *Hopscotch Around the World.* **Illustrated by Karen Milone. New York: Morrow, 1992. ISBN 0-688-08419-2. 47 pages. Grades 3–7**
Milone's pencil and watercolor illustrations and maps indicating the origins of the games

complement Lankford's careful research and step-by-step directions for 19 variations of hopscotch from countries including Aruba, Nigeria, Bolivia, and China.

**Lankford, Mary D.** *Jacks Around the World.* **Illustrated by Karen Dugan. New York: Morrow, 1996. ISBN 0-688-13707-5. 40 pages. Grade 3–7**
Games of jacks, called by local names, exist in most countries. Lankford includes games for Brazil, Israel, Trinidad and Tobago, Zimbabwe, New Zealand, and Somalia. Colorful pencil and watercolor illustrations, maps marking the geographic area of each game, the games' histories, facts about the country of origin, and detailed directions for playing make this a wonderful resource.

**Lauber, Patricia.** *What You Never Knew About Fingers, Forks, and Chopsticks.* **Illustrated by John Manders. New York: Simon and Schuster, 1999. ISBN 0-689-80479-2. 40 pages. Grade 1+**
When did people stop eating with their fingers? What did people do with greasy fingers? How do people show pleasure with their food? This informative and often humorous book surveys international eating customs and table manners from the Stone Ages to today. The illustrations are cartoonish and exaggerated and add to the fun of the journey through the ages. The closing double-page spread of table manners and modern cookout will elicit chuckles. An extensive bibliography follows.

**Levinson, David, and Karen Christensen, eds.** *The Encyclopedia of World Sport: From Ancient Times to the Present*, **3 volumes. Santa Barbara: ABC-CLIO, 1996. ISBN 0-87436-819-7. 1,317 pages. Grade 7+ and Teacher Reference**
The editors emphasize the globalization of sports, teamwork, dynamics, trends, and sportsmanship in this tour de force three-volume guide. They provide in-depth coverage and scholarly essays on more than 300 sports. The essays analyze the origin, significance, training, development, and future of the sports. Essays address every aspect of the sport—from the physical logistics to the psychological and social implications. The inclusion of some entries initially gave me pause until I made the connections to sports. (For example, I found "animal rights" an unusual topic until I read about the concerns about animal-baiting, greyhound racing, and hunting as sports.) I am not a sports enthusiast, but I found these encyclopedia entries compelling and fascinating.

**Livingston, Myra Cohn.** *Festivals.* **Illustrated by Leonard Everett Fisher. New York: Holiday House, 1996. ISBN 0-8234-1217-2. 32 pages. Grades K–3**
Respected poet Livingston captures the essence of each multicultural holiday with her vivid images and powerful rhythms. Master artist Fisher showcases different styles of art to match each culture. Chinese New Year, Tet Nguyen-Dan, Purim, Cherry Blossom Festival, Now-Ruz, Ramadan and Eid-ul-Fitr, Diwali, the Day of the Dead, and Las Posadas are among the holidays featured. A glossary explains the background and importance of each.

**Markel, Michelle.** *Cornhusk, Silk, and Wishbones: A Book of Dolls From Around the World.* **Boston: Houghton Mifflin, 2000. ISBN 0-6180-5487-1. 48 pages. Grade K+**
Whether fashioned from high-tech synthetics or rags and fruit, dolls are a universal symbol of childhood and joy. Children through all times in all countries have loved and collected them. Markel shares her affection for and fascination with dolls through fabulous

color photography and lively text. Enter into the world of memories and dreams as Markel examines traditional dolls and unique ones made from unlikely materials like chicken bones and sealskin.

**Markham, Lois.** *Harvest.* **World celebrations and ceremonies series. Woodbridge, CT: Blackbirch, 1999. ISBN 1-56711-275-7. 24 pages. Grades 3–7**
In most countries there are harvest festivals or special celebrations for the gathering of crops. Learn about celebrations in Brazil, England, India, Israel, Japan or China, Mexico, Nigeria, Puerto Rico, Russia, and the United States, such as the Festa da Uva (Festival of the Grapes) in January in Brazil, the Mid-Autumn Festival in the fall in China, Pongal in January in India, Sukkot in the fall in Israel, and the New Yam Festival in July or August in Nigeria. For each country, Markham includes a country map, a global map to show the country in context of the world, and color photos of the customs, foods, dance, costumes, and rituals of the holiday. These comparisons of cultures are a wonderful springboard for multicultural studies and awareness activities.

**Marks, Diana F.** *Let's Celebrate Today: Calendars, Events, and Holidays.* **Englewood, CO: Libraries Unlimited, 1998. ISBN 1-56308-558-5. 337 pages. Teacher Reference**
Marks includes movable and fixed-date world celebrations by month and suggests activities for each event, along with Web sites and other resources.

**Milord, Susan.** *Hands Around the World: 365 Creative Ways to Build Cultural Awareness and Global Respect.* **Milwaukee: Gareth Stevens, 1999. ISBN 0-8368-2231-5. 160 pages. Grades 3–6**
Did you know field hockey originated in Asia, spinach came from Persia, and children play Cossacks and Robbers in Russia? In Java, children straddle bamboo poles and fight with pillows. In West Africa, they play hide-and-seek in the sand. Learn these and many more unusual things about the world's agriculture, games, calendars, celebrations, language, and life, all interwoven into narratives for each day of the year. Although it is cumbersome to locate details about specific countries from indexed pages, this lively resource is well worth exploring.

**Moehn, Heather.** *World Holidays: A Watts Guide for Children.* **New York: Franklin Watts, 2000. ISBN 0-531-11714-6. 123 pages. Grades 2–8**
Introduce children to celebrations around the world from Adults' Day to Yom Kippur in this alluring encyclopedia of religious, national, and seasonal holidays. Search the contents page or the index and explore the cross-references. Be sure to read the explanations of the Roman, Julian, Gregorian, Jewish, Hindu, Chinese, and Islamic calendars. Another valuable feature is the holiday calendar, showing key holidays by month for the years 2001 through 2005.

**Nelson, Wayne E. and Henry "Buzz" Glass.** *International Playtime: Classroom Games and Dances from Around the World.* **Carthage, IL: Fearon Teacher Aids, 1992. ISBN 0-86653-990-5. 239 pages. Grades K–8**
Nelson and Glass's treasury of games and dances helps children learn about the people and cultures of Africa, Asia, Caribbean, Central America, Middle East, Pacific, and South America.

**Oakley, Ruth.** *Games with Rope and String.* **Illustrated by Steve Lucas. Games children play around the world series. Tarrytown, NY: Marshall Cavendish, 1989. ISBN 1-8543-5081-1. 48 pages. Grade 3+**
Create a magical world from string. See how children around the world tell stories and play games using rope and string.

**Robins, Deri.** *Kids Around-the-World Cookbook.* **Illustrated by Charlotte Stowell. New York: Kingfisher, 1994. ISBN 1-85697-627-0. 40 pages. Grades 3–6**
Colorful illustrations of children and animals and signs and symbols of the varying countries enhance this easy, step-by-step cookbook for kids. Recipes include hummus from Turkey, Smetana mushrooms from Russia, banana raitha from India, chicken satay from Indonesia and Thailand, tortillas from Mexico, pineapple ice cream from the Caribbean, bobotie from Africa, pavlova from Australia, and borek from the Middle East.

**Rufus, Anneli S.** *The World Holiday Book: Celebrations for Every Day of the Year.* **San Francisco: HarperSanFrancisco, 1994. ISBN 0-06-250912-8. 374 pages. Grade 3+**
Rufus includes information about 365 holidays, including well-known ones like New Year's Day and Christmas, lesser-known days like Ladies' Day, and celebrations from around the world like Big Kite Flying (Odakaoge) and Warriors' Memorial (Gishi-sai).

**Sita, Lisa.** *Coming of Age.* **World celebrations and ceremonies series. Woodbridge, CT: Blackbirch, 1999. ISBN 1-56711-276-5. 24 pages. Grades 3–7**
In most countries, there are special celebrations when a child comes of age. Learn about these rites in Brazil, England, India, Israel, Japan or China, Mexico, Nigeria, Puerto Rico, Russia, and the United States, including the Upanayam ceremony in India. Join the hunting party for Yanomami boys in Brazil, Quince Anos in Mexico, and the Coming-of-Age ceremony in Japan. For each country, Sita includes a country map, a global map to show the country in context of the world, and color photos of the customs, foods, dance, costumes, and rituals of the holiday. These comparisons of cultures serve as an effective springboard for multicultural studies and awareness activities.

**Solheim, James.** *It's Disgusting—And We Ate It! True Food Facts from Around the World—And Throughout History!* **Illustrated by Eric Brace. New York: Simon and Schuster, 1998. ISBN 0-689-80675-2. 44 pages. Grades K–3**
The title says it all. If horse blood and earthworm soup are your cup of tea, you'll gobble up this history. Readers, especially boys, will revel in fascinating food facts. Solheim spans cultures and times, examining tastes, unusual dishes, and the scoop on some of today's favorites.

**Spirn, Michele.** *Birth.* **World celebrations and ceremonies series. Woodbridge, CT: Blackbirch, 1999. ISBN 1-56711-277-3. 24 pages. Grades 3–7**
Spirn examines ways people celebrate the birth of babies in Brazil, England, India, Israel, Japan, China, Mexico, Nigeria, Puerto Rico, Russia, and the United States. For each country, she includes a country map, a global map to show the country in context of the world, and color photos of the ritual of celebration. Travel to Brazil for a drum ceremony to announce the birth of the baby, attend a naming party in India or Africa, or

visit a Shinto shrine in Japan. These comparisons of cultures are a wonderful springboard for multicultural studies and awareness activities.

**Spirn, Michele.** *New Year.* **World celebrations and ceremonies series. Woodbridge, CT: Blackbirch, 1999. ISBN 1-56711-249-8. 24 pages. Grades 3–7**
Not everyone celebrates the new year on the first of January. Spirn explains how the different calendars determine the holidays and shares the ways people celebrate the new year in Brazil, England, India, Israel, Japan or China, Mexico, Nigeria, Puerto Rico, Russia, and the United States. For each country, she includes a country map, a global map to show the country in context of the world, and color photos of the customs, foods, dance, costumes, and rituals of the holiday. Celebrate the Chinese New Year Lantern Festival, the Hindu holiday of Diwali, Rosh Hashanah in Israel, and New Year's Day in England and Russia. These comparisons of cultures facilitate multicultural studies and awareness activities.

**Swain, Gwenyth.** *Carrying.* **Small world series. Minneapolis: Carolrhoda Books, 1999. ISBN 1-57505-359-8. 24 pages. Grades K–1**
Children take carrying things for granted. Swain shows how what people carry and how they carry it can reflect their culture and country. Discuss ways children of the world are alike and different through the brilliant color photos of girls carrying babies and dolls in Cameroon, a boy carrying a fish to market in the Philippines, girls carrying jars of water on their heads in India, and a clown carrying a child in Wisconsin.

**Swain, Gwenyth.** *Celebrating.* **Small world series. Minneapolis: Carolrhoda Books, 1999. ISBN 1-57505-258-X. 24 pages. Grades K–1**
This simple rhymed verse and color photos reveal some of the things and ways people celebrate around the world. Share the joy with children celebrating such times as the 50th anniversary of the Workers' Party, a girl in Mali boasting a new hairdo for a special day, a day in the park in Hanoi, and a day with friends in Nebraska.

**Swain, Gwenyth.** *Eating.* **Small world series. Minneapolis: Carolrhoda Books, 1999. ISBN 1-57505-257-1. 24 pages. Grades K–1**
Children will enjoy this simple rhymed verse book about food. The expressive, colorful photos capture people in the joyful act of eating in places like the Philippines, India, Mexico, Morocco, Antarctica, and Moldova.

**Swain, Ruth Freeman.** *Bedtime!* **Illustrated by Cat Bowman Smith. New York: Holiday House, 1999. ISBN 0-8234-1444-2. 32 pages. Grades K–3**
What did people wear to bed in ancient Egypt? Who invented pillows? How can astronauts sleep in zero gravity? Explore some of these questions in this delightful history of sleeping customs from around the world. Smith's cartoon illustrations and Swain's striking tidbits make this a book kids will want to share.

**Vaughan, Marcia.** *How to Cook Gooseberry Fool: Unusual Recipes from Around the World.* **Easy menu ethnic cookbooks series. Photos by Robert L. and Diane Wolf. Minneapolis: Lerner, 1993. ISBN 0-8225-0928-8. 47 pages. Grade 3+**
The recipes in this book are as enticing as the title. In a fascinating introduction, Vaughan explains how some world recipes originated and how they got their funny

names. Experiment with beverages like spiders from Australia, appetizers like ants-on-a-log from the United States, soups like pick-a-pepper soup from Equatorial Guinea, side dishes like wow-wow sauce from England, main dishes like little shoes from Greece, and desserts like donkey ears from Mexico.

*Vegetarian Cooking Around the World*. **Photos by Robert L. and Diane Wolfe. Easy menu ethnic cookbooks series. Minneapolis: Lerner, 1992. ISBN 0-8225-0927-X. 47 pages. Grade 3+**

As more children explore options of vegetarian eating, this book discusses the philosophy and healthfulness of vegetarian food. It features easy-to-follow recipes for beverages, breads and staples, breakfast, lunch, dinner, and dessert. Try dishes like rice pancakes from Kenya, fruit muesli from Australia, and cornmeal coo-coo from Barbados.

**Vezza, Diane Simone.** *Passport on a Plate: A Round-the-World Cookbook for Children.* **Illustrated by Susan Greenstein. New York: Simon and Schuster, 1997. ISBN 0-689-80155-6. 150 pages. Grade 4+**

Despite the use of only minimal b&w illustrations, this cookbook is a wonderful resource for the regions of the world. There is an introduction to each country, including the characteristic foods and spices. The recipes are fabulous, including groundnut stew from Africa, curried coconut vegetables from the Caribbean, blushing pears from China, pillow bread from India, Christmas salad from Mexico, strawberries Romanoff from Russia, and parent and child rice bowl from Japan.

**Webb, Lois Sinako.** *Holidays of the World Cookbook for Students.* **Phoenix, AZ: Oryx, 1995. ISBN 0-89774-884-0. 297 pages. Grade 5+**

This cookbook, one of the most comprehensive collections of world recipes, offers far more than cooking tips. It is a treasury of world traditions and festivals and foods with a wealth of information about local holidays, customs, and the foods that are special to each. Webb includes 388 recipes from more than 136 countries. Although there are no illustrations, b&w maps highlight the region of the recipes. The glossary is one of the best available.

**Webb, Lois Sinako.** *Multicultural Cookbook of Life-Cycle Celebrations.* **Phoenix, AZ: Oryx, 2000. ISBN 1-57356-290-4. 473 pages. Grade 5+**

Webb shares more than 30 years of research and experience in this priceless collection of recipes updated and modernized for today's cooks and fat-conscious society. Webb explains that food is far more than life-sustaining. It marks all of life's passages and "communicates many things: a family's wealth and success, status within the society, family ties, and religious devotion." Learn about cultures of the world as Webb visits 145 countries. She introduces us to the location, history, ethnic and religious make-up of each country, and examples of local celebrations. The easy-to-follow recipes use common ingredients so anyone can make them. I've learned so much about world cultures from this cookbook!

**Wilcox, Jane.** *Why Do We Celebrate That?* **Why do we series. New York: Franklin Watts, 1996. ISBN 0-531-14393-7. 32 pages. Grades 4–7**

Wilcox looks at holidays, festivals, fasts, and feasts around the world in this valuable multicultural resource. Double-page spreads with color illustrations (some cartoons) look at celebrations for birth, coming of age, and death; for the four seasons; for birthdays; and for farming and harvest. Wilcox also shares national holidays (like Columbus Day, Independence Day, and Bastille Day) and "fantastic festivals" (like the running of the bulls in Pamplona, Red Nose Day, and Well-Dressing in England). The book is filled with interesting and fun facts, followed by a quiz.

**Wilcox, Jane.** *Why Do We Use That?* **Why do we series. New York: Franklin Watts, 1996. ISBN 0-531-14395-3. 32 pages. Grades 4–7**
Journey through time with Wilcox with this intriguing look at inventions and practicality. Learn how men and women used ingenuity to devise better ways for cleaning, cooking, shopping, and gardening. Double-page spreads with color illustrations (some cartoons) look at the origins of some of our favorite inventions for entertainment, comfort, and protection.

**Wilkinson, Philip.** *A Celebration of Customs and Rituals of the World.* **Illustrated by Robert R. Ingpen. New York: Facts on File, Inc., 1996. ISBN 0-8160-3479-6. 224 pages. Grades 5–8**
Wilkinson chronicles fascinating contemporary and traditional customs and rituals around the world with rich, colorful illustrations by Ingpen. The book highlights ceremonies of birth, death, coming-of-age and initiation, marriage, hunting, harvesting, eating and drinking, and healing.

**Wukovits, John.** *The Encyclopedia of World Sports.* **New York: Franklin Watts, 2001. ISBN 0-531-11777-4. 186 pages. Grades 4+**
Explore the world of sports from alpine skiing to yacht racing, from the popular to more specialized. The introduction by sports reporter Michael Freeman emphasizes sports as a "global community." Analysis of each event includes the origin, development, rules, history, key moments, greats, equipment, event, and best of the bests. The overview, complete with b&w and color photos, also gives the date and place of organization, governing body, legendary performers, championship events, and place of competition.

**Zaslavsky, Claudia.** *Math Games and Activities from Around the World.* **Chicago: Review Press, 1998. ISBN 1-5565-2287-8. 160 pages. Grades 4–7**
Entice students with more than 70 exciting activities from Japan, China, Africa, Australia, and other countries around the world. While students discover math can be fun, they will also learn about geography, art, and history.

# *Flags, Anthems, and Foreign Languages*

**Bukiet, Suzanne.** *Scripts of the World.* **Illustrated by Helene Muller and Christian Lai Cong Phuoc. Cincinnati: Multi-Cultural Books and Videos, Inc., and AIMS International Books, Inc., 1997. ISBN 0-9656274-1-1. 91 pages. Grades 5+**
Bukiet begins with a tale of how a young boy, Ajjar, created the first hand-drawn message. She gives an overview of the beginning of writing, the role of schools and libraries, and the five dominant language families today. B&w illustrations show

children against a background of the script of their language. Double-page-spread watercolors and pen-and-ink illustrations of the characteristic scripts introduce each of the five tales told, one from each language family. Although there is no introduction to the legends, they can stand alone as representatives of their cultures. Bukiet features "The Silken Beard" (Chinese), "Baba-Yaga" (Russian), "The Shepherd" (Arabian), "The Eclipse of the Sun" (Indian), and "The Flash of Lightning" (Celtic).

**Evans, Lezlie.** *Can You Count Ten Toes? Count to 10 in 10 Different Languages.* **Illustrated by Denis Roche. Boston: Houghton Mifflin, 1999. ISBN 0-395-90499-4. Grades K–3**
In this charming and colorful collaboration of rhyme, Evans and Roche unite the countries, their flags, and their people. Children will have fun speaking in different languages and deciphering the author's and illustrator's biographies by using numbers. Languages include Spanish, Japanese, Russian, Tagalog, and Hebrew.

*Flags of the World.* **Danbury, CT: Grolier Educational, 1997. ISBN 0-7172-9159-6 set. 64 pages per volume. Grade 3+**
This nine-volume encyclopedia of flags of the world offers the traditional features of flag information and country maps and facts. One of the most appealing features of this set is the inclusion of a traceable full-page color flag for each country. Regional color bands aid students in placing the country in the context of the world. The data file box includes land area, climate, major physical features, population, form of government, armed forces, largest cities, official language, ethnic composition, official religion, religious affiliations, currency, gross national product, gross domestic product, and major resources.

*Going to Grandma's Around the World* **[videorecording]. A Sing, Color 'n Say World of Languages Fun Video. Directed by Phillip Siadi. Troy, MI: Worldkids Press, 1998. ISBN 1-880449-21-8. 20 minutes. Grades K–2**
In this charming animated film, children sing the popular title song and travel to 10 different countries. Fun Facts sections introduce them to each country's culture, customs, and traits. Children will also learn to say "I love you Grandma" in Arabic, Hebrew, Japanese, French, Spanish, Polish, Hungarian, Russian, and Italian.

## *Folktales, Fairy Tales, Myths, and Legends*

**Barchers, Suzanne I.** *Multicultural Folktales: Readers Theatre for Elementary Students.* **Englewood, CO: Teacher Ideas Press, 2000. ISBN 1-56308-760-X. 188 pages. Teacher Reference for Grades 1–5**
How can children be actively involved in sharing world cultures? This collection of reproducible scripts from more than 30 countries and regions of the world is one answer. Introduce children to the joys of performing without the burdens of memorizing lines, expensive sets, and elaborate costumes. Readers' theater scripts are organized by recommended grade level and include brief plot summary, presentation and delivery suggestions, props, and characters. Present plays like "The Peach Boy" from Japan, "Baba-Yaga" from Russia, "Gifts of Love" from Korea, "Spider Flies to the Feast" from

Liberia, "The Tree That Bled Fish" from Micronesia, "Water, Water Will Be Mine" from Kenya, and "The Legend of the Feathered Serpent" from Mexico.

**Baumgartner, Barbara.** *Crocodile! Crocodile! Stories Told Around the World.* **Illustrated by Judith Moffatt. New York: Dorling Kindersley, 1994. ISBN 1-56458-463-1. 45 pages. Grades K–3**
Baumgartner retells popular stories in her own style, with deft narratives, catchy refrains, and clever animals. She encourages children to act out their own stories and includes instructions for making puppets. Moffatt's cut-paper illustrations are expressive, colorful, and fun. Share stories like the title story and "Crocodile Hunts for the Monkey" from India and "The Grateful Snake" from China.

**Baumgartner, Barbara.** *Good as Gold: Stories of Values from Around the World.* **Illustrated by Amanda Hall. New York: Dorling Kindersley, 1994. ISBN 0-7894-3482-2. 48 pages. Grades K–3**
All that glitters is not gold in this collection of tales about greed and worth. Baumgartner suggests it is not necessary to read each moral to children. Ask them to create tags for "Why the Beetle Has a Golden Coat" from Brazil, "Maria and the Stingy Baker" from Peru, "The Bird with Golden Feathers" from southern Africa, and "Two Brothers and the Pumpkin Seeds" from Korea.

**Brill, Marlene Targ.** *Tooth Tales from Around the World.* **Illustrated by Katya Krenina. Watertown, MA: Charlesbridge, 1998. ISBN 0-88106-398-3. 32 pages. Grades K–2**
Did you know evil witches steal teeth? Has the tooth mouse come to your house? Did the tooth fairy leave food under your pillow? Children will be fascinated with other countries' customs for lost teeth.

**Brown, Mary Ellen, and Bruce A. Rosenberg, eds.** *Encyclopedia of Folklore and Literature.* **Santa Barbara, CA: ABC-CLIO, 1998. ISBN 1-57607-003-4. 784 pages. Teacher Reference**
This comprehensive guide to folklore is impressive in scope (global and historical) and content. In a thought-provoking introduction, Brown shows how folklore is literature. She suggests that folklorists place more emphasis on the oral tradition, performance, and artistry than on the mechanics of composition. The more than 350 entries (arranged alphabetically) profile authors, works, scholars, movements, concepts, motifs, and terms that have shaped the rich heritage of folklore. Each offers cross-references and references to foster further study. A list of entries, entries arranged by category, and an index make this volume user-friendly.

**Caduto, Michael J.** *Earth Tales from Around the World.* **Illustrated by Adelaide Murphy Tyrol. Golden, CO: Fulcrum, ISBN 1-55591-968-5. 192 pages. Teacher Reference**
These tales of Earth, Sky, Fire, Water, Seasons and Weather, Plants, Animals, Circle of Life, Stewardship, and Wisdom come from all around the world and vary in their degrees of sophistication. Determine which to share with classes. "Lessons" follow each chapter with summaries of the key ideas of each story. Experiment with some of Caduto's "Activities" about the Earth and about Stories and Cultures. Caduto shows the depths of his research with detailed source notes.

**Climo, Shirley.** *A Pride of Princesses: Princess Tales From Around the World.* **Collected, retold, and annotated by Shirley Climo. Illustrated by Angelo Tillery. New York: HarperTrophy, 1999. ISBN 0-06-442101-3. 106 pages. Grades 4–7**
Girls hear fairy tales about princesses and dream of the happily-ever-after. Some of these stories are variations of familiar ones, like "Prince Ivan and the Frog Princess" and "King Thrushbeard" (*Taming of the Shrew* theme). Most, however, will be delightfully new. Learn about Mpunzanyana, the brave princess of the South African Xhosa, who marries a five-headed serpent to save her sister in "Two Brides for Five Heads" and Maix, a stubborn princess of the Central American Maya, who is captured by an ogre when she runs away with Tepe, the man she loves in "The Princess and the Music-Maker."

**Climo, Shirley.** *A Serenade of Mermaids: Mermaid Tales From Around the World.* **Collected, retold, and annotated by Shirley Climo. Illustrated by Lisa Falkenstern. New York: HarperTrophy, 1999. ISBN 0-06-442103-1. 101 pages. Grades 4–7**
Climo explains that most of the mermaid tales were of European origin and that now more non-Western tales are surfacing. She introduces tales from Japan, New Zealand, Iceland, Greece, Switzerland, Ireland, Scotland, and Alaska in this collection. My personal favorite is "The Listening Ear" from Japan, a variation of "The Listening Cap" (*See* DeSpain, Pleasant, page 39), in which a person is rewarded with the gift of the language of creatures of nature and earns riches and joy.

**Climo, Shirley.** *A Treasury of Mermaids: Mermaid Tales From Around the World.* **New York: HarperCollins, 1997. ISBN 0-06-023876-3. 80 pages. Grades 1–5**
Climo shows the importance of the sea in cultures of the world. Trace these compelling legends from Japan, New Zealand, and other countries through Jean and Mou-sien Tseng's evocative watercolors and pen-and-ink sketches.

**Creeden, Sharon.** *In Full Bloom: Tales of Women in Their Prime.* **Little Rock, AR: August House, 1999. ISBN 0-87483-576-3. Grade 7+**
In this fascinating collection, Creeden selects 30 tales from around the world and pairs them with biographies of mature women who embody matching traits and strengths. Part I, "Roses" ("beloved, idealized mothers, matriarchs, and saints"), includes "Grandmother Death" from Mexico, "Beruriah's Jewels" from Israel, "The Lion's Whiskers" from Ethiopia, "The Lady and the Unjust Judge" from Turkey, "Holding Up the Sky" from China, "The Old Woman and Tengu" from Japan, "Why Cat Lives with Woman" from Africa, and "Aunt Misery" from Puerto Rico. Part II includes biographies of American women who reveal the spirit of the stories and are the "Not Roses" ("women who are not the norm, unrestrained as wildflowers").

**Crossley-Holland, Kevin, ed.** *The Young Oxford Book of Folk Tales.* **New York: Oxford University Press, 1999. 213 pages. Grade 4+**
Travel the world through these 33 tales. Crossley-Holland shows the similarities among motifs and applauds the differences among customs and cultures. He divides his tales by Asia and India, the Near and Middle East, Europe, Africa, the Pacific, Central and South America, and North America. Some stories, like Iran's "The Forty Thieves" and Germany's "The Pied Piper of Hamelin," will be familiar. Some, like Japan's "The Tongue-cut Sparrow" and China's "The Magic Brocade," are frequently anthologized. Finds like

Romania's "Stan Bolovan" (who has 100 children) and Turkey's "Trousers Mehmet and the Sultan's Daughter" make this a valuable addition to a collection. Includes a glossary.

**DeSpain, Pleasant.** *Thirty-Three Multicultural Tales to Tell.* **Illustrated by Joe Shlichta. American storytelling series. Little Rock, AR: August House, 1993. ISBN 0-87483-265-9. 126 pages. Grade 3+**

Master storyteller DeSpain gathered 33 folktales from around the world (Guatemala, India, China, Germany, Africa, Russia, Fiji, Korea, Japan, Mexico, the United States, Holland, France, Greece, and Native America) and performed his magic on them. He retells them in lively language and a conversational format so they are easy to either read aloud or to learn. Personal favorites include "The Listening Cap" from Japan, "The Magic Pot" from China, and "The Mirror" from Korea. (Other collections by DeSpain are available in print and nonprint. *Multicultural Tales to Tell: Twenty Concise Folktales from Around the World* is available on audiocassette: 1994. ISBN 0-87483-345-0.)

**Doherty, Berlie, ed.** *Tales of Wonder and Magic.* **Illustrated by Juan Wijngaard. Cambridge, MA: Candlewick, 1998. ISBN 1-56402-891-7. 110 pages. Grades 5–8**

In this masterful collection, Doherty gathers nine magical tales from Africa, Australia, Europe, and North America and adds her own original tale, "The Girl Who Couldn't Walk." The rather sophisticated stories can nevertheless be told to younger children. The most unusual is "Chura and Marwe," a story from Africa told by Humphrey Harman. It is about two slaves, a beautiful girl and a toad-face boy, who are separated when they fear punishment from their owner. Marwe jumps into a pool, but enters the Underworld instead of drowning. Here she lives for years until she begs to return home. Chura proves himself among the Masai warriors and begins a new life, too. Their reunion and the happy ending will charm readers and listeners. The gouache paintings by Juan Wijngaard seem almost photographic in their detail and intensity. The story borders, appropriate for each culture, add a complementing touch.

**Evetts-Secker, Josephine.** *The Barefoot Book of Father and Son Tales.* **Illustrated by Helen Cann. Brooklyn, NY: Barefoot Books, 1999. ISBN 1-902283-32-5. 80 pages. Grades 1–5**

The relationship between a father and a son can be positive or negative, strong or weak, nurturing or hostile. In these 10 tales from around the world, the author examines the bond between father and son. She looks at the expectations and challenges of the father, his guidance, and the journey his son must take toward maturity and knowledge. "The Prodigal Son" is a familiar story from the Bible. This facile retelling and Cann's extraordinary watercolors with symbolic borders make it a new experience. Other favorites include the Chilean story "The Little Frog," in which three sons must complete tasks for their father, and the Polynesian tale "Maui-of-a-Thousand Tricks" in which Maui discovers fire and brings it back to man.

**Evetts-Secker, Josephine.** *The Barefoot Book of Mother and Son Tales.* **Illustrated by Helen Cann. Brooklyn, NY: Barefoot Books, 1999. ISBN 1-902283-05-8. 80 pages. Grades 1–5**

The relationships between mother and daughter and father and son are often explored. In this unusual collection, the author examines the bonds between mothers and sons and how some sons go on to become husbands and fathers and others remain immature sons. Helen Cann creates spectacular watercolors on each page with exquisite borders that echo the motifs of the country of origin. The infinitely patient deities in the Nepalese "The Goddess of Luck" reward a young boy. The Maori "The Boy and the Seedpod Canoe" shows the affinity between man and nature. The Greek "Cinderello" is a satisfying tale of magic. Enjoy these and other stories. Be sure to read Evetts-Secker's wonderful "Notes" where she analyzes the stories by themes of mother-son bond, mother and luck, separation, son's journey, heroes and magic, recurring symbols, son's bride, and autonomy.

**Ford, Linda M.** *Musings: Tales of Truth and Wisdom.* **Golden, CO: Fulcrum, 2000. ISBN 1-55591-980-4. 264 pages. Teacher Reference for Grade 4+**
This multicultural treasure has stories to fulfill all needs and occasions. The more than 300 folktales capture the hopes, fears, and dreams of people of more than 80 world cultures. Ford divides the stories by themes, including "Community," "Love and Family," "Resources," "Room for Improvement," "Beauty and Virtue," and "Wisdom and Foolishness." Story Themes and Cultures Cited indexes are helpful, as are detailed source notes. Select stories and help the children prepare and tell them.

**Forest, Heather.** *Wisdom Tales from Around the World.* **Little Rock, AR: August House, 1995. ISBN 0-87483-479-1. 156 pages. Grade 3+ and Teacher Reference**
The subtitle of this book read "Fifty Gems of Story and Wisdom From Such Diverse Traditions As Sufi, Zen, Taoist, Christian, Jewish, Buddhist, African, and Native American." Forest retells tales from around the world with her characteristic flair and poetry. In her introduction, she addresses the multiple levels of stories and their use as teaching tools. Children and adults will enjoy a wide range of tales including the Ashanti "Why Wisdom Is Everywhere," the Taoist parable "Blinded by Greed," the Jakata tale "The Talkative Turtle," and the Middle Eastern "Feeding His Clothes." All are designed for delivery to audiences and require little preparation.

**Forest, Heather.** *Wonder Tales from Around the World.* **Illustrations by David Boston. Little Rock, AR: August House, 1995. ISBN 0-87483-422-8. 155 pages. Grade 3+ and Teacher Reference**
Storyteller Heather Forest knows stories must be heard. She builds on the oral tradition with rhythms, repetitions, and dramatic tension to create this exceptional collection of world stories. Personal favorites for telling to classes include "The Talking Skull" from West Africa, "The Sad Story of Stone Frogs" from Australia, "The Tiger, the Brahman, and the Jackal" from India, and "The Boy Who Drew Cats" from Japan.

**Garrity, Linda K.** *The Tale Spinner: Folktales, Themes, and Activities.* **Golden, CO: Fulcrum, 1999. ISBN 1-55591-970-7. 192 pages. Grades 3–6**
Garrity's bountiful teacher's resource has stories, background information, and activities based on eight different themes. The Cinderella theme includes "Kongjee" from Korea and "Cam and the Magic Fish" from Vietnam. "Don't Believe Everything You Hear" includes "The Hare and the Rumor" from India.

**Gavin, Jamila, and Barnabas and Anabel Kindersley.** *Children Just Like Me: Our Favorite Stories From Around the World.* **Illustrated by Amanda Hall. New York: Dorling**

**Kindersley, 1997. ISBN 0-7894-1486-4. 79 pages. Grades 2–5**
Gavin retells stories introduced by 10 children from different countries of the world that first appeared in the Kindersleys' *Children Just Like Me*. Their stories show the universality of fears, dreams, imagination, and humor. Selections include "The Whistling Monster" from Brazil, "The Corn Maidens" from Mexico, "Witch of the Sands" from Botswana, "The Paradise City" from Morocco, "The Birth of Krishna" from India, "Gulnara the Warrior" from Mongolia, and "Rona and the New Moon" from New Zealand.

**Hamilton, Martha, and Mitch Weiss.** *How and Why Stories: World Tales Kids Can Read and Tell*. **Illustrations by Carol Lyon. Little Rock, AR: August House, 1999. ISBN 0-87483-562-3. 96 pages. Grade 3+**
Master storytellers Hamilton and Weiss, also known as "Beauty and the Beast," collected 25 pourquoi tales from around the world. Discover "How Tigers Got Their Stripes" (Vietnam), "How Brazilian Beetles Got Their Gorgeous Coats" (Brazil), and "Why Ants Are Found Everywhere" (Burma). The stories are designed for delivery and are followed by notes about the stories and tips for telling.

**Hamilton, Martha, and Mitch Weiss.** *Noodlehead Stories: World Tales Kids Can Read and Tell*. **Little Rock, AR: August House, 2000. ISBN 0-87483-584-4. 96 pages. Grade 3+**
This latest collection from storytellers Hamilton and Weiss ("Beauty and the Beast") is full of fools and folly from such places as Uruguay, Lebanon, Indonesia, Ghana, and Iceland. Each brief story is intended for telling and is followed by notes about the story and tips for telling. Try to top the noodleheads in "What a Bargain!" from Arabia, in which the husband ends up selling his cow to himself and the wife adds her silver bracelet to a sale of thread to increase the weight and price! Or try "The Donkey Egg" from Algeria, in which a boy pays 100 coins for a watermelon he thinks is a donkey egg. The authors point out that "these noodle stories are not meant to be told for the purpose of making fun of others, but rather in the spirit of laughing at the noodlehead in all of us."

**Harrison, Michael, and Christopher Stuart-Clark, eds.** *The Oxford Treasury of World Stories*. **New York: Oxford University Press, 1998. ISBN 0-19-278144-8. 144 pages. Grades 4–8**
Although I would have liked an introduction to this collection of 23 global stories (each from a different country), the stories themselves will fill a gap in your collections. The volume includes retellings of classics like "Cinderella" from the United States, "The Fox and the Tomten" from Sweden, and "Momotaro the Peach Boy" from Japan. Other familiar characters, like Anansi and Robin Hood, appear with a new cast of characters. Students will enjoy lesser-known stories like "The Lake Lovers," a happily-ever-after Maori tale from New Zealand; "The Barber's Wife," a tale from India about the worst barber and his clever wife; and "The Seven Baldies and One Shorty," a humorous story from Mongolia. The source notes are personalized and interesting.

**Hausman, Gerald and Loretta.** *Dog Myths from Around the World*. **Illustrated by Barry Moser. New York: Simon and Schuster, 1999. ISBN 0-689-80696-5. 96 pages. Grades 4–7**
These 13 stories from 13 cultures center around man's best friend. "The Gift of Fire: A Basenji Tale," from Africa, explains how Rukuba stole fire from his master to give to

mankind. As punishment, he lost his voice. The Hausmans offer trickster tales (like "How Dog Brought Death into the World: A Husky Tale"), enchanted dog tales (like "The Ghostly Weaver: A Retriever Tale"), guardian dog tales (like "The Seven Sleepers: A Saluki Tale"), super dog tales (like "The Dog Who Married a Princess: A Shar-pei Tale"), and treasure dog tales (like "The Dog, the Cat, the Snake, and the Ring: A Bichon Frise Tale"). Moser's watercolors capture the spirit, loyalty, and soul of the indispensable canines.

**Hausman, Loretta, and Gerald Hausman.** *Cats of Myth: Tales from Around the World.* **Illustrated by Leslie Baker. New York: Simon and Schuster, 1999. ISBN 0-689-82320-7. 96 pages. Grade 1+**
Many people think of cats as sleek, sassy, proud, or aloof. These nine stories from places like East India, Japan, Egypt, and Southeast Asia will expand the description. Add the words regal, magical, and cunning. The authors classify these diverse tales as "The Creation Cat," "The Trickster Cat," "The Goddess Cat," "The Monster Cat," and "The Guardian Cat." Purr with contentment as you read these stories and their illuminating afterwords. Leslie Baker can win over even the most resistant as cat-lovers with her engaging watercolors. I just wish there were more of them!

**Hazell, Rebecca.** *The Barefoot Book of Heroic Children.* **Illustrated by Helen Cann. Brooklyn, NY: Barefoot Books, 2000. ISBN 1-902283-23-6. 96 pages. Grades 1–5**
Children can be heroic in many different ways, Hazell tells us. Some are brave, some overcome physical disabilities and social conditions, and some make the best of what they have. Hazell introduces each of her heroic children and sets the stage for the child to tell his or her own story. Each is followed by an epilogue detailing the rest of the life of the child. Cann's eye for detail and her signature borders enrich the stories of Anne Frank, Pocahontas, Milarepa, Sundiata, Fanny Mendelssohn, Anne Sullivan and Helen Keller, Wilma Rudolph, Alexander Graham Bell, Louis IX, David (Bible), and Sadako Sasani. The final portrait is the compelling story of Iqbal Masih, a Pakistani boy sold at the age of four to a carpet factory owner. His work to free children from bondage and his murder at the age of 12 is a tale that will provoke discussions on many fronts.

**Hoffman, Mary.** *The Barefoot Book of Brother and Sister Tales.* **Illustrated by Emma Shaw-Smith. Brooklyn, NY: Barefoot Books, 2000. ISBN 1-84148-029-0. 64 pages. Grades 1–5**
Although rivalry and jealousy can color relationships, siblings forge indestructible bonds. There is no fiercer protector than a sibling. Hoffman retells traditional brother-and-sister stories like the German "Hansel and Gretel" and explores thematic variations of stepfamilies in the Armenian "The Red Cow" and the Sudanese "Achol and Maper." The unusual Russian tale, "Alionushka and Ivanushka," is one of enchantment and a wicked sorceress who turns the princess's brother into a kid goat and disposes of the princess in the sea. Girls will love the Japanese "Trampling the Demons" with its spunky heroine. Shaw-Smith's lush border and page illustrations will captivate readers.

**Hoffman, Mary.** *A First Book of Myths: Myths and Legends for the Very Young from Around the World.* **Illustrated by Roger Langton and Kevin Kimber. New York: Dorling Kindersley, 1999. ISBN 0-7894-3973-5. 48 pages. Grades K–3**
Introduce children to classical figures like Icarus, Hanuman, Toyotama, Andromeda,

Midas, and Odin with these retellings designed for children. Hoffman incorporates dialogue and location into these short, simple retellings of myths that beg to be read aloud. The fluid illustrations of Langton and Kimber reflect the culture and customs of the country of origin. Hoffman includes a Who's Who in First Myths that identifies the characters and type of myth or legend and source notes.

**Hoffman, Mary.** *A Twist in the Tail: Animal Stories from Around the World.* **Illustrated by Jan Ormerod. New York: Henry Holt, 1998. ISBN 0-8050-5946-6. 69 pages. Grades K–4**

Hoffman's lively retellings of 10 multicultural tales are perfect for storytelling with groups or for children reading alone. Ormerod's vibrant and sometimes-sassy illustrations are captivating. "A Birthday Surprise" from the Caribbean is an Anancy (Anansi) the Spider trickster tale variant. "The Fox and the Crab Have a Race" from China lends itself well to comparison with Aesop's fables. "The Bright Blue Jackal" (and they do mean BRIGHT blue) is a popular Indian tale. Other countries featured include Cape Verde, Turkey, Malaysia, North America, Nigeria, Venezuela, and Australia. Hoffman provides source notes.

**Holt, David, and Bill Mooney, eds.** *More Ready-to-Tell Tales from Around the World.* **Little Rock, AR: August House, 1994. ISBN 0-87483-592-5. 256 pages. Grade 4+ and Teacher Reference**

The dynamic storytelling duo serves up 46 tellable tales from their colleagues, dividing the stories by comic tales ("The Barking Mouse" from Cuba), wise fools ("Juan Bobo's Pig" from Puerto Rico), trickster tales ("How Hare Drank Boiling Water and Married the Beautiful Princess" from Benin), tall tales ("The Snake and the Frog" from North America), how-and-why tales ("How the Rabbit Lost Its Tail" from Haiti), served with a twist ("The Tail of the Linani Beast" from Kenya), codes of conduct ("Deer and Jaguar Share a House" from Brazil), wheel of fortune ("The Kiss of Evil" from Iraq), family and community ("Sweet and Sour Berries" from China), and benediction ("The Ruby" from Hindu tradition). Storytelling tips, source and story notes, and recommended audience and age levels enhance this international collection.

**Holt, David, and Bill Mooney, eds.** *Ready-to-Tell Tales: Sure-fire Stories from America's Favorite Storytellers.* **Little Rock, AR: August House, 1994. ISBN 0-87483-381-7. 224 pages. Grade 4+ and Teacher Reference**

Holt and Mooney claim the difference between their collection and others is that these stories are "tried and true." They have been honed by storytellers and include telling tips and source notes from each contributor. Personal favorites for storytelling to audiences of children and adults include "The Magic Pot" from China, "Lazy Jack" from England, "The Wise Judge" from Japan, and "The Freedom Bird" from Thailand.

**Hopkins, Lee Bennett.** *Mother Goose Around the World.* **New York: Sadlier-Oxford, 1999. ISBN 0-8215-0491-6. 20 pages. Grades K–3**

Hopkins' collection guarantees a pleasurable journey into the world of nursery rhymes. He features China's "Wee Little Boy," Japan's "Wild Geese Flying," Russia's "Clapping Hands," and other Mother Goose rhymes. The illustrators capture the joy and whimsy of the tales. The inclusion of the original language of the tale is a wonderful way to introduce children to other languages. Paul and Jan Silversten perform the nursery rhymes on an audiocassette (ISBN 0-8215-0493-2).

**Keenan, Sheila.** *Gods, Goddesses, and Monsters: An Encyclopedia of World Mythology.* **New York: Scholastic, 2000. ISBN 0-439-04289-5. 128 pages. Grade 3+**
Explore the mythology of India, China, Japan, Southeast Asia, Africa, Egypt, the Near East, Greece, Rome, Celtic Lands, Norse Lands, North America, Central America, South America, and Oceania and Australia. The entries are clear and concise. Each is presented with fascinating sidebar narratives and color photos of artifacts, paintings, and sites. Unlike other compilers, Keenan chose to index the mythology figures alphabetically by country of origin. This results in an encyclopedia that is both informative and easy-to-use.

**Koenig, Viviane.** *A Family Treasury of Myths from Around the World.* **Retold by Viviane Koenig. Illustrated by Véronique Ageorges, Viviane Koenig, and Daniel Hénon. New York: Harry N. Abrams, 1998. ISBN 0-8109-4380-8. 168 pages. Grade 4+**
Koenig gathers familiar and new world stories for family telling in this collection, including "Izinagi and Izanami" from Japan, "How the Elephant Was Punished" from India, Egyptian myths, African animal stories, and a Senegalese flood myth. (*Note*: In the Greek myth of Helios' Chariot, Koenig's explanation of how Africans' skin became dark is disquieting.)

**Leeming, David Adams, ed.** *The Children's Dictionary of Mythology.* **New York: Franklin Watts, 1999. ISBN 0-531-11708-1. 128 pages. Grades 4–8**
This is a much-needed resource for upper elementary and middle school students. The scope encompasses world cultures, including summaries of familiar myths; mythological characters, locations, objects, and motifs; and introductions to great sagas of the world. The format is appealing with purple headings, pronunciation, summary, and cross-references for each entry. The text is well-written, and color photos and informative green sidebars enhance the volume. Capitalize upon the students' interest in heroes and heroines, gods and goddesses, and monsters.

**Leeming, David Adams, and Marion Sader, eds.** *Storytelling Encyclopedia: Historical, Cultural, and Multiethnic Approaches to Oral Traditions Around the World.* **Phoenix, AZ: Oryx, 1997. ISBN 1-57356-025-1. 560 pages. Teacher Reference**
This valuable resource of world folklore and storytelling throughout the ages offers a history of storytelling in America, cultural meanings, universal themes, and an extensive bibliography and index. The more than 700 entries include anthologists, critics, and storytellers, characters and places from folklore and mythology, types of folklore, and motifs. Travel from Verna Aardema to Zoroastrian Creation in this encyclopedia of storytelling elements and techniques from around the world.

**Livo, Norma J., ed.** *Moon Cakes to Maize: Delicious World Folktales.* **Golden, CO: Fulcrum, 1999. ISBN 1-55591-973-1. 192 pages. Grade 5+**
Livo unfolds more than 40 stories with a theme of food. Legends, fables, rhymes, and folktales include "Moon Cakes" and "The Pear Tree" from China; "Legend of the Rice Seed," "The Orphan Boy and the Monkeys," and "Why Farmers Have to Work So Hard" from the Hmong; "The Dumpling" and "The Peachling" from Japan; "The Origin of

Maize" from Mexico, and "The Night It Rained Bagels" from Russia. Extension activities entitled "Food for Thought" follow each chapter.

**Livo, Norma J., ed. *Troubadour's Storybag: Musical Folktales of the World*. Golden, CO: Fulcrum, 1996. ISBN 1-55591-953-7. 152 pages. Grade 6+**
Livo brings her knowledge and her passion to this book, examining the origins and role of music. Her retelling of these tales includes "Suggestions for Extended Activities." She exhorts teachers to use the natural links between music and storytelling to enhance the experience for children. Personal favorites include "The Talking Bird and the Singing Tree" from Russia, "A Shepherd Wins His Bride" from Turkey, and "The Dance of the Monkey and the Sparrow" from Japan.

**Lupton, Hugh. *Tales of Wisdom and Wonder*. Illustrated by Niamh Sharkey. New York: Barefoot Books, 1999. ISBN 1-901223-09-4. 64 pages. Grades 3–7**
These stories unfold in the traditional form, but the endings of each give the reader pause. One of the best examples of this is the French "The White Rat." See if you predicted the ending to this variation of the Mouse Bridegroom legend. The illustrations are angular and exaggerated and fun. Poor monkey misunderstands the word "misery" in the Haitian "Monkey and the Papa God." My favorite is "The Blind Man and the Hunter," from West Africa, which conveys the wisdom of men who see with the heart.

**MacDonald, Margaret R. *Shake-It-Up Tales! Stories to Sing, Dance, Drum, and Act Out*. Little Rock, AR: August House, 2000. ISBN 0-87483-590-9. 176 pages. Teacher Reference**
The stories people remember most are the ones that involved them as participants, not as passive listeners. MacDonald exhorts teachers to play with the language, sounds, and movement of these 20 multicultural stories and shares tips on effective storytelling. She organizes the dynamic stories by types of participation: chanting, singing, dancing, drumming (including chants, claps, motions, and sound effects; singing tales; dancing tales; and drumming tales), and talk-back tales (including stories with improvisation slots, riddle stories, actors-from-the audience, tandem telling, story theatre, and act-out-tales). MacDonald offers simple and effective methods to enliven classes and presentations. So get up and Shake-It-Up!

**Mama, Raouf. *The Barefoot Book of Tropical Tales*. Illustrated by Deirdre Hyde. New York: Barefoot Books, 2000. ISBN 1-902283-21-X. 64 pages. Grades 3–7**
Mama regrets the erosion of the storytelling tradition among today's youth. Here he gathers some of his favorite trickster, pourquoi, and cautionary tales to share, and sweetens the pot with ghost and spirit stories. Students will recognize recurring story motifs and variations on familiar stories. "The Magic Drum" from Benin, a variation of "Toads and Diamonds," pits a kind son against his greedy stepbrother. In "The Wise Man and the Thief" from Sri Lanka, Appuhami uses flattery and invention to expose a villager who has been stealing melons from his neighbor's farm. The colorful, bold illustrations and borders complement this multicultural anthology.

**Mayer, Marianna. *Women Warriors: Myths and Legends of Heroic Women*. Illustrated by Julek Heller. New York: Morrow, 1999. ISBN 0-688-15522-7. Grade 4+**
Mayer pays tribute to "the commitment and courage of each heroine, as well as an

exploration of the nature and uses of the innate power of womanhood" in this intriguing collection. Featured women of power include the Amazon Queen Hiera and the goddess of war Morrigan.

**Matthews, Caitlin.** *The Barefoot Book of Princesses.* **Illustrated by Olwyn Whelan. New York: Barefoot Books, 1997. ISBN 1-901223-74-4. 65 pages. Grades 3–7**
In this anthology, princesses show that resourcefulness and their own strength of character are better than magic. Matthews' narratives are fluid, and Whelan's watercolors are like brilliant textured fabrics. Tales include the Persian "The Mountain Princess," the Chinese "The Beggar Princess," and the Kalmuck "The Birdcage Husband" (from Central Asia). Sampling these stories from diverse cultures offers students opportunities to compare and contrast their own princess tales.

**Matthews, Caitlin.** *While the Bear Sleeps: Winter Tales and Traditions.* **Illustrated by Judith Christine Mills. New York: Barefoot Books, 1999. ISBN 1-902283-81-3. 80 pages. Grades 3–7**
A little girl stumbles into the cave of a hibernating bear. Join her and her new special friend for winter stories. Read about Christmas, Hanukkah, winter solstice, New Year customs, Twelfth Night, and Kwanzaa in this illuminating collection. The expressive acrylics and the recurring onlookers add to the delight of the stories.

**McCarthy, Tara.** *Multicultural Myths and Legends: Stories and Activities to Promote Cultural Awareness.* **New York: Scholastic Professional Books, 1994. ISBN 0-590-49645-X. 127 pages. Grades 2–6**
McCarthy retells stories from Mongolia, Africa, Persia, Japan, and China and suggests cross-curricular connections. My personal favorites include "How the Horse-Head Fiddle Came To Be" from Mongolia, "Daughter of the Star" from Zaire, "The Crane Wife" from Japan, "Chih-nii The Heavenly Spinner" from China, and "The Talking Bird" from Persia.

**McCaughrean, Geraldine.** *The Bronze Cauldron: Myths and Legends of the World.* **Illustrated by Bee Willey. New York: McElderry Books, 1998. ISBN 0-689-81758-4. 130 pages. Grade 4+**
McCaughrean offers 27 myths and legends that enrich understanding of other cultures. She interweaves dialogue and action in her retellings, making the stories perfect for performance or read-aloud. Willey's distinctive watercolors help visualize the tale and echo the motifs of the country of origin. Non-Western stories include "Young Buddha" and "The Armchair Traveler" from India, "Ragged Emperor" from China, and "Biggest" from Japan.

**McCaughrean, Geraldine.** *The Crystal Pool: Myths and Legends of the World.* **Illustrated by Bee Willey. New York: McElderry Books, 1999. ISBN 0-689-82262-9. 144 pages. Grade 4+**
This fourth happy marriage of the writing of McCaughrean and artistry of Willey makes 28 more world trickster and creation tales accessible to middle readers. The title story is a Melanesian myth. Other myths include "The Gods Down Tools" (Sumeria), "A Bouquet of Flowers" (Aborigines), " Race to the Top" (Maori), "Isis and Osiris"

(Egypt), "Dear Dog" (Japan), "The Curious Honeybird" (Bantu), "Monkey Do: The Story of Hanuman" (Hindu), and "Thunder and Smith" (China). Legends include "Lamia" (India), "The Alchemist" (China), "Gull-Girl" (Siberia), "Work Shy Rabbit" (West Africa), "Cat v. Rat" (Congo), and "The Sky-Blue Storybox" (Ghana).

**McCaughrean, Geraldine.** *The Golden Hoard: Myths and Legends of the World.* **Illustrated by Bee Willey. New York: McElderry Books, 1996. ISBN 0-689-80741-4. 130 pages. Grade 4+**
McCaughrean offers 22 tales from around the world, with brief notes about each, and wonderful mixed-media illustrations by Willey. Stories include "The Man Who Almost Lived Forever" (Sumeria); "The Admirable Hare" (Ceylon); "Skinning Out" (Ethiopia); "Quetzalcoatl" (Mexico); and trickster tales of Maui (Polynesia) and Anansi (West Africa).

**McCaughrean, Geraldine.** *The Silver Treasure: Myths and Legends of the World.* **Illustrated by Bee Willey. New York: McElderry Books, 1997. ISBN 0-689-81322-8. 130 pages. Grade 4+**
McCaughrean includes 23 myths and legends told with rich background culture. Non-Western culture stories include "The Men in the Moon" from Kenya, "Babushka" from Russia, "The Silver-Miners" from Bolivia, "The Lighthouse on the Lake" from Japan, "Can Krishna Die?" from India, and "A Nest and a Web" from the Middle East.

**Muten, Burleigh.** *Grandmothers' Stories: Wise Woman Tales from Many Cultures.* **Illustrated by Sian Bailey. Brooklyn, NY: Barefoot Books, 1999. ISBN 1-902283-32-5. 80 pages. Grades 1–5**
In these tales, older women are strong, wise, and resourceful. Bailey's watercolors and bottom borders are stories unto themselves. Although "Grandmother's Basket" from Russia does feature an old woodwitch who eats children, it is Tanya and Vanya's grandmother who gives them the tools they need to escape. In the Senegalese "The Midwife and the Djinn," Old Fatu is whisked off to assist in the childbirth of sextuplets to the wife of the magical creature. Her wisdom and kindness are rewarded. The story of "The Old Woman Who Was Not Afraid" from Japan is a familiar one of a woman who outwits the oni (ogres).

**Olson, Arielle North, and Howard Schwartz.** *Ask the Bones: Scary Stories from Around the World.* **Illustrated by David Linn. New York: Viking, 1999. ISBN 0-670-87581-3. 145 pages. Grade 4+**
Olson and Schwartz selected and retell 21 eerie, gruesome, mystical, or gory stories for the stalwart. Students will enjoy bone-chilling stories like "The Haunted Forest" from Uzbekistan, "The Bloody Fangs" from Japan, "Beginning with the Ears" from Iraq, "Nowhere to Hide" from Russia, and "The Black Snake" from Persia. The authors include bibliographical references.

**Osborne, Mary Pope.** *Mermaid Tales from Around the World.* **Illustrated by Troy Howell. New York: Scholastic, 1993. ISBN 0-590-44377-1. 84 pages. Grades 4–7**
Osborne skillfully adapted 12 mermaid stories from around the world. Howell captures the artistic flavor of each country in stories from Iran, Japan, China, Ukraine, and

Africa. Personal favorites include "Serpent and the Sea Queen" from Japan and "Fish Husband" from Africa.

**Pepper, Dennis.** *The Oxford Book of Animal Stories.* **New York: Oxford University Press, 1994. ISBN 0-19-278134-0. 304 pages. Grade 4+**

This valuable collection draws on world legends and storytelling and includes a wide range of authors, including Isaac Bashevis Singer and Rudyard Kipling.

**Philip, Neil.** *The Illustrated Book of Fairy Tales.* **Illustrated by Nilesh Mistry. New York: Dorling Kindersley, 1998. ISBN 0-7894-2794-X. 160 pages. Grade 4+**

Dr. Philip introduces these 52 classic tales from around the world with an overview of the genre and a reminder that fairy tales were often didactic. (*Note:* Some are quite graphic and gruesome as are the original Grimm tales.) He examines recurring themes, fairy-tale justice, and characterization, and he looks at the original storytellers (Charles Perrault, the Brothers Grimm, and Hans Christian Andersen). Beautifully illustrated stories are arranged by theme (Under a Spell, Riches and Rags, Heroes and Heroines, and True Love Conquers All) and beg for comparison with other anthologized tales. Personal favorites include "Three Magic Oranges" from Costa Rica, "The Girl Who Combed Pearls" from Portugal, and "The Unknown Sister" from Suriname.

**Philip, Neil.** *Myths and Legends.* **DK Annotated guides. New York: Dorling Kindersley, 1999. ISBN 0-7894-4117-9. 128 pages. Grade 5+**

Dr. Philip, expert on mythology and folklore, discusses the meaning and history of mythology and shares more than 50 world myths and legends. Many are familiar, but readers will experience them in a new way with the opulent double-page spreads for each myth from the ancient Egyptians and Sumerians, West Africa, the Caribbean, Central America, Australia, Polynesia, India, China, Japan, Northern Europe, and Greece and Rome. Famous artworks from museums around the world decorate the legends. For example, the Chinese legend of the Eight Mortals is illustrated with a plate, and the Ten Suns of Heaven with a second 2nd century BC funeral banner. These artworks serve as the focus of annotations, bombarding the senses with little-known details relevant to each myth. The only downside is that art credits are difficult to access.

**Pilling, Ann.** *Creation: Read-Aloud Stories from Many Lands.* **Illustrated by Michael Foreman. Cambridge, MA: Candlewick, 1998. ISBN 1-56402-888-7. 96 pages. Grades 2–6**

Address age-old questions of our origins with these retellings of pourquoi tales perfect for reading aloud. Stories like the Australian Aboriginal "How the World Was Lit Up by a Bonfire" and the Ashanti "Why the Snake Has No Legs" will entertain and enlighten.

**San Souci, Robert D.** *A Terrifying Taste of Short and Shivery: Thirty Creepy Tales.* **New York: Delacorte, 1998. ISBN 0-385-32635-1. Grade 3+**

Every country has its ghost stories, and San Souci retells some of the more bizarre and frightening in this collection. Read captivating tales like the Chinese "The Tiger Woman" about revenge from a hunter's prey. Older readers might enjoy the anthropological and ethnic insights these ghost stories reveal.

**San Souci, Robert D.** *Even More Short and Shivery: Thirty Spine-tingling Stories.* Illustrated by Jacqueline Rogers. New York: Bantam Books, 1997. ISBN 0-385-32252-6. 176 pages. Grades 4–8

San Souci gathers short and spooky folktales from Iceland, Ireland, France, China, Mexico, Poland, Nigeria, Martinique, and the United States in this satisfying multicultural collection. Enjoy adaptations of favorites by Washington Irving and Charles Dickens or new treasures like "The Skull That Spoke," "The Monster of Baylock," and "The Blood-Drawing Ghost."

**Sherman, Josepha.** *Told Tales: Nine Folktales from Around the World.* Illustrated by Jo-Ellen Bossun. New York: Silver Moon Press, 1995. ISBN 1-881889-64-5. 73 pages. Grades 3–5

Folklorist Sherman shows the universality of storytelling in this collection of creation tales ("Why the Sky Is Separate from the Earth" from Botswana), hero tales ("Li Chi and the Serpent" from China), moral tales ("Necessity" from Romania), and a silly tale ("Hiding the Bell" from Germany). Recommended activities include tracking down tales and mask making.

**Sierra, Judy.** *Multicultural Folktales For the Feltboard and Readers' Theater.* Phoenix, AZ: Oryx, 1997. ISBN 1-57356-003-0. Grades K–6

Sierra includes 20 short folktales from around the world, including "Kancil and the Crocodile" from Indonesia and "Eat. Coat. Eat!" from Turkey. Use the suggestions and traceable patterns following each story to experiment with storytelling techniques.

**Sierra, Judy.** *Nursery Tales Around the World.* Illustrated by Stefano Vitale. New York: Clarion, 1996. ISBN 0-395-67894-3. 114 pages. Grades K–3

Vitale's colorful, inventive borders, designed with motifs of the story's country, enrich Sierra's lively and sometimes humorous retelling in this rich collection of tales that beg to be heard and shared. Personal favorites include "The Fox and the Crab" from China, "Odon the Giant" from Philippines, "The Boy Who Tried to Fool His Father" from Zaire, and "Anansi and the Pig" from Jamaica.

**Stryer, Andrea Stenn.** *The Celestial River: Creation Tales of the Milky Way.* Little Rock, AR: August House, 1998. ISBN 0-87483-528-3. 80 pages. Grades 3–8

Stryer explains man's fascination with the Milky Way galaxy (a.k.a. Celestial River, Star-Filled Basket, Path to the Place of Abundance) and culls stories of its origin from different cultures. She also provides an illuminating introduction to each story. Share these captivating stories from ancient Japan, ancient Greece, the Navajo, Aborigines of Australia, Maori, the San of the Kalahari, and Argentina. Use the stories as springboards for discussion of the solar system.

**Walker, Paul Robert.** *Little Folk: Stories From Around the World.* Illustrated by James Bernardin. San Diego: Harcourt Brace and Company, 1997. ISBN 0-15-200327-4. 72 pages. Grade 4+

Journey into the world of the little folk (fairy, dwarf, elf, leprechaun, pixie, brownie, hobgoblin, nisse, Menehane, and nunu) and share their legends. "People of the Rock" is an African tale, and "One-Inch Boy" is a retelling of "Issun Boshi" about a tiny boy similar to Tom Thumb. Bernardin matches the artistic style of the illustrations to the appropriate country.

**Walker, Richard.** *The Barefoot Book of Pirates.* **Illustrated by Olwyn Whelan. New York: Barefoot Books, 1998. ISBN 1-91223-79-5. 64 pages. Grades 3–7**
Students will be surprised to discover stories about female pirates like Grace O'Malley and legendary heroes like Robin Hood. There are even pirate stories from Japan, Morocco, and Germany. Some pirates can be tamed, as in the Japanese "Music Charms the Pirates." Sometimes a pirate's treasure is his downfall, as in the Scottish "The Abbey Bells." Take a titillating journey through the imagination of Whelan, from the skull-and-crossbones endpapers to stormy seas, rocking ships, and grinning skeletons.

**Walker, Richard.** *The Barefoot Book of Trickster Tales.* **Illustrated by Claudio Munoz. New York: Barefoot Books, 1998. ISBN 1-902283-08-2. 80 pages. Grades 3–7**
Trickster tales tickle the funny bone. The characters, whether animal, human, or inanimate, elicit a begrudging nod of respect for their cleverness. This collection features familiar tricksters like Ananse the Spider, Brer Rabbit, and the Three Sillies. Some are variations of other stories. Compare the Swiss "Nail Soup" with the Russian "Stone Soup." Compare the Bengali story "The Frail Old Woman" with *No Dinner: The Story of the Old Woman and the Pumpkin* by Jessica Souhami. My favorite, the Kampuchean "The Spirits in the Leather Bag," reminds us "stories can live only when they are told." Keep these stories alive through telling.

**Weber, Judith Eichler.** *Melting Pots: Family Stories and Recipes.* **Family ties series. Illustrated by Scott Gubala. New York: Silver Moon Press, 1994. ISBN 1-881889-53-X. 54 pages. Grades 3–5**
Weber introduces each story with interesting facts about ways people celebrate around the world with food. Food is the focus of each simple story, including "The Noodle" about Chinese-American Hua Chang's first birthday noodle from her Chinese grandmother, "Fried Plantains" from Cuba, and "Bean Soup" from Greece. Weber's guidelines for original melting pot recipes are the best part of the book. Use this as a springboard for other tasty explorations in literature and culture studies.

**Yolen, Jane.** *The Fairies' Ring: A Book of Fairy Stories and Poems.* **Collected and adapted by Jane Yolen. Illustrated by Stephen Mackey. New York: Dutton Books, 1999. ISBN 0-525-46045-4. 96 pages. Grades K–5**
Surely the fairies themselves have sprinkled some magic dust on this enticing collection. Older students will appreciate Yolen's lyrical language and Mackey's luminous and lavish oils. The full-page illustrations take one's breath away. The more than two dozen stories and poems capture fairies at their best and worst and expose the foibles and follies of mankind. Personal favorites include "The Peri Wife," a Persian tale, and "The Stolen Wife," a Maori tale from New Zealand.

**Yolen, Jane, ed.** *Gray Heroes: Elder Tales from Around the World.* **New York: Puffin, 1999. ISBN 0-14-027618-1. 256 pages. Grade 8+**
Yolen recognizes the importance and continuing contributions of the elderly in these 75 tales from around the world. Some use old age as metaphor. Divided by wisdom, trickery, adventure, and love, the stories include "A Clever Old Bride" from Korea; "Empty-Cup Mind," "The Old Woman and the Rice Cakes," and "Lump Off, Lump On" from Japan; "An Old Man's Wisdom," "The Old Woman and the Fox," "The Lord of Death," and "The Clever Old Man" from India; and "The Silver Swindle" from China.

**Yolen, Jane.** *Not One Damsel in Distress: World Folktales for Strong Girls.* **Illustrated by Susan Guevara. San Diego: Harcourt, Inc., 2000. ISBN 0-15-202047-0. 116 pages. Grades 3–7**

Yolen collected and told these 13 traditional world folktales that focus on girls and women of strength, courage, and resourcefulness. Explore the realm of damsels who confront danger through stories of heroines like Atalanta the Huntress (Greek patron of women warriors), Nana Miriam (African warrior), Senorita Maldonada (fought for rights in Argentina), and Li Chi (Chinese queen and serpent slayer). Yolen begins with an open letter to her daughter and granddaughters in which she discusses the book's heroines and the lack of female models in ages past. She concludes by saying, "But this book is for you because it is important to know that anyone can be a hero if they have to be. Even girls. Especially you." Use these inspiring stories to encourage young girls to stand up for their beliefs.

**Zeitlin, Steve.** *The Four Corners of the Sky: Creation Stories and Cosmologies from Around the World.* **Pictures by Chris Raschka. New York: Henry Holt, 2000. ISBN 0-8050-4816-2. 135 pages. Grade 4+**

What made night and day? What was the power of the sun? Where did rain and snow originate? From earliest time, man struggled to make sense of his universe. In this illuminating collection, Zeitlin gathers myths and legends from the Ancient Egyptians, Maori, Hebrews, Greeks, Hindus, Norse, Incas, Jains, Haitians, Desana Indians, Africans, Chinese, Europeans, and from contemporary science. He divides them by common themes: Between Two Parents, Earth and Sky; Something Out of Nothing; Cycles of Creation and Destruction; At the Center of the Universe; Mirroring the Cosmos; A Universe of Animals and Plants; and the Cosmic Egg. Raschka modeled his b&w illustrations on each country's artifacts, objects, and designs.

## Folktales, Fairy Tales, Myths, and Legends: Videos

***Fairy Tales from Around the World: Beauty and the Beast and Other Animated Fables*** **[videorecording]. Hosted by Pat Morita. Chicago: Encyclopedia Britannica, 1990. ISBN 1-56020-316-1. 60 minutes. Grades K–4**

These retellings in color animation are a perfect multicultural lesson. Children can compare versions of "Beauty and the Beast" and "Rumpelstiltskin" from France, China, Germany, Norway and Israel.

***Fairy Tales from Around the World: Cinderella and Other Animated Fables*** **[videorecording]. Hosted by Pat Morita. Chicago: Encyclopedia Britannica, 1990. ISBN 1-56020-316-1. 60 minutes. Grades K–4**

Use these animated fairy tales to help children understand how stories originate in one country and are shared around the world. They will enjoy sharing different versions of familiar fairy tales. The selections include interpretations of "Cinderella" from France, Chile, and Africa, and versions of "Hansel and Gretel" from Germany, Syria and the Philippines. Stories average 12 minutes in length.

***Fairy Tales from Around the World: Sleeping Beauty and Other Animated Fables*** [videorecording]. Hosted by Pat Morita. Chicago: Encyclopedia Britannica, 1990. ISBN 1-56020-316-1. 60 minutes. Grades K–4

Morita serves as an inviting host for this series video. Children will enjoy seeing how different cultures have similar themes and stories as they compare and contrast interpretations of "Sleeping Beauty" and "Rapunzel" from France, Bangladesh, Italy, Germany, Malta and Israel.

## *Geography and Maps*

**Adams, Simon.** *The DK Geography of the World*. New York: Dorling Kindersley, 1996. ISBN 0-7894-1004-4. 304 pages. Grade 3+

DK assembles an impressive array of color maps of all types, with hundreds of color illustrations, fact boxes, and clear text to provide physical geography and key places of countries around the world. The most fascinating sections explain how the landscape or climate has shaped the country's development. It examines the lifestyles of the inhabitants and gauges the country's place in today's world.

***Atlas of the Earth***. Scholastic First Discovery Books. New York: Scholastic, 1997. ISBN 0-590-96211-6. 24 pages. Grades K–2

Children will delight in the overlays and exquisite color illustrations as they learn about the changes in the earth's formation through the ages. The authors tell about continents, land formations, oceans, and the North and South Poles. The acetate transparencies help children visualize changes like the effects of erosion on the earth and a mountain transformed into an active volcano.

**Bieniek, Denise.** *The World Around Us: Geography Projects and Activities*. Mahwah, NJ: Troll Creative Teacher Ideas, 1996. ISBN 0-8167-3882-3. 96 pages. Teacher Reference

Bieniek offers project ideas and extended activities for elementary school classes centered on geography standards. Reproducible unit pages will be helpful to teachers. Units can be adapted for older students.

***Biomes of the World***. Danbury, CT: Grolier Educational, 1999. ISBN 0-7172-9341-6. Grade 4+

This nine-volume set examines the biotic communities of the world. The maps, color photography, and facile text help children to understand the animals and environmental issues of the major ecological regions of the world, including polar regions, deserts, oceans, wetlands, mountains, temperate and tropical forests and grasslands.

**Chambers, Catherine.** *All About Maps*. Illustrated by David Cockcroft. Hello out there series. New York: Franklin Watts, 1998. ISBN 0-531-14471-2. 32 pages. Grades 4–8

Maps, keys, charts, cross-sections, satellite images, color illustrations, and a glossary accompany simple text in this educational volume. Chambers reviews every aspect of mapping, including distance, plotting and drawing, locations skills, city maps, and world maps. "Hello," "Spot It," and "Treasure Trek" insets provide interesting facts and lesson extensions.

**Chicola, Nancy A., and Eleanor B. English.** *Discovering World Geography with Books Kids Love.* **Golden, CO: Fulcrum, 1999. ISBN 1-55591-965-0. 166 pages. Teacher Reference for Grades K–6**

Address national academic standards and integrate geography into literature strands with this ambitious resource. As Chicola and English explore "realms" of the world, they survey location, topography, climate, flora and fauna, and unique features in "Getting Your Bearings" to place the area in global perspective. In "Mapping," they summarize the book and include key understandings, knowledge, skills, perspectives, activities, and questions to ask for each. "Charting with More Books" includes additional titles to develop with the geographical region.

**Chrisp, Peter.** *The Search for a Northern Route.* **Exploration and encounters series. New York: Thomson Learning, 1993. ISBN 1-5684-7122-X. 48 pages. Grades 3–6**

Woodcuts, period maps, and historical illustrations document the early searches for Cathay (China) by explorers from Holland, England, France, Spain, and Portugal. Chrisp helps to explain the riches and mystery the East possessed and the value to the world that incited so many costly and dangerous expeditions to search for a northern route.

***DK Student Atlas.*** **New York: Dorling Kindersley, 1998. ISBN 0-7894-2399-5. 160 pages. Grade 3+**

All atlases are not created equal. In its novel approach, this student atlas approaches geography both regionally and thematically, making global, continental, and regional connections. Introductory map skills sections are comprehensive and clear. Maps of world population, climate and life zones, world economy, and borders and boundaries encourage students to compare places and features. Each map also features text summaries of industry, landscape, farming and land use, climate, population, and environmental issues.

**Delafosse, Claude.** *Atlas of People.* **Created by Gallimard Jeunesse. Illustrated by Denise Millet. First discovery book series. New York: Scholastic, 1996. ISBN 0-590-58281-X. 24 pages. Grades K–3**

This appealing introduction to cultures around the world offers simple text and vibrant illustrations. It looks at some of the world's people, customs, cultures, and countries. The most popular feature will be the acetate overlay pages that transform pages into new images.

**Fowler, Allan.** *Let's Visit Some Islands.* **Rookie read-about science series. New York: Children's Press, 1998. ISBN 0-516-20807-1. 32 pages. Grades K–2**

Help children understand what an island is, how islands are formed, and what it is like to live on an island. Fowler shows the difference between a continent and an island. He uses color photos and simple text to illustrate examples of islands and groups of islands such as Greenland, Japan, Liberty Island, and Venice. He also looks at Hawaii and volcanoes, Manhattan Island, and plants and animals of islands. A pictorial glossary follows.

**Fowler, Allan.** *Living in a Desert.* **Rookie read-about geography series. New York: Children's Press, 1998. ISBN 0-516-21560-4. 32 pages. Grades K–2**

Fowler includes a map and color photos to show children where to find the earth's deserts. He features the Bedouins in the Sahara and Arabian deserts, the people of the Gobi Desert in Asia, and adobe homes in North American deserts. Discussion of life in the desert includes irrigation in North Africa and salt mines in South America. A pictorial glossary follows.

**Fowler, Allan.** *Living in a Rain Forest.* **Rookie read-about geography series. New York: Children's Press, 2000. ISBN 0-516-21555-8. 32 pages. Grades K–2**
Introduce children to the location, structure, plants and animals, climate, and people of the world's rain forests with this simple text book. Fowler concludes with mention of attempts to protect the rain forests. A pictorial glossary follows.

**Fowler, Allan.** *Living in the Mountains.* **Rookie read-about geography series. New York: Children's Press, 2000. ISBN 0-516-21563-9. 32 pages. Grades K–2**
With simple text and color photos, Fowler introduces children to the geography of mountains, plateaus, valleys, islands, and volcanoes. A pictorial glossary follows.

**Fowler, Allan.** *Living Near a River.* **Rookie read-about geography series. New York: Children's Press, 2000. ISBN 0-516-21556-6. 32 pages. Grades K–2**
From blue lines on maps to historic paintings to color photos of the Hudson and Mississippi rivers, Fowler shows children the role of the river. He discusses farming needs, transportation, and the harnessing of energy in this simple book. A pictorial glossary follows.

**Fowler, Allan.** *Living Near the Sea.* **Rookie read-about geography series. New York: Children's Press, 2000. ISBN 0-516-21562-0. 32 pages. Grades K–2**
Fowler examines the joys and dangers of living near the sea. He shows how floods affect people, large dams protect people, and the sea provides a living. The author looks at types of boats and ships and kinds of houses near the sea. A pictorial glossary follows.

**Fowler, Allan.** *Living on Farms.* **Rookie read-about geography series. New York: Children's Press, 2000. ISBN 0-516-21564-7. 32 pages. Grades K–2**
With simple text and color photography, Fowler takes children from traditional farms of the past to specialized farms of today. He emphasizes the hard work of farming and shows planting, irrigation, and harvest. A pictorial glossary follows.

**Fowler, Allan.** *Living on the Plains.* **Rookie read-about geography series. New York: Children's Press, 2000. ISBN 0-516-21565-5. 32 pages. Grades K–2**
Help children understand the geography of the world with the map, color photography, and simple text of this series book. Fowler shows the forming of plains from glaciers, rolling plains, and plains between mountains or rivers. He takes children back in time to the settling of the West and compares life then and now for the farmers. A pictorial glossary follows.

**Grant, Donald, ed.** *Atlas of Islands.* **Created by Gallimard Jeunesse and Donald Grant. Illustrated by Donald Grant. First discovery book series. New York: Scholastic, 1999. ISBN 0-439-04402-2. 24 pages. Grades K–3**
This fabulous introduction to islands around the world offers simple text and vibrant illustrations. It looks at islands famous in history, pirates, and wildlife, plants, and

lifestyles on the islands. The real treasure of the book is the acetate overlay pages that transform frozen islands to tropical islands and Man-a-hat-ta Island into modern New York City.

**Gresko, Marcia S.** *A World of Communities.* **Woodbridge, CT: Blackbirch Press, Inc., 1998. ISBN 1-56711-297-8. 79 pages. Grades 3–5**

This book is claimed to be "a unique text for social studies," and it is. The logical approach addresses elementary school teachers' long-standing concerns of relevance and teachability. Gresko begins with the landscape of each part of the world and how it and the climate affect the way people live. She looks at each community and studies ways in which people all over the world are both different and the same. She ends each chapter with a focus on a particular city of the country. The book has color photos, charts, maps, and wonderful insets, including Helpful Hint, Key Map Terms, Word Watch, At a Glance, Brainstorm, Geography Skill Builder, and Community Project. After an examination of the world of maps, Gresko profiles India (Bombay), China (Guangzhou), Russia (Moscow), South Africa (Johannesburg), Israel (Jerusalem), England (London), Puerto Rico (San Juan), and the West Indies (St. Vincent). A bibliography, glossary, and index are included.

**Hook, Sue, and Angela Royston.** *A First Atlas.* **Illustrated by Mel Pickering and Lindy Norton. Scholastic first encyclopedia series. New York: Scholastic, 2000. ISBN 0-590-47528-2. 93 pages. Grades K–5**

What a wonderful introduction to the world! It is filled with intriguing facts and inviting visuals. The large bold type, vivid pictorial maps, colorful legends, "animals and plants" boxes, and "Did You Know?" insets are superb. But it is Hook and Royston's regions-of-the-world approach that makes this a rare find. The top border cross-references are an added bonus.

**Howarth, Sarah.** *The Children's Atlas of the Twentieth Century.* **Brookfield, CT: Millbrook, 1995. ISBN 1-56294-563-7. 95 pages. Grade 4+**

Color illustrations, concise maps, and pictorial symbols chronicle the 20th century in this historical political atlas. Howarth spans World War I to the Persian Gulf War and highlights people who have made their mark on history, from United States President Theodore Roosevelt to South African President Nelson Mandela.

**Jeunesse, Gallimard.** *Atlas of Countries.* **Created by Gallimard Jeunesse and Claude Delafosse. Illustrated by Donald Grant. First discovery book series. New York: Scholastic, 1996. ISBN 0-590-58282-8. 24 pages. Grades K–3**

Children will enjoy the interactive acetate overlays that allow them to change night to day, rotate the earth, and see landscapes of other languages. It is not the best book for content, but it is a book that will excite children and encourage them to learn more about the countries of the world.

**Johnson, Sylvia A.** *Mapping the World.* **New York: Atheneum, 1999. ISBN 0-689-81813-0. 32 pages. Grade 3+**

Place the 20th century in historical perspective with this cartography treasure. Johnson reveals how changes in the geographical world alter man's perception of the world.

**Kottke, Jan.** *Living in a Desert.* Communities series. New York: Children's Press, 2000. ISBN 0-516-23300-9. 24 pages. Grades K–3

Meet Hala and Abbas of the Syrian Desert, Tarik of the Sahara Desert, and Batu of the Gobi Desert. Compare their homes and lifestyles through Kottke's brief, large-print text and color photos. A glossary, index, and a few related titles follow. Pair this with Fowler's *Living in a Desert* (pages 53–54) which gives a geographical overview of deserts.

**Leedy, Loreen.** *Mapping Penny's World.* Illustrated by the author. New York: Henry Holt, 2000. ISBN 0-8050-6178-9. 32 pages. Grades K–3

When Lisa's class is learning about maps, she decides to map the world of her dog Penny. After mapping the familiar places, she and Penny plot their future world travels. They take readers on a trip around the world as Penny rides an elephant and plays with a panda in Asia, barks at a giraffe in Africa, hides in a kangaroo's pouch in Australia, surfs in the Pacific, pulls a sled in Alaska, and visits with the penguins in Antarctica. Leedy helps children make the connection between world maps and local places in this delightful story.

**Llewellyn, Claire.** *Our Planet Earth.* Scholastic first encyclopedia series. New York: Scholastic, 1997. ISBN 0-590-87929-4. Grades 2–5

This valuable reference work features two-page spreads with maps, color photos, illustrations, and diagrams of specific topics. The volume is organized by themes: the history of the earth, the earth's surface, the changing planet, and life on earth. Insets for the "Did You Know?" section offer fascinating facts, for instance, "Earth's center is about 100 times hotter than the hottest desert!"

*National Geographic Beginner's World Atlas.* Washington, DC: National Geographic Society, 1999. ISBN 0-7922-7502-0. Grades K–3

National Geographic Society's reputation for quality nonfiction and photography is well earned. This is the definitive world atlas with its easy-to-read maps, glorious pictures, and engaging seven-continent content. A child in native costume introduces each continent. Political and physical maps, facts and figures charts, and glossary and pronunciation guide accompany statistics on the land (land regions, water, climate, plants, and animals) and the people (countries, cities, people, languages, and products) for each continent.

*Our World: A Child's First Picture Atlas.* Washington, DC: National Geographic Society, 2000. ISBN 0-7922-7576-4. 32 pages. Grades K–2

The concept of the round earth is a difficult one for children to comprehend. This wonderful over-sized atlas has spare but clear text and clearly defined illustrations and maps to help children see both sides of the globe, the earth as a map, land, land and water, and where people live. The two-page spreads of the continents and regions have large colorful maps and drawings of representative flora and fauna.

**Pickering, Mel.** *Picture Reference Atlas.* Princeton, NJ: Two-Can, 1996. ISBN 1-58728-651-3. 48 pages. Grades K–5

What a visual delight for children and a factual feast for teachers! This book includes continent and region maps. In addition to the map indicators of mountains, rivers, borders, and the like, children can explore pictures identifying crops, buildings, animals, local people, and other features. Each page has bold Fact Finder and Factfile boxes to help children understand the continent or region and place it in perspective to the world.

**Pope, Joyce.** *The Children's Atlas of Natural Wonders.* **Brookfield, CT: Millbrook Press, 1995. ISBN 1-56294-886-5. 91 pages. Grade 4+**

Comparative graphics, bold cross-sections, color photos, relief maps, and straightforward text make this an appealing resource. Pope examines the geography, geology, and natural history of natural wonders in North, Central, and South America, Europe, Asia, Africa, Australia and the Pacific, and the polar regions. Some of the 36 featured wonders include the Amazon, the Dead Sea, the Nile River, the Sahara Desert, the Great Barrier Reef, and Antarctica.

**Rogers, Linda K.** *Geographic Literacy Through Children's Literature.* **Englewood, CO: Teachers Idea Press, 1997. ISBN 1-56308-439-2. 161 pages. Teacher Reference**

Rogers skillfully discusses the five themes of the geography standards developed by the Geographic Education National Implementation Project and offers practical hands-on activities centering on quality children's literature. The annotated bibliography includes flexible activities and extensions by grade level (K–3, 4–6, and Jr/Sr High).

**Sammis, Fran.** *Maps and Mapmaking.* **Tarrytown, NY: Benchmark Books, 2000. ISBN 0-7614-0367-1. 64 pages. Grade 4+**

Sammis offers a history of mapmaking and an overview of the how's and why's of mapping. She includes historical maps and looks at the changes in maps today based on new technologies.

**Steele, Philip.** *The Children's Atlas of the World.* **New York: Franklin Watts, 2000. ISBN 0-531-11775-8. 128 pages. Grade 3+**

Steele offers an overview of the planet, mapmaking, and the political and physical world. His coverage of each continent includes an introduction, statistics (general facts, vegetation, language, religion, resources, climate, and farming), and lands and people, followed by detailed geographical regions of the continent. Relief maps are strategically placed on one page for tracing and reproducing. The atlas is enriched by the many sidebars with country flags, "Peoples of the Region," and Did You Know? notes, the Fact File, and index.

**Steele, Philip.** *The Kingfisher Young People's Atlas of the World.* **New York: Kingfisher, 1997. ISBN 0-7534-5086-0. Grade 3+**

Steele examines the vastness and variety of earth and provides facts and figures for 200 countries and map study. This atlas for children is replete with color relief maps, flags, photos, and illustrations.

**Winne, Joanne.** *Living on an Island.* **Communities series. New York: Children's Press, 2000. ISBN 0-516-23305-X. 24 pages. Grades K–3**

Large, sparse text and contemporary photos take children to visit Peter and his brothers on an ice island in Iceland, Hasani on the African island Madagascar, and Laila on an island in Fiji. Children can compare their homes and lifestyles. A glossary, index, and a few related titles follow. Pair this with Fowler's *Let's Visit Some Islands* (page 53) that gives a geographical overview of islands.

Yorinks, Arthur. *The Alphabet Atlas.* Illustrated by Adrienne Yorinks. Letter art by Jeanyee Wong. New York: Winslow Press, 1999. ISBN 1-890817-14-7. 64 pages. Grades K–3

Yorinks collaborated with his wife, Adrienne, quilter and textile artist, and Wong, a gifted calligrapher, to create a unique alphabet tour around the world. The quilted art of the world map end pages introduces us to the medium that will lead us through 26 countries. Wong's embellished letters share a page with the author's brief fact about each country and hidden glimmering animals, plants, or designs symbolic of the country. It is Adrienne Yorinks' exquisite quilt art illustrations that tell us most about each country. Created from fabrics indigenous to the country, each page conveys additional information through the interwoven flora, fauna, animals, and geography. With its padded cover and stunning, vibrant format, this is a book to treasure. I only wish Adrienne Yorinks had provided more detailed notes for what she included for each page and why. Visit the interactive web site (http://www.winslowpress.com) for games, links, and information about the author and illustrator.

## *Geography and Maps: CDs*

*3D Talking Globe: The "See and Hear" Atlas Gazetteer* [interactive multimedia]. Small blue planet series. San Francisco: Now What Software, 1996. Grade 3+

The world is literally brought alive for children with this spectacular CD-ROM virtual reality globe, 3D atlas, and almanac. With a click, children can also access the interactive gazetteer of three million place names, hear the pronunciations of place names, enter their own notes, and measure distances with a special ruler tool. I especially enjoy scanning and viewing the world through the magnifying glass. Younger children can enjoy many of these features with guidance. Older students will benefit most from the more sophisticated features that require computer literacy.

*GeoHistory Maps: Europe to Eurasia* [interactive multimedia]. New York: GeoHistory, Inc., 1998. Grade 5+

GeoHistory offers up-to-date resources through a combination of their online Internet databases resources (http://www.geohistory.com/) and their CD-ROM program. *Europe to Eurasia* includes the civilizations of the Mediterranean basin, Europe, the Near East, and the Balkans from 3000 BC to the present. The format encourages users to compare and contrast political, cultural, religious, and ethnic influences throughout the ages. The map views and text articles are excellent, but teachers and students will most appreciate the capability of manipulating maps. They can sort them by region, chronology, or theme; create overlays or slide shows; and save, print, or paste maps into other programs for special effects and multimedia presentations. *GeoHistory* also provides curriculum suggestions and bibliographies. (Other titles, *The Americas* and *The World*, were not available for review.)

## *Human Rights, Racism, and Social Issues*

Allison, Anthony. *Hear These Voices: Youth at the Edge of the Millennium.* New York: Dutton, 1999. ISBN 0-525-45353-9. 170 pages. Grade 7+

The honest text and revealing b&w photos explore the lives of at-risk teenagers around the world, describing what it is like to become an adult in this society. The teenagers speak conversationally, in their own voices, with no censorship. Some of their answers are raw, shocking, painful, and sad. The portraits are unflinching, including the story of Muay, a 14-year-old girl from Thailand, sold into prostitution by her drug-addicted stepfather; 18-year-old Irina, a recovering alcoholic from the Ukraine; and boys aged 10 to 19 from the Streetwise Shelter in South Africa. Allison does emphasize that all of the teens have received help and are optimistic about the future.

**Birdseye, Debbie Holsclaw and Tom Birdseye.** *Under Our Skin: Kids Talk About Race.* **Photos by Robert Crum. New York: Holiday House, 1997. ISBN 0-8234-1325-X. 32 pages. Grade 3+**
The authors hope reading the words of six young people of different ethnic backgrounds will help others see the universality of man. These teens talk about the impact of race on their lives and friendships. Thirteen-year-old Rosa is Mexican, Akram is a Muslim from North Africa, Jenny is from China, Tad is Caucasian, Janell is Native American, and Jason is African American. Use this book for a sensitivity awareness session or a springboard for discussion of prejudice and tolerance.

**Bradley, Catherine.** *Freedom of Movement.* **What do we mean by human rights? series. New York: Franklin Watts, 1998. ISBN 0-531-14447-X. 46 pages Grades 4–8**
Americans travel freely. It is difficult for them to imagine countries that restrict or forbid movement. Bradley introduces readers to key articles of the Universal Declaration of Human Rights concerned with freedom of movement. Color photos, quotes, and text are interspersed with startling cases of violations of human rights, reported on brown paper background with black-highlighted type. Bradley cites examples including Cambodia depriving people of their nationality in 1993; effects of immigration controls by the United Kingdom in 1985; the curbing of people's freedom to travel to Berlin in 1961; and Rwandan prevention of people from returning home in 1994. She features many other violations of human rights. A glossary, useful addresses, and an index complete this persuasive resource.

**Brownlie, Alison.** *Crime and Punishment: Changing Attitudes 1900–2000.* **20th century issues series. Austin, TX: Raintree Steck-Vaughn, 1999. ISBN 0-8172-5573-7. 64 pages. Grades 6–8**
Narratives, historical photos, magazine covers, and color photos help chronicle crime and punishment in the 20th century. Brownlie examines genocide in Rwanda, punishment in Iran, criminal political leaders (Jean-Paul Akayesu, Kofi Annan, Yasser Arafat, Fidel Castro, Mao Zedong, Pablo Escobar), famous criminals and organized crime (Al Capone), murderers (Gary Gilmore), types of punishment, and the judicial system. She analyzes the internationalization of crime and the challenges of terrorism, genocide, drugs, and street crime. Key Moment and Opinion boxes offer food for thought. The bibliography, glossary, and useful addresses encourage further study.

**Charney, Israel W., ed.** *Encyclopedia of Genocide.* **Santa Barbara, CA: ABC-CLIO, 1999. ISBN 0-87436-928-2. 718 pages. Grade 6+ and Teacher Reference**
This remarkable two-volume encyclopedia opens with Elie Wiesel's words from his acceptance speech for the Nobel Peace Prize in 1986: "Because if we forget, we are guilty, we are

accomplices." Archbishop Desmond Tutu and Simon Wiesenthal establish the purpose of the encyclopedia in the forewords entitled, "Why Is It Important to Learn About the Holocaust and the Genocides of All Peoples?" Many students think the Holocaust is a thing of the past. They are oblivious to modern-day atrocities. The scope and depth of this project elucidate the sad realities of today's genocide. There are more than 90 respected contributors, with more than 200 entries, primary source documents and newspapers, photos, art, tables, and maps. Charny, executive director of the Institute on the Holocaust and Genocide in Jerusalem, begins with definitions of genocide and democide and the comparative study of genocide. The second part begins the alphabetical entries for "Genocidal Events, Intervention, and Prevention" from the Adana massacre of Armenians to genocide in Yugoslavia. Each entry includes a brief bibliography.

*Ethics and values*, 8 volumes. Danbury, CT: Grolier Educational, 1998. ISBN 0-7172-9274-6. Grade 4+ and Teacher Reference

This encyclopedia focuses on issues of ethics, morality, and values for world societies. Issues include affirmative action, anti-Semitism, bias, censorship, cooperation, environment, family, freedom of the press, free speech, global obligations, hate, prejudice, racism, rights, stereotypes, tolerance, universal values, and women's rights. B&w illustrations may discourage readers' use, but the text is handled well.

Garlake, Teresa. *Poverty: Changing Attitudes 1900–2000*. 20th century issues series. Austin, TX: Raintree Steck-Vaughn, 1999. ISBN 0-8172-5894-9. 64 pages. Grades 6–8

Every country of the world suffers from poverty, homelessness, and population growth, but the percentages are higher for Third World or developing countries. Garlake examines problems of population growth, immigration, refugees, malnutrition, disease (plague), famine (in China, Ethiopia, Russia), drought, prejudice (apartheid, caste system), and those who worked to ease poverty. Narratives, historical photos, magazine covers, and color photos affirm the extent of poverty and related suffering in the 20th century. Garlake spans the history of poverty to a look at the future. Key Moment and Opinion boxes offer food for thought. The bibliography, glossary, and useful addresses encourage further study.

Grant, R.G. *Racism: Changing Attitudes 1900–2000*. 20th century issues series. Austin, TX: Raintree Steck-Vaughn, 1999. ISBN 0-8172-5567-2. 64 pages. Grades 6–8

If your students think the Holocaust was the only time men faced prejudice and racism, this book will open their eyes. Narratives, historical photos, magazine covers, and color photos affirm the existence of racism in every country of the world in the 20th century. Grant's scope is universal. He discusses the Aborigines, Africa, Afrikaner, Amritsar massacre, Kofi Annan, apartheid, Arab people, Ashanti, and Asians. Key Moment and Opinion boxes offer food for thought. The bibliography, glossary, and useful addresses encourage further study.

Green, Jen. *Dealing with Racism*. How do I feel about series. Brookfield, CT: Copper Beech, 1998. ISBN 0-7613-0810-5. 24 pages. Grades 1–3

Children from different races are shown with cartoon bubble sayings: "We should be nice to each other." "Everyone's different—I think that's super." "Say 'No!' to racism." "Racism can be really hurtful." These serve as the perfect framework for discussion of the book's message. Green presents a straightforward treatment of the meaning and history of racism, racism today, how people feel about racism, and how to stop racism.

**Green, Jen.** *Talking About Racism.* **Talking about series. Austin, TX: Raintree Steck-Vaughn, 2000. ISBN 0-7398-1375-7. 32 pages. Grades K–3**

This bold-print book is a good introduction for children about ways in which people are different and the need to respect each other. Green speaks directly to the children, explaining in words and terms they can understand racism, gangs, and overcoming prejudice. The color photos of children affirm the book's message of acceptance.

**Grunsell, Angela.** *Racism.* **Let's talk about series. New York: Gloucester, 1991. ISBN 0-531-17279-1. 32 pages. Grades 2–5**

How did racism begin? What makes people racists? Grunsell addresses these questions and discusses stereotypes, prejudice, myths of racial superiority, effects of racism, racism in schools, and ways children can cope with and combat racism.

**Haughton, Emma, and Penny Clarke.** *Rights in the Home.* **What do we mean by human rights? series. New York: Franklin Watts, 1997. ISBN 0-531-14436-4. 46 pages Grades 4–8**

The authors chronicle why people are forced from their homes, from natural disasters to evictions to spousal or parental abuse. They share the articles of the Universal Declaration of Human Rights related to rights in the home. Color photos, quotes, and text are interspersed with profiles of related issues, reported on brown paper background with black-highlighted type. Haughton and Clarke discuss nuclear families, arranged marriages, gay marriages, controls on family size, children's rights, parenting, domestic violence and self-protection, abuse of the elderly, standards of living, and the right to dignity and privacy in one's own home. A glossary, useful addresses, and an index round out this illuminating resource.

**Hirst, Mike.** *Freedom of Belief.* **What do we mean by human rights? series. New York: Franklin Watts, 1998. ISBN 0-531-14435-6. 46 pages Grades 4–8**

Children in the United States find it difficult to imagine persecution in other countries for religious and political beliefs. Hirst explains Article 18 of the Universal Declaration of Human Rights and offers compelling examples of violations of human rights, the right to freedom of belief. Color photos, quotes, and text are interspersed with startling cases of violations of human rights, reported on brown paper background with black-highlighted type. Hirst profiles a Buddhist monk tortured and beaten by the Chinese Communist forces for his beliefs; Copernicus, who suffered for freedom of thought; Russian authors sentenced to labor camps for expressing their ideas; a Nigerian hanged for his belief in freedom; and more. A glossary, useful addresses, and an index complete this potent resource.

**MccGwire, Scarlett.** *Censorship: Changing Attitudes 1900–2000.* **20th century issues series. Austin, TX: Raintree Steck-Vaughn, 1999. ISBN 0-8172-5574-5. 64 pages. Grades 6–8**

Censorship and freedom of speech are interwoven. Narratives, historical photos, magazine covers, and color photos affirm the repression of freedom of speech around the world in the

20th century. MccGwire gives an overview of the history of censorship and the legacy of the Victorian era. She considers how the media have impacted censorship, censorship in wartime, and censorship and religion, sex, and national security. Topics she addresses include apartheid, the Gulf War, the Bolsheviks, the Ethiopian famine, Tiananmen Square, the Vietnam War, and the Falklands War. MccGwire profiles victims (Nelson Mandela, Alexander Solzhenitsyn, Stephen Biko, Salman Rushdie) and enforcers of censorship (Ayatollah Khomeini, Saddam Hussein, Mao Zedong, Juan Peron, Augusto Pinochet). Key Moment and Opinion boxes offer food for thought. The bibliography, glossary, and useful addresses encourage further study.

**O'Connor, Maureen. *Equal Rights*. What do we mean by human rights? series. New York: Franklin Watts, 1998. ISBN 0-531-14448-8. 46 pages. Grades 4–8**

In the past, the term "equal rights" has been most associated with women in the work place. This volume makes important strides in educating children about the fuller scope and meaning of the term. Color photos, quotes, and text are interspersed with startling cases of violations of human rights, reported on brown paper background with black-highlighted type. O'Connor profiles the Kurds in Iran, Anne Frank in Amsterdam, Aung San Suu Kyi in Myanmar, and Stephen Biko in South Africa, all actual instances where people were singled out because of their race, creed, age, or gender. She discusses apartheid, massacres in East Timor, and ethnic cleansing in Bosnia. This volume surveys abuses of equal rights for women, gays, and children. It examines equal rights to medical treatment, to vote, and equal opportunities, regardless of religion or political belief. O'Connor also includes a glossary, useful addresses, and an index.

**Prior, Katherine. *Workers' Rights*. What do we mean by human rights? series. New York: Franklin Watts, 1997. ISBN 0-531-14434-8. 46 pages. Grades 4–8**

The Universal Declaration of Human Rights was adopted by the United Nations in 1948 to protect people of all countries, races, beliefs, religions, ages, and genders. Prior highlights the key clauses of the declaration concerned with work and shows the wide gap in workers' rights around the world. She shares people's struggles to gain and keep employment, unfair labor practices, safety on the job, unfair and unequal pay, child labor, trade unions, and modern slavery. Prior concludes this informative work with a glossary, useful addresses, and index.

**Stearman, Kaye. *Slavery Today*. Talking points series. Austin, TX: Raintree Steck-Vaughn, 1999. ISBN 0-8172-5320-3. 64 pages. Grades 6–8**

Most students are shocked to learn slavery exists today. They think the Emancipation Proclamation freed slaves. Stearman presents many conditions in which someone is denied freedom and is "wholly or partly owned by another person or organization." She explores topics like debt bondage, child laborers, child servants, sale of people, migrant workers, forced labor, and gaining freedom. Useful addresses and a bibliography encourage further study of human rights violations such as slavery.

**Stearman, Kaye. *Women's Rights: Changing Attitudes 1900–2000*. 20th century issues series. Austin, TX: Raintree Steck-Vaughn, 1999. ISBN 0-8172-5892-2. 64 pages. Grades 6–8**

The fight for equal pay and equal rights for women is not limited to the United States.

Narratives, historical photos, magazine covers, and color photos affirm the injustices suffered by women in every country of the world in the 20th century. Stearman looks at the treatment of women in Russia, Communist China, and Africa. She discusses purdah (keeping women indoors) and sati (burning of widow with husband's body) in India, footbinding in China, and female genital mutilation in Africa. She applauds the efforts and progress of groups like the Women's International League for Peace and Freedom and the silent protests of the Mothers of the Plaza de Mayo in Argentina. She disparages groups like the Taliban in Afghanistan who continue to restrict women's rights. Key Moment and Opinion boxes offer food for thought. The bibliography, glossary, and useful addresses encourage further study.

**Steele, Philip.** *Freedom of Speech.* **What do we mean by human rights? series. New York: Franklin Watts, 1997. ISBN 0-531-14433-X. 46 pages Grades 4–8**
Steele examines man's need to communicate and the right to freedom of speech asserted by the Universal Declaration of Human Rights. Color photos, quotes, and text are interspersed with startling cases of violations of human rights, reported on brown paper background with black-highlighted type. Steele profiles the condemnation of Socrates for teaching dangerous ideas; censorship of art in Melbourne, Australia, in 1995; Bowdlerization of Shakespeare's plays in England in 1818; censorship of writing as blasphemous in Bangladesh in 1993; and speaking up for change by Dr. Martin Luther King, Jr. in Washington, DC, in 1963. He addresses issues of racism, controlling information, censorship of media, arresting and jailing dissidents, propaganda, and more. A glossary, useful addresses, and index follow.

**Stern-LaRosa, Caryl, and Ellen Hofheimer Bettmann.** *The Anti-Defamation League's Hate Hurts: How Children Learn and Unlearn Prejudice.* **New York: Scholastic, 2000. ISBN 0-439-21121-2. 332 pages. Teacher Reference**
If you have only one book to guide children from prejudice, this is the one. It is comprehensive and sensitive. The authors explain prejudice and hurt in terms children can understand. The examples they choose are ones with which children (and adults) can identify. In the first section, they examine how children learn hate, things that make people different from one another, why people hate, and what to do to combat and erase hate. Part Two is a question-and-answer section, divided by age groups, and followed by analyses of name-calling, joking, excluding, crimes of hate, and key diversity skills and concepts. The third section addresses what parents and children can do to combat hate in schools, the media, and on the Internet. Finally, the authors consider how people can work toward change in the community, workplace, and house of worship. A bibliography and list of organizations and Web sites encourage further study.

**Weatherford, Doris.** *Women's Almanac 2000.* **Phoenix, AZ: Oryx Press, 2000. ISBN 1-57356-341-2. 370 pages. Grade 6+**
Students trying to assess the strides forward and steps backward for women in the last two millennia will find this text concise, informative, and indispensable. Weatherford analyzes women and their social, religious, and political issues. She documents her data, offers a country-by-country global snapshot of the condition of women, and highlights women in the United States. The profiles and time lines of notable women in U.S. and world history will be essential for Women's History Month studies.

# The Immigrant Experience

**Bode, Janet.** *The Colors of Freedom: Immigrant Stories.* **New York: Franklin Watts, 1999. ISBN 0-531-11530-5. 144 pages. Grade 7+**

Named as a 2000 New York Public Library Best Books for the Teen Age, this book offers both a history of immigration and a testimonial to the spirit and strength of immigrants from around the world. Bode explains the process of researching and writing the featured stories from Mayflower ancestors to the early 1900s. The remainder of the book includes interviews of immigrant teenagers who talk about their homelands and the immigrant experience, including their photos, poems, and recipes. Read stories of the Americas and the Caribbean nations; Mexico; Eastern Europe, the Middle East, and Africa; and Asia and the Subcontinent. Finally, try recommended student activities.

**Bunting, Eve.** *How Many Days to America? A Thanksgiving Story.* **Illustrated by Beth Peck. New York: Clarion, 1998. ISBN 0-899-19521-0. 32 pages. Grades K–3**

When refugees in this poignant story survive a perilous boat trip from the Caribbean to America, they show the true meaning of giving thanks.

**Bunting, Eve.** *A Picnic in October.* **Illustrated by Nancy Carpenter. San Diego: Harcourt Brace, 1999. ISBN 0-15-201656-2. Grades K–3.**

It is time for the family's yearly trip to Ellis Island on October 28. Reluctantly, the young boy attends the celebration of the birthday of the Statue of Liberty. As he watches his grandmother and new immigrants to the United States, he finally understands what Lady Liberty means and why this picnic is so important.

**Gallo, Donald, ed.** *Join In: Multiethnic Short Stories by Outstanding Writers for Young Adults.* **New York: Laurel Leaf, 1995. ISBN 0-440-21957-4. Grade 7+**

Gallo understands teenagers and their concerns and needs. He elicited 17 stories by famous Young Adult authors (including Julius Lester, Rita Williams-Garcia, Jean Davies Okimoto, and Linda Crew) that show struggles with identity, acceptance, family, and assimilation into American culture. Gallo includes brief author biographies.

**Lawlor, Veronica, and Rudolph W. Giuliani.** *I Was Dreaming to Come to America: Memories from the Ellis Island Oral History Project.* **Selected and illustrated by Veronica Lawlor; foreword by Rudolph W. Giuliani, Mayor, New York City. New York: Viking, 1995. ISBN 0-670-86164-2. 40 pages. Grades 3–6**

Lawlor's original collage illustrations accompany the memories of immigrants who arrived at Ellis Island.

**Maestro, Betsy.** *Coming to America: The Story of Immigration.* **Illustrated by Susannah Ryan. New York: Scholastic, 1996. ISBN 0-590-44151-5. Grades K–4**

From the first double-page spread of the "Around the World Dinner" to the final "melting pot" fair, Maestro and Ryan celebrate the diversity of the United States. This history of immigration is my favorite book for teaching children about sameness and differences.

**Rebman, Renee C.** *Life on Ellis Island.* **The way people live series. San Diego: Lucent Books, 2000. ISBN 1-56006-533-8. 95 pages. Grades 6+**

The series succeeds in its goal to "flesh out the traditional, two-dimensional views of people in various cultures and historical circumstances." Rebman takes us on an unforgettable journey to "the island of hope, island of tears." She chronicles the various immigrant movements, the circumstances that led people to leave their homelands, the difficulties and dangers of getting to America, and the actual immigration experience. Sidebars offer insights into daily activities and adjustments (including the changing of names, quotas, and confusing "modern" conveniences in America). Rebman incorporates primary and secondary materials and includes b&w maps, photos, and illustrations to examine the lives of those who came to America, those who were detained, groups who offered support, and present-day immigration. The chronology, glossary, and bibliographies encourage further research.

**Stein, R. Conrad.** *Ellis Island*, **2nd ed. Cornerstones of freedom series. New York: Children's Press, 1992. ISBN 0-516-06653-6. 31 pages. Grades 3–5**
Stein provides an introduction to the history, closing, and restoration of the Ellis Island immigration center. The simple text and photos of the turn of the 20th century help children understand the life of the immigrants who came to America from around the world.

# *Religion and Philosophy*

**Aiyengar, Devi S.** *I Am Hindu*. **Religions of the world series. New York: PowerKids Press, 1997. ISBN 0-8239-2381-9. 24 pages. Grades K–3**
Anil, from Houston, shares the rudiments of his faith. The colorful photography and large print make this an appealing introduction to Hindu rituals, customs, history, and holy days, including Hindu temples, Diwali, Krishna's birthday, Dussehra, Ganesh, marriage, India, Bhagavad Gita, and home shrines. A glossary follows.

**Bowker, John.** *World Religions: The Great Faiths Explored and Explained*. **New York: Dorling Kindersley, 1996. ISBN 0-7894-1439-2. 200 pages. Grade 5+**
This comprehensive study transcends the traditional narrative and color photos. It is a work of art with its religious artifacts, sacred texts, and magnificent paintings and architecture of the world. The annotations are an added adventure, introducing readers to fascinating details about rites, customs, and culture. Bowker features chapters on the meaning of religion, ancient religions, Hinduism, Jainism, Buddhism, Sikhism, Chinese religions, Japanese religions, Judaism, Christianity, Islam, Native religions, the Golden Rule, religious time line and maps, and a bibliography.

**Chalfonte, Jessica.** *I Am Muslim*. **Religions of the world series. New York: PowerKids Press, 1997. ISBN 0-8239-2375-4. 24 pages. Grades K–3**
Ahmet, from Detroit, shares the rudiments of his faith. The colorful photography and large print make this an appealing introduction to Islamic rituals, customs, history, and holy days, including Allah, Muhammed, the Qur'an, Islamic law, mosques, prayer, Hajj, almsgiving, and Ramadan. A glossary follows.

**Ganeri, Anita.** *Growing Up: From Child to Adult*. **Illustrated by Jackie Morris. Life times series. New York: Peter Bedrick, 1998. ISBN 0-87226-287-1. Grades K–3**
Ganeri explores the initiation rituals or special ceremonies for children who embrace the

faiths of Hinduism, Buddhism, Sikhism, Judaism, Christianity, and Islam. The photos of the children are charming and joyful.

**Ganeri, Anita.** *Religions Explained: A Beginner's Guide to World Faiths.* **Your world explained series. New York: Henry Holt, 1997. 72 pages. Grade 3+**
This series offers more detail than most to help children understand the tenets, scriptures, rites, feast days and festivals of the world's religions. The book is replete with color photos and illustrations. Ganeri examines traditional religions (Judaism, Islam, Catholicism, Christianity, Hinduism, and Buddhism) as well as lesser-known religions (Sikhism, Jainism, Rastafarianism, Bahaism, Hare Krishna and New Age movements, and spirit religions of South and North America, Africa, and Australasia).

**Ganeri, Anita.** *What Do We Know About Buddhism?* **What do we know about series. New York: Peter Bedrick, 1997. ISBN 0-8722-63859-4. 48 pages. Grades 3–7**
In this series that includes color photos and illustrations to guide children through various religions, this volume traces the origins of Buddhism through the life and teachings of Gautama or Buddha. It answers questions about lifestyle, worship, monasteries, sacred texts, holy places, and festivals. One of the most interesting sections depicts the most important times in a Buddhist's life. Ganeri shows the rise of Buddhism in Asia, highlights Tibetan Buddhism, and looks at Buddhist art and literature. Ganeri includes a glossary and index.

**Ganeri, Anita.** *What Do We Know About Hinduism?* **What do we know about series. New York: Peter Bedrick, 1996. ISBN 0-8722-6385-1. 40 pages. Grades 3–7**
In this series that includes color photos and illustrations to guide children through various religions, this volume shows Hindu gods and goddesses, festivals, history, and beliefs.

**Jacobs, William Jay.** *World Religions: Great Lives.* **New York: Atheneum, 1996. ISBN 0-689-80486-5. Grade 7+**
Jacobs' fine collection of biographies includes Jesus, Moses, Muhammad, Confucius, Buddha, Mahatma Gandhi, and others. He includes Golda Meir and Mother Teresa among other female founders and proponents of religion in the Eastern and Western worlds.

**Kadodwala, Dilip.** *Holi.* **A world of holidays series. Austin, TX: Raintree Steck-Vaughn, 1997. ISBN 0-8172-4610-X. 32 pages. Grades 3–6**
Celebrate Holi, the Hindu Festival of Color, with this fascinating study of the traditions, ceremonies, and foods of the day. Learn about the power of good over evil, Vishnu the Protector, and how the holiday is celebrated in other countries.

**Kimmel, Eric A.** *Be Not Far From Me: The Oldest Love Story, Legends From the Bible.* **Illustrated by David Diaz. New York: Simon and Schuster, 1998. ISBN 0-689-81088-1. Grade 4+**
Kimmel weaves his magic touch on these accounts of the lives of Abraham, Moses, Deborah, Elijah, and other heroes and heroines of the Bible and the Midrash. Diaz's striking silhouettes and the vibrant maps and time line make this a keepsake book.

**Langley, Myrtle.** *Religion.* **Eyewitness books. New York: Knopf, 1996. ISBN 0-679-98123-9. 59 pages. Grade 3+**
Prepare for an amazing visual experience. Langley's intriguing details about the world's

religions jump off the page with the stunning, colorful illustrations and photos characteristic of the Eyewitness series books. Study the history, beliefs, and practices of the Hindu way, the Buddhist path, Shinto harmony, Jain respect for life, Sikh teaching, Zoroastrianism, Confucianism, Taoism, Islam, Judaism, and Christianity.

**Maestro, Betsy.** *The Story of Religion.* **Illustrated by Giulio Maestro. New York: Mulberry Books, 1999. ISBN 0-688-17146-X. 48 pages. Grade 2+**
The Maestros emphasize sharing the earth and respecting differing beliefs. They introduce young readers to both primitive and organized religions with appealing color illustrations for aspects of each faith, from the Buddhists of China to the Muslims of the Middle East.

**Marchant, Kerena.** *Id-ul-Fitr.* **Festivals series. Brookfield, CT: Millbrook Press, 1998. ISBN 0-7613-0963-2. Grades 2–6**
Contemporary photos and simple large-print text introduce children to the Muslim festival of Id-ul-Fitr, the Islamic calendar, and other festivals like Al-Hegira and Meelad-ul-Nabal.

**Matthews, Mary.** *Magid Fasts for Ramadan.* **Illustrated by E.B. Lewis. New York: Clarion Books, 1996. ISBN 0-395-66589-2. 48 pages. Grades 3–6**
In this wonderful introduction to the customs of the Muslims, eight-year-old Magid, living in contemporary Cairo, decides he will fast for Ramadan, even though his family feels he is too young. He discovers how difficult it is and that he must be honest. The family's compromise is a poignant scene, enhanced by Lewis's soft, sympathetic watercolors.

**Nomura, Noriko S.** *I Am Shinto.* **Religions of the world series. New York: PowerKids Press, 1997. ISBN 0-8239-2380-0. 24 pages. Grades K–3**
Yasuko, from Honolulu, shares the rudiments of her faith. The colorful photography and large print make this an appealing introduction to Shintoism, the official religion of Japan. Nomura describes rituals, customs, history, and holy days, including being Shinto, Kami, purification, shrines, New Year's Day, Hina Matsuri, marriage, 7-5-3 Festival, and Seyin-no-Hi. A glossary follows.

**Osborne, Mary Pope.** *One World, Many Religions: The Ways We Worship.* **New York: Knopf, 1996. ISBN 0-679-93930-5. 86 pages. Grade 3+**
With its articulate text, stunning photography, and sweeping panoramas, this is my favorite book on religions of the world. The photography captures unusual moments as well as the joy and awe of rituals for Judaism, Christianity, Islam, Hinduism, Buddhism, Confucianism, and Taoism.

**Penney, Sue. Discovering Religions series. Austin, TX: Raintree Steck-Vaughn. 48 pages. Grades 4–7**
Penney provides a clear, user-friendly approach to the principles and practices of each faith. Colorful photos of contemporary children who practice the faith help children become more aware and accepting of other faiths. *Buddhism* (1997; ISBN 0-8172-4395-X) includes Siddhartha Gautama, the Eightfold Path, the role of pilgrimages, and Buddhist philosophies. *Christianity* (1997; ISBN 0-8172-4396-8) includes the life and

teachings of Jesus Christ, the Bible, and rituals. *Hinduism* (1997; ISBN 0-8172-4397-6) includes the Vedas, god and goddesses, and holy days. *Islam* (1997; ISBN 0-8172-4394-1) includes Muhammed and the role of family and women. *Judaism* (1996; ISBN 0-8172-4393-3) includes worship in synagogues, holy days, and readings. *Sikhism* (1996; ISBN 0-8172-4398-4) includes celebrations and the five Ks.

**Quinn, Daniel P. *I Am Buddhist*. Religions of the world series. New York: PowerKids Press, 1997. ISBN 0-8239-2370-7. 24 pages. Grades K–3**
Yeyen, a Chinese Buddhist from San Francisco, shares the rudiments of her faith. The colorful photography and large print make this an appealing introduction to Buddhist rituals, customs, history, and holy days, including prayer, Karma, Guan Yin, Buddha Day, sutras, honoring the ancestors, and refuge in the Buddha, the Dharma, and the Sangha. A glossary follows.

**Ray, Jane. *Let There Be Light: Bible Stories*. Illustrated by the author. New York: Dutton, 1997. ISBN 0-525-45925-1. Grades K–3**
Ray's gold borders and glittering folk art symbolize the light of the universe. Her unique art and gentle retellings from the Old and New Testaments, stories of Creation, Noah's Ark, and Christmas will delight readers of all ages.

**Sanderson, Ruth. *Tapestries: Stories of Women in the Bible*. Illustrated by the author. Boston: Little, Brown and Co., 1998. ISBN 0-316-77093-0. Grades 3–5**
Noted biblical women come alive through Sanderson's facile text and evocative oils. Share these brief biographies of Eve, Sarah, Rebekah, Miriam, Rahab, Deborah, Jael, Ruth, Hannah, The Witch of Endor, Abigail, Bathsheba, and the Queen of Sheba from the Old Testament and Mary of Nazareth, Elizabeth, Anna, Mary and Martha, Procula, Mary Magdalene, Lydia, Priscilla, Phoebe, and Tabitha from the New Testament.

**Sevastiades, Philemon D. *I Am Eastern Orthodox*. Religions of the world series. New York: PowerKids Press, 1997. ISBN 0-8239-2377-0. 24 pages. Grades K–3**
Anastasia, from Chicago, shares the rudiments of her faith. The colorful photography and large print make this an appealing introduction to Eastern Orthodox rituals, customs, history, and holy days, including being Eastern Orthodox, traditions and the Bible, Jesus Christ, the Trinity, holidays, and sacraments. A glossary follows.

**Sevastiades, Philemon D. *I Am Protestant*. Religions of the world series. New York: PowerKids Press, 1997. ISBN 0-8239-2377-0. 24 pages. Grades K–3**
Yvonne, from Atlanta, shares the rudiments of her faith. The colorful photography and large print make this an appealing introduction to Protestant rituals, customs, history, and holy days, including being Protestant, Protestant sects, Jesus Christ, prayer, Baptism, and salvation. A glossary follows.

**Sevastiades, Philemon D. *I Am Roman Catholic*. Religions of the world series. New York: PowerKids Press, 1997. ISBN 0-8239-2376-2. 24 pages. Grades K–3**
Victor, from Los Angeles, shares the rudiments of his faith. The colorful photography and large print make this an appealing introduction to Roman Catholic rituals, customs, history, and holy days, including Jesus Christ, the Pope, the Trinity, holidays, and sacraments. A glossary follows.

**Sita, Lisa.** *Worlds of Belief: Religion and Spirituality.* **Our human family series. Woodbridge, CT: Blackbirch, in cooperation with the Denver Museum of Natural History, 1996. ISBN 1-56711-125-4. 80 pages. Grade 4+**

The power of religion envelops all cultures of the world. Sita explores the religious beliefs, manners, and customs of Americas, Africa, Europe and the Middle East, Asia, and Australia and the South Pacific in this beautifully written and visually appealing volume.

**Sturges, Philemon.** *Sacred Places.* **Illustrated by Giles Laroche. New York: Putnam, 2000. ISBN 0-399-23317-2. 40 pages. Grade 3+**

In this spectacular book, Sturges and Laroche created "a celebration of the many different ways people have found to use the language of architecture to praise their Creator and to express their feelings about the mystery of life and death." They explore the special places of worship of Hindus, Buddhists, Abraham's God ("People of the Book"), Jews, Christians, and Muslims. "Sites of Sacred Places" locates the featured mosques, churches, temples, shrines, cathedrals, and personal sacred places around the world. The paper relief illustrations by Laroche are intricate and exquisite; Sturges' text is lyrical.

**Weiss, Bernard P.** *I Am Jewish.* **Religions of the world series. New York: PowerKids Press, 1997. ISBN 0-8239-2349-5. 24 pages. Grades K–3**

David, from St. Louis, shares the rudiments of his faith. The colorful photography and large print make this an appealing introduction to Judaic rituals, customs, history, and holy days, including being Jewish, the Sabbath, synagogue, Bar Mitzvah, High Holy Days, the Hebrew Bible, and Jerusalem. A glossary follows.

# *Religion and Holiday: Videos*

*Chinese New Year* **[videorecording]. Holidays for children video series. Bala Cynwyd, PA: Schlessinger Video Productions, 1994. ISBN 1-57225-013-5. 25 minutes. Grades K–4**

Michael Keck hosts this interactive series that captures for children the excitement and the significance of holidays. He leads children to an understanding of the symbols, customs, rituals, and folklore of Chinese New Year. Through colorful footage, children experience an actual celebration of Chinese New Year in Chinatown and then travel back to 1975 for a traditional celebration in Peking, China. The zodiac quiz and a Chinese dragon-making project draw the children into the festivities.

*Ramadan* **[videorecording]. Holidays for children video series. Bala Cynwyd, PA: Schlessinger Video Productions, 1996. ISBN 1-57225-098-4. 25 minutes. Grades K–4**

Michael Keck hosts this interactive series that captures for children the excitement and significance of holy days. He leads children to an understanding of the symbols, customs, rituals, and folklore of the Ramadan. Through color footage, music, and narration, children will travel to the Middle East to see how people celebrate this month-long holiday. They will learn about the Five Pillars of Islam, Muhammed, the Koran, prayer, fasting, and sacrifice. Children can participate with a diorama project.

# Science and Nature

*Atlas of Animals.* Created by the Scholastic Staff, Rene Mettler, and Claude Delafosse. First discovery book series. New York: Scholastic, 1996. ISBN 0-590-58280-1. 24 pages. Grades K–3

This is an appealing introduction to more than 50 animals of the world. It shows animals like the panda in China and the elephant in Africa, all in their natural habitats. The acetate overlay pages are the most popular feature of the book.

Baines, John. *Coasts.* Ecology Alert! series. Austin, TX: Raintree Steck-Vaughn, 1999. ISBN 0-8172-5370-X. 32 pages. Grades 4–6

This series emphasizes the partnership among nations to preserve the world's resources and harmony. The activities and case studies are valuable teaching tools. This volume focuses on resources of the coasts, the animals and plants, and how people around the world can act responsibly to prevent the extinction of endangered species.

Baird, Nicola. *A Green World?* Viewpoints series. New York: Franklin Watts, 1998. ISBN 0-531-14451-8. 32 pages. Grades 4–8

This worthy series presents opposing views on contemporary social issues, encourages debate, and leaves questions for the reader to answer. Use "Facts to think about" as a springboard for discussion of ecology. With introductory text, opposing viewpoint quotes, and color photography, Baird provokes discussion of pollution, global warming, wildlife protection, organic food, population, recycling, survival, and proactive protests. She includes a glossary and a list of contacts for further information.

Bang, Molly. *Common Ground: The Water, Earth, and Air We Share.* New York: Scholastic, 1997. ISBN 0-590-10056-4. 32 pages. Grades K–3

Through simple vignettes, Bang shows how man has overused and abused the resources of the earth. The illustrations are vibrant and telling. This is a perfect introduction to a lesson on ecology and global responsibility.

Barish, Wendy. *Endangered Animals.* Created by Sylvaine Perols and Gallimard Jeunesse. First discovery book series. New York: Scholastic, 1997. ISBN 0-590-96214-0. 24 pages. Grades K–3

This spectacular book introduces young readers to four endangered creatures from each of the continents. The environmental message is conveyed visually with the startling contrasts between the giant panda, the red throat parrot, the slow-moving sloth, and other special creatures in their destroyed homes and then in their colorful natural environments. The overlays are nothing special, but playing with them will enchant children.

Beecroft, Simon. *The New Book of El Niño.* Brookfield, CT: Copper Beech Books, 1999. ISBN 0-7613-0797-4. 32 pages. Grades 3–8

What is El Niño? Is El Niño responsible for extremes in weather? Explore these questions through fascinating text and sidebars, striking computer illustrations, satellite photos, color photos and illustrations, and cut-aways.

**Brown, Paul.** *Energy and Resources.* **Living for the future series. New York: Franklin Watts, 1998. ISBN 0-531-14483-6. 32 pages. Grades 4–8**

This easy-to-use resource helps students understand how energy is produced, the limitations on today's resources, and ways we can achieve "sustainable development" as recommended by Agenda 21 of the Earth Summit. Color photos abound. A glossary, list of organizations and agencies, and index round out this useful volume.

**Butterfield, Moira.** *Animals in Hot Places.* **Looking at series. Austin, TX: Raintree Steck-Vaughn, 1999. ISBN 0-7398-0112-0. 32 pages. Grades 2–4**

Butterfield features animals that live in deserts around the world. Each double-page spread boasts a full-page color photograph of the animal and a page of large-print text about its habits and habitats. The microscopic photography captures wonderful moments of animals like the Moloch lizard, sand cat, fennec, and tarantula. A color map of the world helps children understand where the animals live in relationship to their own world.

**Butterfield, Moira.** *Animals in Trees.* **Looking at series. Austin, TX: Raintree Steck-Vaughn, 1999. ISBN 0-7398-0110-4. 32 pages. Grades 2–4**

Butterfield features animals from around the world that live in trees. Each double-page spread boasts a full-page color photograph of the animal and a page of large-print text about the habits and habitats. The microscopic photography makes the koala, red-eyed tree frog, bush baby, and other animals look as if they could climb onto the reader's lap. A color map of the world helps children understand where the animals live in relationship to their own world.

**Cassie, Brian.** *Say It Again.* **Illustrated by David Mooney. Watertown, MA: Charlesbridge, 2000. ISBN 0-88106-341-X. 32 pages. Grades K–2**

This will be one of the children's favorite books. "Some creatures, from Peru to Ghana,/ And Madagascar to Guyana,/ Have names that have a double sound./Here are a few that we have found." Fabulous watercolors take children around the world to meet these creatures with names like coro coro, killy killy, frou frou, and wonga wonga. Cassie describes the habitat and habits of each at the end of the book.

**Church, Andrew and Amanda.** *Transportation.* **Ecology Alert! series. Austin, TX: Raintree Steck-Vaughn, 1999. ISBN 0-8172-5372-6. 32 pages. Grades 4–6.**

This series emphasizes the partnership among nations to preserve the world's resources and harmony. The activities and case studies are valuable teaching tools. This volume shows the development of modes of transportation around the world and these vehicles' impact upon the environment.

**Cranfield, Ingrid.** *100 Greatest Natural Wonders.* **100 Greatest series. Danbury, CT: Grolier, 1997. ISBN 0-7172-7685-6. 111 pages. Grade 3+**

This volume of the series includes one-page profiles and color photography and illustrations of wonders of the world. Explore the wonders of space (Auroras), volcanoes (Mount Fuji), minerals (Lakes Natron and Magadi), saltwater (Great Barrier Reef), freshwater (Victoria Falls), marshes (The Pantanal), ice (The Ross Ice Shelf), mountains (Mount Everest), caves (The Mulu Caves), valleys (Yangzi Gorges), rocks (Ayers Rock), trees (Amazon Rainforest), and deserts (The Namib Desert).

**Delano, Marfe Ferguson.** *Animal Safari: Tree Frogs.* Washington, DC: National Geographic Society, 2000. ISBN 0-7922-7127-0. Grades K–1

This board book with simple text will delight children with the vivid close-up photography of the fascinating tree frog. The back cover features tree frogs from Australia, Ecuador, Malaysia, Mexico, and the United States, and will help children understand how nature's creatures are both alike and different.

**Dudzinski, Kathleen.** *Meeting Dolphins: My Adventures in the Sea.* Washington, DC: National Geographic Society, 2000. ISBN 0-7922-7129-7. 64 pages. Grade 3+

Dolphins are amazing mammals. In this magnificent book, marine biologist Dudkinski shares her life's study of dolphin communication around the world. She explains the listening device she invented to monitor dolphin vocalizations. With the help of IMAX photography, she takes readers into the undersea world for a journey they won't forget.

**Dunn, Andrew.** *The Children's Atlas of Scientific Discoveries and Inventions.* Brookfield, CT: Millbrook Press, 1996. ISBN 0-7613-0241-7. 96 pages. Grades 4–8

Dunn makes the distinction between discoveries (finding things already there) and inventions (using things in a new way) in this attractive and educational resource. He organizes the collection by technology and the birth of ideas, communications and travel, learning about life, and astronomy and cosmology. Abundant color maps, diagrams, illustrations, and photos help students visualize man's understanding and use of his world.

*The Encyclopedia of the Environment.* New York: Franklin Watts, 1999. ISBN 0-531-11709-X. 160 pages. Grades 4–8

Search this invaluable resource from acid rain and adaptation to zooplankton and zoos and aquariums. The more than 300 environmental topics are arranged alphabetically with color illustrations and photos. Concise text is accompanied by cross-references, keywords, fast facts, and profiles. The volume addresses ways to protect the environment and includes an extensive bibliography and lists of environmental organizations and agencies.

**Featherstone, Jane.** *Energy.* Ecology Alert! series. Austin, TX: Raintree Steck-Vaughn, 1999. ISBN 0-8172-5374-2. 32 pages. Grades 4–6

This series emphasizes the partnership among nations to preserve the world's resources and harmony. The activities and case studies are valuable teaching tools. This volume explains sources of energy and the effects on the environment. It recommends the use of solar, wind, and geothermal power, all of which are renewable energy sources.

**Featherstone, Jane.** *Farming.* Ecology Alert! series. Austin, TX: Raintree Steck-Vaughn, 1999. ISBN 0-8172-5371-8. 32 pages. Grades 4–6

This series emphasizes the partnership among nations to preserve the world's resources and harmony. The activities and case studies are valuable teaching tools. This volume shows how man struggles to feed the world and how agriculture has had to change to create sustainable farming. It also considers arable and livestock farming.

**Fowler, Allan.** *It Could Still Be Endangered.* Rookie read-about science series. New York: Children's Press, 2000. ISBN 0-516-21208-7. 32 pages. Grades K–2

Charming color photos of the giant panda, sea otter, black-footed ferret, and mother manatee with her calves, as well as less cuddly animals like the cheetah, gray wolf, and poison-dart frog will draw children to this simple book. Here they will discover the meaning of endangerment. A pictorial glossary follows.

**Fowler, Allan.** *Save the Rain Forests.* **Rookie read-about science series. New York: Children's Press, 1996. ISBN 0-516-20029-1. 32 pages. Grades K–2**
Fowler shows animals and plants in their natural habitat in the rain forest with color photos and simple text. He includes a world map to teach children both the location and disappearance of rain forests. Finally, he explains the uses and impact of cutting down trees. A pictorial glossary follows.

**Fyson, Nance.** *World Population.* **Living for the future series. New York: Franklin Watts, 1998. ISBN 0-531-14479-8. 32 pages. Grades 4–8**
This easy-to-use resource helps students understand how the world is in crisis with six billion people, how there are limited resources to share, why people must control the size of families, and ways we can achieve "sustainable development" as recommended by Agenda 21 of the Earth Summit. Color photos abound. A glossary, list of organizations and agencies, and index round out this useful volume.

**Gallant, Roy A.** *Dance of the Continents.* **Tarrytown, NY: Benchmark, 1999. Story of science series. ISBN 0-7614-0962-9. Grade 5+**
Trace the fascinating history of plate tectonics with brilliant photography and interesting text. Gallant also projects future geological changes.

**Gifford, Clive.** *How the Future Began: Everyday Life.* **New York: Kingfisher, 2000. ISBN 0-7534-5268-5. 64 pages. Grade 3+**
This provocative book surveys the technologies that have advanced man to the present and projects his future. It speculates about homes and cities, transportation, work and play, and healthy living of the 21st century. Gifford also addresses environmental concerns and man's global responsibilities. The time lines bounce from a tennis racket, rise with a glass elevator, soar with a jet, and climb a thread of DNA across the double-page spreads. Color montages superimpose images on buildings. Aerial photography and macroscopic images abound in this exceptional book.

**Gold, Susan Dudley.** *Blame It On El Niño.* **Austin, TX: Raintree Steck-Vaughn, 1999. ISBN 0-7398-1376-5. 96 pages. Grade 4+**
Gold debunks the myth of El Niño as the cause for weather-generated destruction. She uses scientific evidence to explain how El Niño works, to evaluate its role in weather changes and devastation, and to speculate about the future of El Niño. Maps, charts, color photos and illustrations complement a lucid, well-organized text. Gold includes source notes, a glossary, bibliography, Web sites, and an index.

**Goodman, Susan E.** *Animal Rescue: The Best Job There Is.* **Ready-to-read series. New York: Simon and Schuster, 2000. ISBN 0-689-81794-0. 48 pages. Grades 2–5**
Who helps the animals in time of disaster and need? Join American John Walsh of the World Society for the Protection of Animals as he travels to South America for a jungle rescue, the Mideast for wartime rescue, and to Japan for an earthquake rescue. The

photos and details of trapped, starving, and suffering animals paint a realistic portrait in this powerful book.

**Hoff, Brent, and Carter Smith III.** *Mapping Epidemics: A Historical Atlas of Disease.* **New York: Franklin Watts, 2000. ISBN 0-531-11713-8. 112 pages. Grade 7+**
Movies have dramatized devastating outbreaks of disease, but students need to go further than the evening news and daily newspapers to hear about new viruses and diseases. The introduction, establishing the immediacy and severity of scope of the epidemics, is followed by a glossary. AIDS, Lyme disease, and West Nile virus are only a few of the 32 contemporary threats to man's immune system featured in this encyclopedia. The authors offer double-page spreads, appropriate for upper middle school students, for each epidemic, with clear color maps showing areas of outbreaks. The sidebar information (including global distribution, causative agent, transmission, symptoms, treatment, and prevention and control) and extended text permit more in-depth study for older readers.

**Hewitt, Sally.** *Time.* **It's science! series. New York: Children's Press, 1999. ISBN 0-516-21655-4. 30 pages. Grades K–3**
This series is specifically designed to appeal to children and introduce them to basic scientific concepts. The bold headings, large concise text, and expressive color photos are appealing. Help children understand time, day, night, measuring time, counting the hours, dates, years, seasons, fast, slow, and natural changes. The valuable "Think About It," "Look Again," and "Try It Out!" insets give suggestions for further discussion and projects. A glossary and index follow.

**Hewitt, Sally.** *Weather.* **It's science! series. New York: Children's Press, 2000. ISBN 0-516-21657-0. 30 pages. Grades K–3**
With this appealing concept book, teach children about rain, sun, hot, cold, air, wind, clouds, snow, ice, storms, differences in weather around the world, and forecasting. Teachers will love "Think About It," "Safety Warning," "Look Again," and "Try It Out!" insets that offer ideas for discussion and activities. A glossary and index follow.

**Jackson, Carolyn.** *Animals.* **Pictures and words series. New York: Franklin Watts, 1999. ISBN 0-531-11712-X. 128 pages. Grades 2–6**
This attractive illustrated volume features 125 wild animals of the world. Entries are arranged alphabetically, divided by animal groups (including mammals, marsupials and monotremes, birds, reptiles, fish, mollusks, crustaceans, amphibians, insects, and arachnids). Each entry is a full page with bold headings color-coded by groups, a brief description of the animal, color photos and illustrations, and engrossing information about the animals' habits and habitat.

**Livo, Norma J.** *Celebrating the Earth: Stories, Experiences, and Activities.* **Englewood, CO: Teacher Ideas Press, 2000. ISBN 1-56308-776-6. 174 pages. Teacher Reference for grades K–8**
Although this book uses world folktales and experiences, I have placed it in the science section because Livo says she wants to develop a naturalist intelligence in children. She explains why she used stories, why animals are important characters in the story, and how Howard Gardner's theory of multiple intelligences is at the center of her work. She

divides the "stories for budding naturalists" by amphibians and reptiles, flying creatures, four-footed animals, constellations, plants, creatures from the water, natural phenomena, and American folklore. After each story, Livo discusses the tale and adds a personal story. The "activities for budding naturalists" section offers a wealth of cross-curricular activities and projects to extend each story or topic and reinforces the science strand of the geography and social studies standards.

**Morgan, Sally. *Acid Rain*. Earth Watch series. New York: Franklin Watts, 1999. ISBN 0-531-14567-0. 32 pages. Grades 4–8**
Replete with photos, a map, and diagrams, this resource offers one of the best discussions of the meaning, causes, and impact of acid rain. Morgan pays close attention to detail, offering visible evidence of the dangers of acid rain, from an eroded statue to damaged conifers to the poisoning of wildlife. Colored insets entitled "Taking Part," "On the Ground" and "Eco Thought" give telling statistics and illuminating facts. A "Fact File," glossary, and index enhance this recommended resource.

**Morgan, Sally. *Changing Climate*. Earth Watch series. New York: Franklin Watts, 1999. ISBN 0-531-14568-9. 32 pages. Grades 4–8**
In this informative volume, Morgan examines trends in climate, the definition and types of climate, climates and oceans, and climate clues. The text is supplemented by "On the Ground" and "Eco Thought" features and is supported by color photos, maps, and illustrations. Other issues addressed include the effects of natural events on climate, greenhouse effect, global warming, effects on animals and plants, finding new fuels, and the role of man.

**Morgan, Sally. *Homes and Cities*. Living for the future series. New York: Franklin Watts, 1998. ISBN 0-531-14478-X. 32 pages. Grades 4–8**
This easy-to-use resource helps students understand how cities are planned and built, the need for responsible action, concerns of waste disposal and destruction of resources, and ways we can achieve "sustainable development" as recommended by Agenda 21 of the Earth Summit. Color photos abound. A glossary, list of organizations and agencies, and index round out this useful volume.

**Morgan, Sally. *The Ozone Hole*. Earth Watch series. New York: Franklin Watts, 1999. ISBN 0-531-14569-7. 32 pages. Grades 4–8**
Morgan helps students understand what the ozone hole is and does for Earth. With maps, diagrams, color photos, and concise text, she shows children how to measure ozone, how to discover a hole, effects of chlorofluorocarbons and other destroyers of ozone, and the effects of the ozone hole on us. The "Fact File," "Eco Thoughts," and glossary help to round out this informative resource.

**Morgan, Sally, and Pauline Lalor. *World Food*. Living for the future series. New York: Franklin Watts, 1998. ISBN 0-531-14477-1. 32 pages. Grade 3+**
The authors look at agriculture, water resources, and marketing of food around the world. They emphasize the need for an action plan to feed the world, for working together, and for environmentally sensitive farming.

**Morgan, Sally.** *Saving the Rain Forests.* **Earth Watch series. New York: Franklin Watts, 1999. ISBN 0-531-14570-0. 32 pages. Grades 4–8**

Articulate text, maps, cross-sections, diagrams, color illustrations, and photos make this an effective rain forest and conservation resource. The author examines the meaning, structure, flora and fauna, and people of the rain forest. She emphasizes the role of nature and man in destroying the habitats of wildlife, plants, and people and considers ways man can work to create sustainable forests. Morgan enhances this text with the thought-provoking statistics and details of "Taking Part," "On the Ground" and "Eco Thought" insets, the "Fact File," glossary, and index.

**Pollard, Michael.** *100 Greatest Disasters.* **100 Greatest series. Danbury, CT: Grolier, 1997. ISBN 0-7172-7684-8. 111 pages. Grade 3+**

This volume of the series includes one-page overviews with color photography and illustrations. Pollard looks at some of the worst manifestations of nature in history. He includes earthquakes (Kobe), volcanoes and tsunamis (Krakatoa), cyclones (Bangladesh), floods (Huang He), fires (Great Fire of London), diseases (AIDS), and manmade and environmental disasters (Chernobyl nuclear accident, Bhopal chemical leak, and acid rain). Try the world string puzzle and travel challenger.

**Rochford, Dierdre.** *Rights for Animals?* **Viewpoints series. New York: Franklin Watts, 1996. ISBN 0-531-14414-3. 32 pages. Grades 4–8**

This worthy series presents opposing views on contemporary social issues, encourages debate, and leaves the questions for the reader to answer. Use the "Facts to think about" as a springboard for discussion of animal rights. With introductory text, opposing viewpoint quotes, and graphic color photography, Rochford elicits discussion of eating meat, cruelty to animals from farming, use of animals for furs and experimentation for cosmetics, animals for research, animals in sports and service, hunting, dangers of extinction, protection of animals, and rights of animals. She also includes a glossary and a list of contacts for further information.

**Royston, Angela.** *100 Greatest Medical Discoveries.* **100 Greatest series. Danbury, CT: Grolier, 1997. ISBN 0-7172-7681-3. 111 pages. Grade 3+**

This volume of the series includes one-page profiles and color photography and illustrations of discoveries in medicine that have improved the quality of life for mankind. Trace medical history from prehistoric trepanning to 20th century laser surgery, CAT scans, and artificial skin. Try the "Medical Madness Quiz."

**Turner, Stephanie.** *Communities.* **Ecology Alert! series. Austin, TX: Raintree Steck-Vaughn, 1999. ISBN 0-8172-5373-4. 32 pages. Grades 4–6.**

This series emphasizes the partnership among nations to preserve the world's resources and harmony. The activities and case studies are valuable teaching tools. This volume discusses where people live, what they eat, how they use and find energy and water, and how they dispose of waste. Turner considers the ongoing and future changes needed for communities to thrive.

**Whiting, Shelagh.** *Rivers.* **Ecology Alert! series. Austin, TX: Raintree Steck-Vaughn, 1999. ISBN 0-8172-5375-0. 32 pages. Grades 4–6**

This series emphasizes the partnership among nations to preserve the world's resources and harmony. The activities and case studies are valuable teaching tools. This volume shows the importance of rivers, riparian flora and fauna, floods, working rivers, rivers for recreation and tourism, and taking care of rivers.

**Wilkinson, Philip.** *100 Greatest Inventions.* **100 Greatest series. Danbury, CT: Grolier, 1997. ISBN 0-7172-7683-X. 111 pages. Grade 3+**
This volume of the series includes one-page features, color photography, and illustrations. Wilkinson examines inventions throughout history and from around the world that have had the most impact on mankind. He includes key discoveries like paper, electric light bulb, microwave oven, fountain pen, and computer.

# Science and Nature: Videos and CDs

*Amazing Animals* **[interactive multimedia]. New York: Dorling Kindersley, 1997. ISBN 0-7894-1718-9. Grades K–6**
Children will love searching for their favorite animals or learning about new ones on this interactive CD-ROM. The "Toy Box," "Amazing Animal Expert," games, contests, and connections to the Internet will add to their hours of fun and education.

*The Animal Kingdom* **[interactive multimedia]. Chicago: World Book, 1997. ISBN 0-7166-2314-5. Grade 5+**
This 10-CD-ROM set offers a visually stunning and scholarly exploration of the lives and habitats of the animal kingdom by classification.

*Blue Planet* **[videorecording]. A presentation of the Smithsonian Institution's National Air and Space Museum and Lockheed Corporation in cooperation with the National Aeronautics and Space Administration; produced by Graeme Ferguson; written, edited, and narrated by Toni Myers. Washington, DC: Smithsonian Institution, 1995. 42 minutes. Grade 4+**
Stunning footage from space helps children realize the vastness of the earth, her changes, and the effects of mankind.

*Discovering Endangered Wildlife: A Multimedia Expedition in Fun and Learning.* **[interactive multimedia]. Cheshire, CT: Lyriq International, 1994. ISBN 1-8824-8619-6. Grade 3+**
This CD-ROM offers a fascinating look at creatures of the world in danger of extinction. It was designed for children and created in conjunction with the National Wildlife Federation. The microscopic color photography, videos, and animal sounds will heighten students' awareness of the world of endangered wildlife. Children will also enjoy the games and puzzles.

*Endangered Animals* **[videorecording]. Distributed by Partridge Films; with voices of Tom Clarke-Hill, Eric Meyers. Amazing animals series. New York: DK Publishing, Inc, 1997. ISBN 0-7894-2156-9. 30 minutes. Grades K–3**
Henry the Lizard takes children on a tour to rescue some of the endangered animals of the world in this episode of the 1997 Golden Gate Award-winning series.

*Eyewitness Encyclopedia of Nature* [interactive multimedia]. New York: Dorling Kindersley, 1995. ISBN0-7894-0041-3. Grades K–4

This easy-to-use CD-ROM takes children on a journey into the world of animals and plants and their habitats. Children will be mesmerized whether they are searching for answers to a particular question or exploring the world of nature for fun.

*Once Upon a Forest* [videorecording]. A Hanna-Barbera production in association with HTV Cymru/ Wales; produced by David Kirschner and Jerry Mills; directed by Charles Grosvenor; written by Mark Young and Kelly Ward; with voices by Michael Crawford, Ben Vereen, and Ellen Blain; Animation director: Dave Michener; art director: Carol Holmes Grosvenor; film editor: Pat A. Foley; music by James Horner. Los Angeles, CA: Fox Video, 1993. ISBN 0-7939-8501-3. 71 minutes. Grades K–3

Heighten children's awareness of ecology and their responsibilities to keep Earth safe with this delightful animated story. Visit Dapplewood, the home of three Furling friends, Abigail the wood mouse, Edgar the mole, and Russell the hedgehog. Life seems wonderful until a chemical spill threatens the health of their friend Michelle. Their teacher Cornelius helps the animals on a dangerous journey to save Michelle and their forest.

*Wide World of Animals* [interactive multimedia]. San Mateo, CA: Creative Wonders, 1995. ISBN 0-7845-0629-9. Grade 1+

This glorious CD-ROM, part of the ABC World Reference series, shows more than 700 species of the animal kingdom in natural habitats.

*Part* **II**

## *World Resources* Web Sites

## *The Arts*

**Aaron Shepard's Reader's Theater Page**
http://www.aaronshep.com/rt/
> Author and performer Aaron Shepard shares his Reader's Theater resources, including original multicultural scripts for classroom use. Teacher Reference

**ArtsEdNet**
http://www.artsednet.getty.edu/
> This Getty's Art Education Web site offers lesson plans and curriculum guides sorted by grade level or listed alphabetically. Search Ancient Worlds, Architecture, Masks, Asian Art, Arts of India, African-American, and Mexican-American Art. Interdisciplinary units include "Our Place in the World," "Worlds of Art," "Understanding Artworlds," and "Exploring an Ancient World." Teacher Reference

**British Museum: Illuminating World Cultures**
http://www.thebritishmuseum.ac.uk/world/world.html
> Explore the world's cultures through their art at this magnificent site. Includes exploration of Africa, Americas, Asia, Egypt, Japan, Near East, and the Pacific. Teacher Reference

**The Children's Literature Web Guide**
http://www.acs.ucalgary.ca/~dkbrown/
> David K. Brown, Director of the Doucette Library of Teaching Resources at the University of Calgary in Alberta, Canada, maintains this internationally recognized and respected Web site devoted to children's and young adult literature. Teacher Reference

**Encyclopedia Mythica**
http://pantheon.org/mythica/
>This award-winning encyclopedia of mythology, folklore, and legends contains more than 5,700 definitions of gods, goddesses, legendary animals, objects, imaginative places, monsters, and supernatural creatures from world cultures. It includes Aboriginal, African, Aztec, Chinese, Egyptian, Haitian, Hindu, Inca, Japanese, Judaic, Korean, Mayan, Mesopotamian, Persian, and Polynesian mythology. Teacher Reference

**Fairrosa Cyber Library of Children's Literature**
http://www.dalton.org/libraries/fairrosa/
>Roxanne Hsu Feldman, a New York middle school librarian, maintains this wonderful resource for children's literature with reviews, articles, discussions, and links. Learn about authors who lived in or traveled to non-Western countries and authors who recreate folktales and stories set in other countries or probing other cultures. The authors include Verna Aardema, Alma Flor Ada, Haemi Balbassi, Katherine Paterson, and Ed Young. Teacher Reference

**Fine Art Resource Directory: Museums and Art History**
http://www.msstate.edu/Fineart_Online/art-resources/museums.html
>Mississippi State offers this valuable site with links to more than 1,000 art resources. Teacher Reference

**Frank Rogers' Enchanted Neighborhood**
http://frankrogers.home.mindspring.com/
>Frank Rogers, media specialist at Gresham Park Elementary School in DeKalb County, Georgia, created this imaginative Web site guide to children's literature. Explore literature sites, sites for kids, and award-winning books. Click on the globe to go to Frank Rogers' Multicultural Neighborhood for links by theme. Click on the blue genie to go to Frank Rogers' Enchanted Neighborhood with links to fairy tales and folktales. Grade 3+

**Gateway to Art History**
http://www.harbrace.com/art/gardner/Anc.html
>Harcourt College Publishers' Art History Resources on the Web is a Web companion to *Gardner's Art Through the Ages* that offers links to information on Ancient Art, Ancient Near and Middle Eastern Art, and Egyptian Art. Grade 6+ and Teacher Reference

**Look in the Mythic Mirror**
http://artsedge.kennedycenter.org/teaching_materials/curricula/curric/mythicmirror/wk7.html
>The ARTSEDGE staff of the Kennedy Center developed this lesson to encourage students to compare and contrast Western and non-Western mythology. Grades 6–8 and Teacher Reference

**Metropolitan Museum of Art**
http://www.metmuseum.org/
>MMA offers one of the finest Web sites for exploring the art of our past and present. Quality educational resources, "Explore and Learn" activities, and ArtiFacts indexed by

country, added to the wealth of art in the collections and exhibits, make this a must-see site for students and educators. Grade 4+

**Museums Around the World**
http://www.icom.org/vlmp/world.html
> This Internet Museum is part of the WWW Virtual Library museums pages maintained by Jonathan Bowen. Search this valuable resource by country to connect to museums around the world. Grade 4+

**Mything Links**
http://www.mythinglinks.org/reference~teachers.html
> Dr. Kathleen Jenks, Mythological Studies Department, Pacifica Graduate Institute, Carpinteria, California, created this fascinating award-winning site that provides an "Annotated and Illustrated Collection of Worldwide Links to Mythologies, Fairy Tales and Folklore, Sacred Arts and Traditions." Plan to get lost for hours in Jenks's commentaries, insights, and delightful links from this and other pages. Explore—for sure! Teacher Reference

**RootsWorld**
http://www.rootsworld.com/rw/rw.html
> Learn about music around the world through this searchable database. Enter search terms or select regional menus for Africa, Europe, Asia, the Americas, and the Pacific to read recording reviews or feature articles about the diverse music of the world. *Note:* Although Webmaster Cliff Furnald encourages subscription, users may search this music resource for free. Because contemporary music is also reviewed and can be explicit or controversial, I recommend teachers select appropriate articles and share these with classes. Teacher Reference

**Tales of Wonder**
http://members.xoom.com/darsie/tales/index.html
> Richard Darsie's award-winning site offers links to Folk and Fairy Tales from Around the World. These include: Africa, Central Asia, China, India, Japan, Middle East, Russia, and Siberia. Teacher Reference

**Teaching Tolerance**
http://www.splcenter.org/teachingtolerance/tt-index.html
> *Teaching Tolerance Magazine* offers this Web site with classroom resources and activities, articles, and teaching tools to help educators "foster equity, respect, and understanding in the classroom and beyond." Teacher Reference

**WebMuseum, Paris**
http://metalab.unc.edu/louvre/
> Search this online museum by artist or theme. Learn about painting styles by accessing the glossary. Nicholas Pioch maintains this illuminating collaborative site with visitors' contributions. Grade 3+

**World Mythology**
http://www.windows.umich.edu/cgi-bin/tour_def/mythology/worldmap_new.html
> Explore world mythology by selecting an area of the world in this amazing University of

Michigan site. Choose from among Aztec, Maya, Amazon, Inca, Sumerian, Hindu, Chinese, Japanese, Egyptian, Yoruba, Fon, and Polynesian mythology. Select Home to explore other features of interest. Grade 6+

# *Biographies*

**4,000 Years of Women in Science**
http://www.astr.ua.edu/4000WS/4000WS.html
This site honors women from En Hedu'Anna (c.2354 BCE) through the 19th century who have contributed to the advancement of mankind through science and mathematics. Dr. Deborah Crocker of the Department of Physics and Astronomy at the University of Alabama developed this site based on lectures by Dr. Sethanne Howard of the National Science Foundation. Grade 4+

**Biographical Dictionary**
http://s9.com/biography/
This award-winning site provides brief biographical statements for 28,000 notable men and women throughout history. Search by year of birth or death, positions held, professions, literary and artistic works, achievements, and other keywords. Search by country as a keyword for a Who's Who list of the country. Scan the Ideas for Students and Teachers. Grade 3+

**Biography.com**
http://www.biography.com/index.html
Biography.com profiles famous people in "Born on This Day" and allows searches of famous people by month and day. BioSearch features 25,000 personalities and 2,500 videos. Each week includes top 10 biographies, people featured on Arts and Entertainment and in the *Biography Magazine*, BioTrivia, and classroom guides and information. "Biography of the Millennium" includes world figures like Suleiman I, Nelson Mandela, Joseph Stalin, Mahatma Gandhi, and Karl Marx. Grade 3+

**Biographies of Jewish Women**
http://www.us-israel.org/jsource/biography/biowomen.html
Detailed biographies of Jewish women include women from ancient to modern times, from ancient Israel to America. The Jewish Student Online Research Center, created by the American-Israeli Cooperative Enterprise (AICE), claims its materials are "designed to give you facts from an unbiased, nonpartisan perspective." Grade 3+

**Lives, the Biography Resource**
http://amillionlives.com/
Kenneth P. Lanxner maintains this ambitious searchable biographical database. He describes it as providing "links to thousands of biographies, autobiographies, memoirs, diaries, letters, narratives, oral histories and more. Individual lives of the famous, the infamous, and the not so famous. Group biographies about people who share a common profession, historical era, or geography. Also general collections, resources on biographical criticism and special collections." Grade 3+

**Newsmaker Bios: Names in the News**
http://abcnews.go.com/reference/newsmakers/newsmakers_index.html

> ABC News provides this searchable ready reference. Select a newsmaker to access to photos, date of birth, birthplace, and education. Gain insights into the shapers of the world through quotes from and about the person. Search World to find raw news by area, 21st century lives, and country profiles. Grade 3+

**Rulers**
http://www.geocities.com/Athens/1058/rulers.html

> This ambitious personal Web site lists heads of state and government of the world from 1800 to the present. Search alphabetically by countries and territories and by foreign ministers. Links are also provided to international organizations. Monthly relevant events are chronicled. Grade 5+

**Zárate's Political Collections (ZPC)**
http://personales.jet.es/ziaorarr/welcome2.htm

> Among Roberto Ortiz de Zárate's collections are Political Leaders 1945–2000, Reliefs and Re-elections, Current Rulers Worldwide, Women World Leaders, and First African Rulers. Grade 5+

## *Country Resources*

**ABC News.com Country Profiles**
http://abcnews.go.com/reference/countryprofiles/countryprofiles_index.html

> Select a country to explore. ABC News offers background on the history, culture, geography, natural resources, government, politics, economics, and demographics of most of the countries of the world. Use the interactive atlas to compare features and statistics of countries. View the color flag and listen to the country's national anthem in RealAudio. Grade 3+

**About.com**
http://geography.about.com/science/geography/msub6.htm

> About.com connects students and teachers to the best resources available on the Net for study about countries and nations. This is a one-stop search that will link you to some of the fine resources listed individually here and some not already listed. Grade 4+

**Adventure Online**
http://www.adventureonline.com/

> This site offers expeditions to the Caribbean for sunken treasure, a Magellan Global Adventure, or Project Central America. Visit Basecamps to read "Live from the Field," "Updates," and "Meet the Team." Read the explorers' journals and complete activities related to the adventure. Follow the links to past explorations with online resources provided. *Note*: Certain features (like lesson plans and special points) require membership and a fee. Grade 4+

**Altapedia Online**
http://www.atlapedia.com/

> Make this statistical overview a first stop for research. Countries A–Z and World Maps sections have political and geographical maps with statistical data for each country of

the world. The Countries A to Z includes facts, figures and statistical data on geography, climate, people, religion, language, history, and economy. The World Maps sections offer physical and political maps for regions of the world. Grade 4+

### Ancient World Web
http://www.julen.net/ancient/
Julia Hayden maintains this treasury of ancient world sites. Search by keyword or by topic, including archaeology, art, history, language and literature, mythology and religion, and science. Grade 6+

### Armed Forces of the World
http://www.cfcsc.dnd.ca/links/milorg/index.html
The Information Resource Centre of Canadian Forces College, Department of National Defence, posts this site that gives official servers and information and archives for the countries of the world. Grade 6+

### Capitals of Every Country
http://geography.about.com/science/geography/library/misc/blnationalcapitals.htm
About.com provides all of the capitals of major countries in one easy listing. Grade 3+

### Centers for Disease Control and Prevention
http://www.cdc.gov/travel/index.htm
Search by destination at this CDC National Center for Infectious Diseases Travelers' Health page to get the most up-to-date information about diseases, vaccinations, special needs, outbreaks, traveling with children, safe food and water, and other health news and concerns. Grade 6+

### Chiefs of State and Cabinet Members of Foreign Governments
http://www.odci.gov/cia/publications/chiefs/
Search alphabetically by country to find the names of the chiefs of state and cabinet members at this site maintained by the Central Intelligence Agency. Grade 6+

### CIA World Factbook
http://www.odci.gov/cia/publications/factbook/
The Central Intelligence Agency offers a searchable listing of country profiles and reference world maps. The CIA updates the *World Factbook* annually. Each profile includes information on the geography, people, government, economy, communications, transportation, military, and transnational issues for the countries of the world. Grade 4+

### CNN CityGuide
http://www.cnn.co.uk/TRAVEL/CITY.GUIDES/
Users can tour Bangkok, Beijing, Hong Kong, Moscow, Singapore, Tokyo, and other major cities of this world at this helpful site. Grade 3+

### Country Profiles: The Spire Project
http://cn.net.au/country.htm
Need information in a hurry? The Spire Project indexes and accesses major world organizations, statistics, document delivery, and research services, and presents them at one

site. Search for general information, travel and health reports, war and justice, economic profiles, and further tools. Grade 5+

**Culture Quest World Tour (Internet Public Library)**
http://www.ipl.org/youth/cquest/
Join Olivia Owl and Parsifal Penguin on a tour around the world. Learn about holidays, cultures, and cuisines as you visit Africa, Antarctica, Asia and the Far East, Australia, Europe, the Middle East, North America, and South and Central America. This delightful site, originally created by students at the University of Michigan's School of Information in 1997, has games, stories, and fun for children of all ages. Grade 3+

**Currency Converter**
http://www.oanda.com/convert/classic
Change American dollars to Algerian dinars, Botswana pulas, Guatemalan quetzals, or Omani rials. Oanda.com provides the latest exchange for 164 currencies at this popular site for travelers and businesses. Grade 3+

**Dewey Browse**
http://www.top.monad.net/~gailgrainger/
Gail Shea Grainger, librarian at Chesterfield School in Chesterfield, New Hampshire, created and maintains this wonderful resource, a searchable database of Web sites arranged by Dewey category. Search the 700s for art; the 800s for literature; the 900s for geography, history, and travel (930s for ancient civilizations, 947 for Russia links, 951 for China links); the 400s for languages; and 92 for biography. Grade 5+

**E-Conflict World Encyclopedia**
http://www.emulateme.com
This site, maintained by David Driggs, provides information by country about economy, defense, geography, government, and people. Information is taken from the *CIA World Factbook, Library of Congress Country Studies*, and the National Archives and Records Administration, and is updated yearly. Links are also provided for country flags, national anthems, and current weather. Grade 5+

**Elections Around the World**
http://www.agora.stm.it/elections/election/main.htm
Wilfried Derksen maintains this searchable site providing up-to-date world elections information. Search alphabetically or by map of the world or by geographic area. Grade 5+

**Electronic Embassy**
http://www.embassy.org/
This site provides information on all of the foreign embassies in Washington, DC. Search alphabetically by the letter of the country or scroll the alphabetical listing to select the desired country. Grade 5+

**Excite Travel: Countries**
http://www.excite.com/travel/regions/
Search more than 5,000 destinations. Travel guides provide factual information, maps, consular and health information, languages, and places to see and stay. Grade 3+

### Exploring Ancient World Cultures
http://eawc.evansville.edu/chpage.htm

Search the ancient wonders of the Near East, India, China, Egypt, Islam, Rome, Greece, and Europe through links provided by the University of Evansville, Indiana. Grade 6+

### Fodor's Travel Guides
http://www.fodors.com/

Although the original intent of Fodor's guides was to help plan trips, this online guide introduces children to countries around the world. They can search for major cities, national parks, and culture and even learn some phrases in a foreign language. Grade 3+

### Foreign Affairs Online
http://www.people.virginia.edu/~rjb3v/rjb.html

Upper-grade students and teachers should search this impressive site, developed by Dr. Robert J. Beck at Tufts University, for links to information on human rights, international law, nongovernmental and governmental organizations, foreign states, the United Nations System, and map resources. Grade 6+

### From Past to Present: A Journey Across the World and Through Time
http://library.thinkquest.org/20176/framesn.htm

Click on the world map to explore continents or step through the door to travel in time in this 1998 ThinkQuest Internet Challenge interactive site. Grade 4+

### Gateway to World History
http://www.hartford-hwp.com/gateway/index.html

Offers links for learning about world history, including electronic documents online, maps, and educational associations. Grade 7+ and Teacher Reference

### Geographia
http://www.geographia.com/

This spectacular site, previously called Interknowledge, provides guides to areas of special interest in Africa, Asia, Caribbean, Europe, and Latin America. Grade 3+

### Global Grocery List
http://landmark-project.com/ggl/

The Landmark Project allows students to gather data about world grocery prices for analysis and comparison for interdisciplinary studies in social studies, science, health, and mathematics. Grade 6+

### Governments on the WWW
http://www.gksoft.com/govt/

Gunnar Anzinger maintains this site of links to governmental institutions, parliaments, ministries, offices, law courts, embassies, city councils, and political parties on the Web. Grade 5+

### Greenpeace
http://www.greenpeace.org/home.shtml

This is the informational site of Greenpeace.org, a nonprofit international organization dedicated to peaceful protection of the environment. Ongoing initiatives include preservation of the rain forest. Grade 4+

**The History Channel**
http://www.historychannel.com/
In addition to the companion materials for its television programming, the History Channel provides a searchable database, "This Day in History," and special features. Students and teachers can also access archived features. Grade 3+

**The History Net**
http://www.thehistorynet.com/
The Cowles History Group offers this searchable site of historical articles. World History, Personality Profiles, and Historic Travel are of special interest in Non-Western studies. Grade 5+

**History/Social Studies Web Site for K–12 Teachers**
http://www.execpc.com/~dboals/boals.html
Dennis Boals maintains this amazing award-winning treasury of resources to promote the use of the Internet as a tool in the teaching of social studies, grades kindergarten through twelve. Teacher Reference

**Horus**
http://www.ucr.edu/h-gig/horuslinks.html
The Department of History at the University of California, Riverside, presents World Wide Web Links to History Resources. Search by alphabetical index, browsing categories, or search engine. Section V provides an extensive alphabetical listing of link collections, including ancient history, history indexes, modern history, and 20th century history. Teacher Reference

**HyperHistory Online**
http://www.hyperhistory.com/online_n2/History_n2/a.html
Andreas Nothiger has brought an interesting concept to life with this collection of more than 1,800 interconnected files documenting the history of the world. Search history, maps, and events by time line, and people alphabetically, by profession, or by time line. People and events are also color-coded by subject on the chronology chart. Grade 5+

**InfoNation**
http://www.un.org/Pubs/CyberSchoolBus/infonation/e_infonation.htm
Select up to seven United Nations member states and then select the geography, economy, population, and social indicators statistics to compare from the data fields. Data provided from *World Statistics Pocketbook* and *Statistical Yearbook*, published by the United Nations. Grade 4+

**Intellicast Weather**
http://www.intellicast.com/
Click on the map to find out weather conditions around the world. Grade 3+

**International Constitutional Law**
http://www.uni-wuerzburg.de/law/home.html

> Dr. Axel Tschentscher of the University of Wurzburg, Germany, maintains this site. Search by Country Index to access constitutional documents and country information for many nations. Teacher Reference

**International Database**
http://www.census.gov/ipc/www/idbnew.html

> The U.S. Census maintains this databank of statistical tables of demographic and socio-economic data for the countries of the world. Statistics include population by age and sex; vital rates, infant mortality and life tables; fertility and child survivorship; migration; marital status; family planning; ethnicity, religion, and language; literacy; labor force, employment, and income; and households. Grade 5+

**International Monetary Fund**
http://www.imf.org/external/country/index.htm

> Access reports about the economic development of countries at this site. The IMF, founded in 1946, is a cooperative group of 182 countries who voluntarily join "to promote international monetary cooperation, exchange stability, and orderly exchange arrangements; to foster economic growth and high levels of employment; and to provide temporary financial assistance to countries under adequate safeguards to help ease balance of payments adjustment." Grade 7+

**Kids' Space**
http://www.kids-space.org/

> This award-winning, commercial-free site has International Kids' Space for Creative Activities, Kids' Space Connection for Communication Activities, and the Guide Bear's Guide Tour to help children learn about the world and share their artwork, writing, and creative projects. Country Search enables children to search the World Wonder Map by region. If children search an alphabetical list by country, they can follow a link for the country (from the *CIA World Factbook* or from a specific country government site) and then select "See other countries" for a color map of all the countries on the continent with links to each. Grade 3+

**Kids Web**
http://www.kidsvista.com/SocialStudies/index.html

> Search geography, government, and history sites targeted for K–12 students and teachers at LearningVista.com. Grade 3+

**Library of Congress Country Studies**
http://lcweb2.loc.gov/frd/cs/cshome.html

> This online site includes versions of books previously published in hard copy by the Federal Research Division of the Library of Congress under the Country Studies/Area Handbook Program sponsored by the U.S. Department of Army. In-depth profiles are presented here for many countries, although the data are being updated. Grade 4+

**Lonely Planet: Destination**
http://www.lonelyplanet.com/dest/
> Choose a region and a country for your search. Each search offers information on the country, travelers' reports, maps, and online resources. Grade 3+

**Microsoft's Expedia**
http://expedia.msn.com
> This site, designed for planning trips, offers valuable information to students. Select Destination Guides to access overviews and facts for countries around the world. Microsoft also provides information on the history, people, food and drink, almanac, highlights, geography, arts and culture, and health and safety for each country. Grade 3+

**Mr. Dowling's Electronic Passport**
http://www.mrdowling.com/
> Mike Dowling, a sixth grade teacher in Florida, has created a virtual tour of the world, complete with downloadable study guides, homework assignments, and tests. Explore Mesopotamia, Ancient Egypt, The Middle East and North America, Ancient Africa, Colonial Africa, Africa Today, India to the Himalayas, Chinese History, China, Southeast Asia, the Caribbean, Mexico and Central America, South America, and World Religions. Grade 4+

**National Geographic Society Xpeditions**
http://www.nationalgeographic.com/xpeditions/
> Xpeditions offers a wide array of cultural, educational, and informational resources for teaching geography and world history. Use the atlas, the 18 US National Geography Standards and Lesson Plans, or Family Xpeditions. Take virtual trips to Places and Regions, Physical Systems, and Environment and Society in Xpedition Hall. Grade 4+ and Teacher Reference

**National Standards for History**
http://www.sscnet.ucla.edu/nchs/hstocb.html
> Includes the National Standards for History K–4 and for United States and World History 5–12. Teacher Reference

**New Countries of the World**
http://geography.miningco.com/library/weekly/aa090197.htm
> With the constant changes in the world, it is reassuring to know we can always access the most up-to-date information through the Mining Company's Geography site. Grade 4+

**Political Resources on the Net**
http://www.politicalresources.net/
> Make this a first stop for searching for resources on governments, ministries, politics, and elections. Search alphabetically or by continent and country. Grade 5+

**The Say Hello to the World Project**
http://www.ipl.org/youth/hello/
> Learn about the languages of the world. Lori Monn, a graduate student at the University

of Michigan's School of Information, developed this exceptional site for the Internet Public Library that provides links to the study of language, characters, and culture. Includes Arabic, Chinese, Hebrew, Hindi, Indonesian, Japanese, Korean, Mayan, Russian, Swahili, Tagalog, Thai, Turkish, and others. Grade 3+

**Seven Wonders of the Ancient World**
http://tqjunior.thinkquest.org/5821/
> This 1999 ThinkQuest Junior site explores the Lighthouse at Alexandria, the Hanging Gardens of Babylon, the Pyramids of Egypt, and other wonders of the ancient world as stories of the Ancient Times Newspaper. Grade 5+

**Travel Warnings and Consular Information Sheets**
http://travel.state.gov/travel_warnings.html
> The U.S. Department of State posts travel warnings, public announcements, and consular information sheets at this site to assist those planning trips to foreign countries. Teacher Reference

**Travel.org**
http://www.travel.org/index2.html
> This online travel directory is a resource for country studies. Click into the globe on the area of study to access links to information on the country, arts and culture, and news. Grade 5+

**UNESCO**
http://www.unesco.org/
> The purpose of the United Nations Educational, Scientific and Cultural Organization, organized in 1945, is "to contribute to peace and security in the world by promoting collaboration among nations through education, science, culture and communication in order to further universal respect for justice, for the rule of law and for the human rights and fundamental freedoms which are affirmed for the peoples of the world, without distinction of race, sex, language or religion, by the Charter of the United Nations." This site includes links to current events, statistics, programs, and information services (including educational database and full-text document access). Grade 5+

**UNICEF: The Progress of Nations**
http://www.unicef.org/pon96/contents.htm
> UNICEF offers reports on women, nutrition, health, education, the Convention of the Rights of the Child, the industrial world, and statistical indicators. Students might find it helpful to access statistical profiles (under statistical indicators) for information on sub-Saharan Africa, the Middle East and North Africa, Central Asia, Asia and Pacific, Americas, and Europe. Grade 5+

**U.S. Census Bureau (World Population Clock Project)**
http://www.census.gov/cgi-bin/ipc/popclockw
> Keep track of monthly population estimates at the U.S. Census Bureau site. Grade 5+

**U.S. Energy Administration Country Analysis Briefs**
http://www.eia.doe.gov/emeu/cabs/contents.html
> Learn about the status of energy resources and utilization for each country at this

government site. Statistics are provided for petroleum, natural gas, coal, nuclear energy, electricity, renewables, and alternate fuels where applicable. Effects on the environment and forecasts are also included. Grade 4+

**U.S. State Department Background Notes**
http://www.state.gov/www/background_notes/index.html

The U.S. State Department updates Background Notes periodically to provide information on geographic regions (including Africa, Middle East and North Africa, East Asia and the Pacific, South Asia, Europe, and Western Hemisphere) and international organizations (including the Association of Southeast Asian Nations, European Community, Organization of American States, and United Nations). Grade 4+

**U.S. State Department: Regions and Country Information**
http://www.state.gov/www/regions.html

From this site, access information from the U.S. State Department about the regional affairs of Africa, East Asia and Pacific, Europe, Near East, new independent states and the former USSR, South Asia, and the Western Hemisphere, and country information (including background notes, educational and cultural affairs, and more). Grade 4+

**United Nations**
http://www.un.org/

This official site explains the goals and main organs of the United Nations and provides information on peace and security, economic and social development, international law, human rights, and humanitarian affairs for the 188 member states. The site can be accessed in Arabic, Chinese, Spanish, Russian, English, and French. Grade 5+

**United Nations CyberSchoolBus Resource Source**
http://www.un.org/Pubs/CyberSchoolBus/menureso.htm

This exceptional site, a Global Teaching and Learning Project designed by the United Nations for children, shows the potential of integrating the Internet into the curricula. Explore the featured topics: Global Trends, City Profiles, Country at a Glance, InfoNation, UN Site-ings, a Virtual Tour, and Parade of Nations. Click into Elementary Planet and the Quiz Quad for puzzles and games. Grade 2+

**The WWW V-L History: Central Catalogue**
http://www.ukans.edu/history/VL/

The University of Kansas maintains this database for historians. Teachers can search by countries and regions, eras and epochs, historical topics, or research methods and materials. Teacher Reference

**The WWW Virtual Library**
http://vlib.org/AlphaVL.html

Pennsylvania State University maintains a mirror site for this database of links, compiled by volunteers who are experts in particular curricula fields. Teacher reference

**WebChron: The Web Chronology Project**
http://campus.northpark.edu/history/WebChron/

This site, developed by the History Department at North Park University in Chicago, offers world history regional and cross-cultural chronologies with related articles written by students. Includes chronologies of Africa South of the Sahara, China and East Asia, India and southern Asia, Central and South America, Mediterranean basin, Russia, Middle East and West Asia, and Christianity, Islam, and Buddhism. Teacher Reference

**Wonders of the World: From the Pyramids to the St. Louis Arch**
http://tqjunior.thinkquest.org/5983/

This 1999 ThinkQuest Junior site teaches about the ancient and modern wonders of the world. Grade 5+

**World Bank Countries and Regions**
http://www.worldbank.org/html/extdr/regions.htm

The World Bank works to fight poverty and provide resources and education to areas in need. Search by country or region to access country briefs, data, and project information. Grade 7+

**The World Conservation Monitoring Centre**
http://www.wcmc.org.uk/

This center monitors conservation and sustainable use of the world's living resources, offering information on endangered species, habitats, forests, protected areas, regions, climate, biodiversity assessment, and environment links. Grade 5+

**World Health Organization**
http://www.who.int/

The World Health Organization maintains this international site with a searchable database of diseases, environment, lifestyles, and world health concerns and goals. Grade 6+

**World Heritage Centre**
http://www.unesco.org/whc/nwhc/pages/home/pages/homepage.htm

World Heritage is a UNESCO program committed to preserving cultural and natural sites of the world. Students can find out which sites are historic and how this program helps. Grade 5+

**World History Compass**
http://www.WorldHistoryCompass.com/

Links are provided to Africa, Ancient Egypt, Asia, Byzantium, Latin America, Middle East, New Zealand, and Persia (Iran). Grade 5+

**World Kid**
http://www.worldkidmag.com

World Kid offers a changing exhibit of Wonders of the World and an art gallery. Nonsubscribers to the magazine may access a few articles and summaries. Features include museums, fashion, languages, cool schools, health and personal care, popular music in literature, illustrations for kids, and space science. Grade 3+

**The World of KruSader**
http://library.thinkquest.org/10898/history.htm

This 1997 ThinkQuest Challenge site shows the wonders of the world. Tour Africa,

Antarctica, Asia, Australia, Europe, the Middle East, North America, and South America with guide KruSader. Grade 5+

**World Surfari**
http://www.supersurf.com
> Brian Giacoppo of Phoenix, Arizona, created this captivating award-winning Web site where each month kids can travel to a different country to learn about its people, society, and history. They can also select a country from the archives to explore. Grade 3+

**World Travel Guide**
http://dir.lycos.com/Recreation/Travel/Destinations/
> Lycos offers Destination Guides to many countries of the world that include overviews of the country, culture, history and government, travel tips, and more. Some are from tour companies, but all can provide insights into the country. Grade 5+

**World Travel Guide**
http://www.enquest.travel-guides.com/navigate/world.asp
> Columbus Publishing provides this World Travel Guide. Select a country or continent or click on the desired area on the world map for general information on area, population, population density, capital, geography, government, language, religion, time, electricity, and communications. Students can extend their searches by clicking on the left query box arrow to select travel information, useful addresses, passport and visa, duty free, money, public holidays, health, getting there, getting around, accommodations, sports and activities, social profiles, business profile, climate, history and government, overview, and map. Grade 4+

**Yahooligans—Around the World: Countries**
http://www.yahooligans.com/Around_the_World/Countries/
> Begin country searches here with sites chosen specifically for children. Select from an alphabetical list of countries. Grade 3+

**Yahooligans—Around the World: Cultures**
http://www.yahooligans.com/School_Bell/Social_Studies/Cultures/
> Yahooligans indexes resources for children related to cultures of the world: African-American, American, Ancient Civilizations and Cultures, Asian-American, Australian, Canadian, Celtic, Chinese, Indian, Japanese, Maya, Mexican, Native-American, and Spanish. Grade 3+

**Your Nation**
http://www.your-nation.com/
> This site allows students to summarize the population, GDP, area, birth rate, life expectancy, and literacy rate of a country and then compare it to another or rank it for a better understanding of the world's nations. Explore the frequently asked questions, too. Grade 7+

**Zip Codes and Postal Codes of the World**
http://www.escapeartist.com/global10/zip.htm
> Open the world of communication to children through the zip codes of the world. Grade 3+

# Current Events and News

**ABC News**
http://abcnews.go.com/
> Browse Headlines for U.S., world, politics, business, technology, science, health and living, travel, sports, and entertainment news or click into Weather.com for up-to-date news reports from around the world. Grade 4+

**CBS News**
http://cbsnews.cbs.com/
> Find the latest local, national, and world news and WeatherWatch online. Select features like CBS MarketWatch, CBS HealthWatch, CBS Sportsline, CBS Entertainment, and CBS News Polls. Grade 4+

**Children's Express**
http://www.cenews.org/
> Children's Express is a nonprofit journalism and leadership organization created in 1975. It is unique in that major newspapers and television networks for adults publish stories by children ages eight to 18 from around the world. The children are the reporters and editors for this innovative online news. Grade 3+

**CNN Interactive News**
http://www.cnn.com/
> CNN has up-to-the-minute world, national, and local news. Special features include Picture of the Day, Link of the Day, and Multimedia Showcase. Users can search current news and archives. Grade 4+

**KidNews**
http://www.kidnews.com/
> Publisher Elaine Floyd offers KidNews as a free news and writing service for students and teachers around the globe. The online service publishes news, features, creative writing, reviews, and sports pieces written by young authors from every continent (except Antarctica). Click in for guidelines for submitting reviews, journalism pieces, short stories, poems, sports critique, real life accounts, or opinions. The staff reviews and edits submissions for content and language before posting. Be sure to read Pen Pal Rules and Surfing Safety. Browse through Classroom Collaborative Projects and Cool Hangouts for more fun. Grade 3+

**MSNBC News**
http://www.nbc.com/msnbc/news/
> Browse News Headlines for key stories or click into Quick News for news, business, sports, local, health, technology, living and travel, and weather news. Grade 4+

**New York Times Learning Network**
http://www.nytimes.com/learning/index.html
> The subtitle of this commendable site is "Connections for Students, Teachers, and Parents." *The New York Times on the Web* provides this free site to encourage students to

be aware of the world around them. Features for students include News Summaries, Daily News Quiz, Word of the Day, Science Questions and Answers, Student Letters, Crossword Puzzle, and Ask a Reporter. Teachers can find a daily lesson plan and lesson plan archives, Education News, and Newspaper in Education (NIE) resources. Other features include Quote of the Day, Site of the Day, and On This Day in History. Grade 4+

**TIME for Kids**
http://www.timeforkids.com/TFK/
This is one of the most valuable resources for children. Show them current events are interesting and important. Help children develop a life-long love of newspapers and magazines through this special version of *Time Magazine*. Grade 4+

**USA Today Education Online**
http://www.usatoday.com/educate/home.htm
*USA Today* offers resources for educators and parents for each day's news, including lesson plans and daily guides.

# *Dates In History*

**AnyDay-in-History**
http://www.scopesys.com/cgi/today2.cgi
This site, created by Scope Systems, is a searchable database providing access to famous events and people by month and day. Grade 3+

**Calendar Zone**
http://www.calendarzone.com/
Calendar Zone offers links to daily, interactive, historic, religious, holiday, and other calendars. Grade 5+

**Connected Teacher**
http://www.connectedteacher.com/calendar/calendar.asp
Classroom Connect, one of the most valued resources for teachers, posts its monthly calendar of important people and events in the past and present. One of the most valuable features is the circled arrow at the end of each date that links the user to a dynamite resource for that person or event. Grade 5+

**Daily Almanacs**
http://www.dailyalmanacs.com/
Michael J. Maggio posts a no-frills monthly calendar. Click on any month and day to see a lengthy list of birth and death dates of noted people and events throughout history. Connect to this site on any day to find out what historical events occurred. The site also includes sunrise, sunset, special events, days until Christmas, phases of the moon, and more. Grade 3+

**The Daily Globe: "J" World**
http://www.dailyglobe.com/
You can access information about days, weeks, months, years, specific days, weekly

holidays, movable holidays, and calendars at this useful personal site. *Note:* Do not send children to this site since some of the biography and linked pages are "informal." Teacher Reference

**This Day in History**
http://www.infoplease.com/cgi-bin/dayinhistory/
Lists important events in history that occurred on this day. Also search other dates and other years in the 20th century. Grade 3+

**This Day in History**
http://www.historychannel.com/tdih/index.html
Find out what happened on this date in history, search your birth date or other date, or read "What Else Happened Today?" at this History Channel site. Search "This Day in Automotive History," "This Day in Civil War History," "This Day in Technology History," and "This Day in Wall Street History." The History Channel presents this searchable database of important dates in world history. Grade 5+

**Today in History Archive**
http://lcweb2.loc.gov/ammem/today/today.html
This American Memory Library of Congress site provides an impressive and lengthy article on a famous person or event, with photos, poems, quotes, and multiple links. Select Archives to search by full text or specific day or browse by month. Grade 3+

**Yahooligans! This Day in History**
http://www.yahooligans.com/docs/tdih/
Each day Yahooligans poses a question of interest to children and answers it. Search any date to read the Q and A. Grade 3+

## *Encyclopedias and Dictionaries*

**Bartleby.com**
http://www.bartleby.com/
Bartleby.com, known for publishing classics of literature, nonfiction, and reference free of charge, also features reference resources, including the 6th edition of *Columbia Encyclopedia*, in addition to *American Heritage Dictionary, Roget's II: The New Thesaurus, American Heritage Book of English Usage, Simpson's Contemporary Quotations, Bartlett's Familiar Quotations,* and *Oxford Shakespeare*. Grade 5+

**Dictionary.com**
http://www.dictionary.com/
Enter your search term in the query box and access definitions and etymologies from major dictionaries in print. This site also offers access to information about words at "Ask Doctor Dictionary," other language dictionaries, a translator, *Roget's Thesaurus,* and more. Grade 3+

**Encarta Learning Zone**
http://encarta.msn.com/
Search the *Encarta Online Encyclopedia* or the *Encarta World English Dictionary* by

keyword, select a map from the atlas drop-down list, or search by categories (physical science and technology; life science; geography; history; social science; religion and philosophy; art, language, and literature; performing arts, or sports, hobbies, and pets). Although the Online Concise Encyclopedia is always free, there is a more in-depth deluxe version available for a fee. Grade 3+

**Encyclopedia Britannica**
http://www.britannica.com

Britannica offers its complete, updated *Encyclopedia Britannica Online*. This free version includes articles from more than 70 magazines, interactive features and spotlights, a guide to the Web's best sites, today's news from the *Washington Post*, markets, sports, and weather. (A special version for schools with additional resources and teaching guides is available for a small charge per student.) Grade 3+

**Encyclopedia Proteus**
http://rtiess.tripod.com/proteus/encyclopedia.htm

Robert J. Tiess maintains this encyclopedia search engine. Enter your keyword in the query box. Select the encyclopedia you wish to search (*Encyclopedia Britannica*, *Encyclopedia.com*, *Encarta*, *Funk and Wagnalls*, *Infoplease*, and *Letsfindout*) or click to display titles next to "Other Enyclopedias" (including *Artcyclopedia*, *Altapedia*, *Compton's*, *Encyclopedia Smithsonian*, *Fairy Tale Encyclopedia*, and others). Grade 4+

**The Free Internet Encyclopedia**
http://www.cs.uh.edu/~clifton/micro.a.html

Clifton Davis maintains this site, providing search by keyword or letter browse and links to familiar resources such as the *Library of Congress Country Studies* and the *CIA World Factbook* and to specialized sites and personal fan sites. Grade 4+

**Funk and Wagnalls**
http://www.funkandwagnalls.com

Funk and Wagnalls.com offers free access to its multimedia encyclopedia, including featured articles and hot topics. Search by keyword, alphabetical article index, and categories. Advanced search enables users to search full text or title by media (all media, photos, animations, music, sound, speeches, virtual tours, maps, flags, and anthems) using multiple words. Other searchable reference databases include *Random House Webster's College Dictionary*, *Roget's 21st Century Thesaurus*, an Interactive World Atlas, World News, and *The Encyclopedia of Animals*. Grade 3+

**Information Please Almanac (Infoplease.com)**
http://www.infoplease.com/

This searchable database is one of the best places to begin research of all topics. It includes general, sports, and entertainment almanacs, *Kids' Almanac*, a dictionary, and the fifth edition *Columbia Encyclopedia*. Grade 3+

**Knowledge Adventure's Let's Find Out Encyclopedia**
http://www.letsfindout.com/

Knowledge Adventure, a multimedia educational software company, provides this online encyclopedia. Children may search by keyword, subject, or browse topics. Grade 3+

**Lycos Zone**
http://lycoszone.lycos.com/
> Select Homework Zone to access *Kids' Almanac*, Encyclopedia, Dictionary, Atlas, Animals, Kids Library, and Homework Help. Select Encyclopedia to access Research Zone to search *Funk and Wagnalls Multimedia Encyclopedia*, *Random House Webster's College Dictionary*, World News, and Media Experience individually or simultaneously through Power Search. Kids can also access more than 500 games. Grades K–8.

**Merriam-Webster Word Central**
http://www.wordcentral.com/
> Merriam-Webster offers an online student dictionary, "Build your own dictionary," a rhyming dictionary in the Music Room, a Teacher's Lounge, and much more at this user-friendly site. Grade 3+

**Refdesk.com**
http://www.refdesk.com/
> Bob Drudge, Webmaster and creator of this comprehensive resource, calls Refdesk.com "the single best source of facts on the Net." Drudge wanted a site that would provide "fast access, intuitive and easy navigation, comprehensive content, rationally indexed." Teachers will agree this site offers that and more. Users can access reference tools, encyclopedias, facts-of-the-day, current news, and facts-at-a glance links. They can search through the facts subject index. Grade 5+

# *Festivals and Foods*

**Christmas Around the World**
http://www.the-north-pole.com/around/index.htm
> Discover how people celebrate Christmas in more than 30 countries, including China, India, Japan, and Russia. Grade 3+

**Diana's Gourmet Corner**
http://belgourmet.com/sitegb/index.html
> Diana van den Broek, of Antwerp, Belgium, maintains this tempting site with international recipes. Select world recipes by country or by category. Diana offers recipes in 25 categories including beverages, appetizers, cold first courses, soups, warm entremets, meat, eggs, rice and grains, vegetables, sauces, bread and more. In addition to this wonderful sampling of foods of the world, Diana provides an essential service with her "International Links." Search by the first letter of the country and then in an alphabetical list of countries beginning with that letter. You will also enjoy exploring "From A to Z" (food glossaries), "Herbs and Spices," and "Flavors." Grade 4+

**The Global Gastronomer: Cuisines of the World**
http://www.cs.yale.edu/homes/hupfer/global/gastronomer.html
> Susanne Hupfer maintains this wonderful site. She says it is "devoted to links to recipes, food history, and food lore of all regions of the globe, with the goal of discovering, sharing, and appreciating the diverse tastes of all the world's people." Grade 4+

### Holidays on the Net
### http://www.holidays.net/
> Learn more about some of the holidays celebrated around the world, including Day of the Dead, Ramadan, Purim, Passover, Shavuot, High Holy Days (Rosh Hashanah, Yom Kippur, Sukkot), and Chanukah. Grade 3+

### International Children's Cookbook
### http://www.b.shuttle.de/ml1000/cookbook.htm
> The Children's Museum in Prenzlauer Berg, Berlin, Germany, encourages children around the world to share family recipes and poetry about food and cooking. Grade 3+

### Multicultural Holidays
### http://www.asianfamily.com/holidays.htm
> FamilyCulture.com, a site providing educational and cultural resources for diverse families, offers this calendar of holidays around the world, arranged by month. Grade 3+

### Multicultural Recipe Book
### http://www.kidlink.org/KIDPROJ/Recipe/contents.htm
> Sixth-grade teacher Florine Nakasone moderates this KIDPROJ Project that collects recipes from children from around the world. Search by country or alphabetically by the name of the recipe. Each recipe includes the name of the country of origin. Grade 2+

### World Wide Holiday and Festival Site
### http://www.holidayfestival.com
> Search by country for national holidays or by religion to learn more about the beliefs of the people of the world. Grade 3+

### WYK's International Food Court
### http://creative-homeliving.com/World_Kitchen/links.stm
> Select International Recipe Links and click on the map region of your choice to locate resources for recipes. Grade 3+

### Yahooligans—Around the World: Food and Eating
### http://www.yahooligans.com/Around_the_World/Food_and_Eating/
> Yahooligans selects resources appropriate for children. From this page, children can access links for agriculture, edible experiments, nutrition, types of food, and recipes and cooking. Grade 3+

## *Flags and Anthems*

### Flags and Anthems
### http://www.lycoszone.com/homework.html
> Lycos Zone offers this useful site. Select Atlas in the Homework Zone and Media to search flags and anthems or maps. Children can browse countries alphabetically within letter groups to locate the flag and anthem for the country. They can also click into map, country information, encyclopedia articles from *Funk and Wagnalls Multimedia Encyclopedia*, and related sites (including Excite travel site and Columbus Travel Guide). Grade 3+

**Flags of All Countries**
http://www.theodora.com/flags/
> This valuable site provides flags and maps for the countries, along with information on geography, people, government, economy, transportation, communications, and defense taken from *The CIA World Factbook*. Grade 3+

**Flags of All Countries**
http://www.wave.net/upg/immigration/flags.html
> Search flags of the world alphabetically by country. Grade 3+

**Flags of the World**
http://cliffie.nosc.mil/~NAFLAG/index.html
> Search by letter of the alphabet or alphabetically by index to access flags of the world. Grade 3+

**Flags of the World**
http://fotw.digibel.be/flags/
> Giuseppe Bottasini developed this site devoted to vexillology, one of the best I've explored. The FOTW staff and contributors have garnered more than 6,900 pages about flags and more than 12,500 images of flags. The historical and design information for each country's flag is fascinating. Grade 4+

**Medals of the World**
http://www.medals.org.uk/
> Ever wonder what a particular medal signifies? Megan Robertson compiled this site, arranged by country (with flag), of orders, decorations and medals, ribbon charts and text lists, and links and references. Grade 5+

**National Anthems**
http://digilander.iol.it/nationalanthems/
> This free site offers MIDI files, anthem words, and flags for 193 countries. The easiest way to search is to click on continents and then country names or flags. Grade 2+

**National Anthems of the World**
http://www.emulateme.com/anthems/index.htm
> Listen to the anthems of the world in MIDI file format. Some include the native text, as well as the MIDI file. Search an alphabetical list of nations or scroll the list. Users are reminded they are not permitted to copy anthems but can purchase them. Grade 3+

**National Anthems of the World**
http://www.imagesoft.net/flags/anthems.html
> Although this is a sales site for a CD-ROM, students can load and listen to anthems from the countries of the world. Grade 2+

**World Flag Database**
http://www.flags.net/
> Graham Bartram maintains this impressive database including more than 260 countries and international organizations with basic information on the country, (its formal name,

capital city, area, population, currency, languages, and religions). The flags include the national and state flags, ensigns, and sub-national flags. Grade 3+

# *Foreign Languages*

**Alta Vista: Live!**
http://world.altavista.com/
What a wonderful option! Alta Vista's World page allows users to enter text to be translated or a URL or Web site to translate. Grade 2+

**Ethnologue: Languages of the World**
http://gamma.sil.org/ethnologue/
Users can access the Internet Version of this world languages resource. The electronic version contains the entire text of the original printed volumes (except language maps). The preface explains how to use this comprehensive resource. Teacher Reference

**Foreign Language for Travelers**
http://www.travlang.com/languages/
Travlang sponsors one of my favorite sites on the Internet. It is simple for children to select the language they speak and then the language they wish to learn. They can listen to and model vocabulary from basic words, numbers, shopping and dining, travel, directions, places, and times and dates. Online translating dictionaries and audio files are available for most languages. (Grade 1+ with guidance) Grade 4+

**The Human Languages Page**
http://www.hardlink.com/~chambers/HLP/
The HLP, a comprehensive catalog of language-related Internet resources, provides links to online dictionaries, translating dictionaries, language lessons, and linguistics resources. Grade 5+

**Language Dictionaries and Translators**
http://rivendel.com/~ric/resources/dictionary.html
This award-winning site, provided by Rivendell International Communications, has key links to multilingual dictionaries and free online translation. Grade 5+

**Travlang's Translating Dictionaries**
http://dictionaries.travlang.com/
Instantly translate a word from English to German, Dutch, French, Spanish, Swedish, Finnish, Norwegian, Hungarian, Africaans, Italian, Portuguese, Czech, and more with these online translating dictionaries. Grade 3+

# *Geography and Maps*

**Atlas of the World**
http://cliffie.nosc.mil/~NATLAS/
This atlas provides maps of the world, Africa, Asia, Central America, Europe, Islands, North America, South America, and selected cities and image maps. Grade 3+

**Bodleian Library Map Room**
http://www.bodley.ox.ac.uk/users/nnj/maproom.htm

> The Bodleian Library in Oxford, England, houses an extensive collection of world maps, journals, gazetteers, and other reference works. This site offers online access to some of these rare resources. Search in the map case or search other map links. Grade 6+

**Compton's 3D Atlas Online**
http://www.3DAtlas.com/main_co.html

> The Learning Company offers this companion site for the 3D Atlas 98 and Compton's 3D Atlas Deluxe CD-ROMs. Search countries of the world, the geographic glossary, and the Educators' Area. Grade 3+

**Geo Game**
http://gsh.lightspan.com/project/gg/index.cfm

> Global Schoolhouse, part of the Lightspan Network, offers this online geography project to help children learn about the world in an interactive game. From this site, click into other projects such as Cyber Fair, Field Trips, Online Expeditions, Newsday, and Make a Difference. This valuable site also offers tools and resources for teachers and students. Grade 3+

**Geography**
http://geography.about.com/science/geography/mbody.htm

> What a spectacular place for geography resources! About.Com indexes links here for blank or outline maps, cartography, census and population, cities and urban geography, climate and weather, geography clip art, coordinates, countries, cultural geography, disasters and hazards, finding places, fun, games and humor, geo education, GPS and GIS, historic maps, homework help, large cities, maps, photos, physical geography, rivers and streams, street and road maps, time and time zones, topographic maps, U.S. and world maps, population of the world, and zip codes. Take the weekly "Geography Quiz." Search the "Geography Glossary." Grade 4+

**GeoWorld**
http://www.geohistory.com/geoworld/default.asp

> The GeoWorld Internet Database makes a wealth of resources available: maps, current events, time lines, history sites, and slide shows. Grade 4+

**The Getty Thesaurus of Geographic Names (TGN)**
http://shiva.pub.getty.edu/tgn_browser/

> The Getty Research Institute provides the TGN, a structured vocabulary containing a million names and other information about continents, nations of the modern political world, and historic places of interest to the art and architecture world. Search by keyword or click on "Browse the World" to access a TGN Hierarchy Display and view the physical features of the continent, general region, or historic region. Grade 6+

**The Great Globe Gallery on the World Wide Web (3G on 3W)**
http://hum.amu.edu.pl/~zbzw/glob/glob1.htm

> View the globe from space, solar eclipses of the world, digital elevation models, global biodiversity, world stress maps, earthquakes, satellites, rotating and spinning globes, ozone,

weather, world heritage maps, and much more at this award-winning site. Explore the natural and modern wonders of the world. The creator, Zbigniew Zwolinski, said his purpose was "to collect examples of the Globe's presentations for…teaching Earth sciences, geography, cartography, and Geographic Information Systems." Grade 4+

### Heritage Map Museum
http://www.carto.com/links.htm

Access more than 1,000 links to maps of the world arranged by geographic region, theme, and historical time line. The museum is located in Lititz, PA. Grade 5+

### Houghton Mifflin Outline Maps
http://www.eduplace.com/ss/ssmaps/index.html

Locate political and physical maps of the world at this site. Houghton Mifflin makes these available to teachers for free to download for classroom or home use. Teachers can also access an interactive geography game, a discussion forum, history update, and current events from this site by clicking into Social Studies Center. Teacher Reference

### Latitude and Longitude Distance
http://www.indo.com/distance/

Enter the latitude and longitude of two places and use this site, "How Far Is It?," to calculate the distance between them. Darrell Kindred created this service using U.S. Census data and supplementary lists from world cities. Grade 5+

### National Geographic Society Map Machine
http://www.nationalgeographic.com/maps/index.html

Type in the name of the place to search in the query box, or click on dynamic maps, flags and facts, atlas maps, or atlas updates at this phenomenal National Geographic site. Students can also view satellite images, night skies maps, or search the National Geographic site from this page. Grade 4+

### World Atlas
http://www.lycoszone.com/homework.html

Lycos Zone offers this serviceable world atlas. Just select Atlas in the Homework Zone. Search by cities or countries. Select media to search flags and anthems or maps. Related sites include Excite travel site and Columbus Travel Guide. Grade 4+

### World Atlas: Maps and Geography of the World
http://geography.miningco.com/library/maps/blindex.htm

Search this About.com page by letter of the alphabet, browse the alphabetical lists, or select links to sites with maps and geographical information by topics (alphabetical list of countries and continents, blank outline maps of each country, countries listed by continent, cities of the world, oceans, and territories and dependencies). Grade 5+

### Xerox PARC Map Viewer
http://pubweb.parc.xerox.com/map

Users can request specific features and design a world-view map at this interactive site. Grade 6+

# Human Rights

**Amnesty International**
http://www.amnesty.org
>This site posts the most recent news releases about human rights investigations, abuses, and political prisoners. Amnesty International, begun in 1961, campaigns worldwide "to promote all the human rights enshrined in the Universal Declaration of Human Rights and other international standards." Grade 6+

**Human Rights Watch**
http://www.hrw.org/
>Human Rights Watch publishes an annual report, current events, and breaking news with a searchable database. Like Amnesty International, HRW was formed "to prevent discrimination, uphold political freedom, and protect people from inhumane conduct in wartime, and to bring offenders to justice." Grade 6+

# Religion and Philosophy

**About Islam and Muslims**
http://www.unn.ac.uk/societies/islamic/
>This site discusses Islamic laws, Jihad, women, practices, the Quran, Sunnah, current issues, and other religions. Teacher Reference

**Al-Islam**
http://www.al-islam.com/
>This searchable database includes Islamic culture, beliefs, holidays, and history, with a dictionary, offered in Arabic, English, French, German, Turkish, Malaysian, and Indonesian. Grade 5+

**Buddha**
http://www.easternreligions.com/text/buddhalife-t.html
>At this site, Ronald Henry Olsommer includes biographical information about the life of Buddha, Siddhartha Gautama (560–480 B.C.), with links to meditations, doctrine, influence, meaning, truths, and commandments. Text is cited: "Socrates, Buddha, Confucius, Jesus," from *The Great Philosophers*, Volume 1" by Karl Jaspers, Verlag, Munich: R. Piper and Co., 1957, pages 41–63. Grade 6+

**Buddhist Information Network**
http://www.buddhanet.net/
>This site is one of the most comprehensive resources on Buddhism and the history and culture of the religion around the world. Grade 5+

**Buddhist Studies WWW Virtual Library**
http://www.ciolek.com/WWWVL-Buddhism.html
>Dr. T. Matthew Ciolek and Professor Joe Bransford Wilson edit this Internet Guide to Buddhism and Buddhist Studies, part of the Asian Studies WWW Virtual Library. Choose from Buddhist electronic resources, Buddhist Art, Tibetan Studies, Zen Buddhism, and resources for other religions. Grade 6+

**Catholic Internet Directory**
http://catholic.net/RCC/Indices/index.html
> Search here for Catholic-related resources, including information about liturgy and worship, Catholic organizations, and scriptures. Grade 5+

**Center for Buddhist Studies Comprehensive Online Buddhist Resources**
http://pears2.lib.ohio-state.edu/e-CBS.htm
> This digital library offers readers access to full-text journals, Buddhist News, scriptures, courses, and resources for the study of Buddhism. Grade 6+

**Confucius**
http://www.friesian.com/confuci.htm
> Learn about the life and teachings of Confucius at this site created and maintained by Dr. Kelley Ross, Department of Philosophy at Los Angeles Valley College. Grade 5+

**Confucius**
http://www.easternreligions.com/text/confucius-t.html
> Ronald Henry Olsommer offers this list of resources on Confucius. Each page of text cites the original source. He offers links about his life, basic ideas, morals, wisdom, influence, and the Analects. Teacher Reference

**Electronic Bodhidharma, International Research Institute for Zen Buddhism**
http://www.iijnet.or.jp/iriz/
> This IRIZ site is maintained by Hanazono University in Kyoto, Japan, an academic research institution devoted to the study of Zen Buddhism. It offers a vast collection of electronic texts, Zen art, and Zen stories. Teacher Reference

**Feasts of the Prophet: Ramadan and Vegetarianism in Islam**
http://www.veg.on.ca/newsletr/janfeb96/Islam_recipes.html
> Julian Bynoe cites "Food for the Spirit: Vegetarianism and the World Religions" by Steven Rosen, *Vegetarian Times*, January 1995, about breaking the fast at the end of Ramadan. He features a few vegetarian recipes. Grade 4+

**Geography of Religion Web Site**
http://www.morehead-st.edu/people/t.pitts/mainmenu.htm
> Professors Timothy C. Pitts and George N. Sharik of Morehead State University created this ambitious project. Click on the symbols bar for the topic of your choice. Search Basics, Buddhism, Confucianism, Hinduism, Humanism, Jainism, Islam, Judaism, Orthodox Christianity, Protestantism, Catholicism, Rastafarianism, Shintoism, Sikhism, Taoism, or other religions. Research for each religion is fully cited. Topics for each include essentials of the faith (founder, adherents, distribution, major teachings, scriptures and significant writings, symbols, major divisions, and major holy days), details about the religion, the geography of the religion, references, and more links. Teacher Reference

**Hindu Kids Universe**
http://www.hindukids.org/
> This interactive site is designed for children to learn about and appreciate their faith. The site features prayers, stories, and comic books for children. Grade 3+

**The Hindu Universe**
http://www.hindunet.org/
>This exceptional searchable site offers Hindu news, Bharat daily news and events as well as the resource center with links to the arts, scriptures, interfaith relations, history, Hindus around the world, worship, customs, and contemporary social issues. Search Hindu Women, Hindu Kids, Hindu Youth, Hindu Links, and much more. Grade 5+

**Hinduism for Schools**
http://www.btinternet.com/~vivekananda/schools1.htm
>The Vivekananda Center in London offers this index and fact finder site. Search topics by primary school or secondary school level for age-appropriate explanations of key ideas of the Hindu faith. Simple terms and festivals are included. Grade 6+

**Interfaith Calendar**
http://www.interfaithcalendar.org/
>Interfaith includes holidays from Baha'i, Buddhism, Christianity, Hinduism, Jainism, Islam, Judaism, Shintoism, Sikhism, Zoroastrianism, and more. Grade 3+

**Islaam.com**
http://www.islaam.com/intro/
>Visit this site to gain a basic understanding of Islam. Pages for Muslims provide updated information and words for reflection. Grade 5+

**IslamiCity**
http://islam.org/Mosque/
>Visit "Virtual Mosque," "100 Mecca City," and "IslamiCity" at this visually appealing and informative site. Click into links about the pillars of Islam, the Islamic history of the Middle East (including Arabic writing, the Crusaders), and Mohammed, the prophet. Grade 5+

**Islamic Gateway**
http://www.ummah.org.uk/
>This site offers articles and links to other resources, including news updates, photos of the Hajj, festivals, and the Islamic calendar. Grade 5+

**The Islamic Interlink**
http://www.ais.org/~islam/
>The Interlink offers links for Islam, Islamic beliefs and practices, the Holy Qur'an, the prophet, history, organizations, comparative religions, and links for audio/video sites. Grade 5+

**Islamic Links**
http://www.irshad.org/pages/islsites.htm
>Explore these varied links to Islamic sites on the Internet. Teacher Reference

**Islamic Studies, Islam, Arabic, and Religion**
http://www.arches.uga.edu/~godlas/
>Links to documents and religious studies are maintained by Professor Alan Godlas, University of Georgia Department of Religion. Grade 6+

### Islamic Voice
http://www.islamicvoice.com/
> This monthly newspaper is about the Islamic world, with features including Children's Corner, Women in Islam, Religion, and In Focus. Grade 6+

### Islamzine
http://www.Islamzine.com/
> This interesting Web site by a Muslim living in the United Arab Emirates teaches about Islam and includes information about women and hijab (covering of the head), marriage, raising children, meanings of names, and current issues. Grade 6+

### Koran Online
http://www.hti.umich.edu/relig/koran
> This is an electronic version of the Holy Qur'an, translated by M.H. Shakir and published by Tahrike Tarsile Qur'an, Inc. Teacher Reference

### Museum of World Religions
http://www.twwrm.org/
> The mission of the Museum of World Religions in Taipei, Taiwan, is "to give people all over the world an opportunity to better appreciate and better understand all human religions." It houses religious art of all faiths, including Tibetan Buddhism, Eastern Orthodox Christianity, Hinduism, Islam, Judaism, Protestant Christianity, and Taiwanese folk religion; a religious music database collection; and links to resources for religious information. Grade 5+

### Muslim Student Association at the University of Buffalo
http://wings.buffalo.edu/sa/muslim/
> MSA is one of the best resources available for the study of Islam. It offers links to introductory texts, scriptures and prophetic traditions, Islamic thought, Islamic language and art resources, and other resources. Grade 6+

### The Qur'an and Sunnah Society
http://www.qss.org/
> This informative site is maintained by al-Qur'an was-Sunnah Society of North America to teach about Islam. Teacher Reference

### Resources for the Study of East Asian Language and Thought
http://www.human.toyogakuen-u.ac.jp/~acmuller/index.html
> Prof. Charles Muller, Toyo Gakuen University in Chiba, Japan, offers links for articles about Buddhism, Confucianism, and Taoism. Teacher Reference

### Taoism
http://www.easternreligions.com/text/taoism-t.html
> Ronald Henry Olsommer offers this list of resources on Taoism. Each page of text cites the original source. He provides links about the master, meaning, power, quietude, values, and Tao Te Ching. Teacher Reference

**Taoism Information Page**
http://www.clas.ufl.edu/users/gthursby/taoism/index.htm
> This World Wide Web Virtual Library site offers links to explore the study of Taoism (Daoisim) and related philosophies. Teacher Reference

**Zen**
http://www.easternreligions.com/text/zen-t.html
> Ronald Henry Olsommer offers this list of resources on Zen. Each page of text cites the original source. He provides links about the enigma of Zen, varieties, definitions, koans (instructive ancient stories and sayings), verses, and more. Teacher Reference.

## *Science and Nature*

**ES 2000: Endangered Species of the Next Millennium**
http://library.thinkquest.org/25014/
> Students from the Netherlands, Singapore, and the United States created this impressive informational 1999 ThinkQuest site. It details endangered species of the world, the threats to their continued existence, and what people can do to help. Share an interactive adventure story, visit the media gallery, and learn fascinating facts and quotes. Grade 4+

**ENDANGERED! Exploring a World at Risk**
http://www.amnh.org/Exhibition/Expedition/Endangered/
> The American Museum of Natural History offers this fabulous interactive tour through the world of endangered animals. Select "endangered animals," scroll the list, and select animals to study. Explore dioramas, endangered habitats, causes of endangerment, and what can be done. Grade 3+

**Endangered Species: An Ongoing SchoolWorld Project**
http://www.schoolworld.asn.au/species/species.html
> John Halse and Karen Walkowiak created this page for SchoolWorld Internet Education as part of the Endangered Species Project. Click on plants and trees, reptiles, insects, amphibians, crustaceans and mollusks, fish, birds, and mammals to read student reports. Grade 3+

**Kids' Corner**
http://www.ran.org/ran/kids_action/index1.html
> The Rainforest Action Network offers this stunning site to teach children about the rain forests, endangered species, and steps kids can take to make a difference. The visuals are lush as you learn about the animals and people of the rain forests. Teachers' Resources include activities and reproducible handouts. Grade 3+

*Part* **III**

# Keypal/Pen Pal Projects and Resources

Educators have always recognized the value of communicating with others through pen pal exchanges. With snail mail, time was often a deterrent to effective research. Today's high-speed educational telecommunications can capitalize on the immediacy of feedback and the spontaneity and excitement of peer response. The Internet is a dynamic, interactive communication tool. Individual students can "talk" electronically with individuals or groups. Classes can communicate with individuals or groups. Teachers can design projects incorporating electronic mail components, using newsgroups, and tapping into Internet-connected bulletin boards. With guidance and monitoring, students can participate in electronic field trips and synchronous discussions on Internet Relay Chat (IRC). Teachers can facilitate group-to-group exchanges called global classrooms. Using e-mail and telecommunications, students can draw upon information access, social studies, and geography standards, as well as hone composition, revision, and editing skills.

Keypal/pen pal project possibilities are limitless. Children can learn about the world around them through their peers. They can establish contact with children in other countries to learn about geography, government, history, festivals, religions, and cultures. They can discuss books, art, music, and politics. They can gain insights and applaud the similarities and respect the differences of others.

In 1996, I received a Cherry Hill (New Jersey) Public Schools district grant for a project entitled "Multicultural Online Resources, Peer Teaching, and Special Students." This project was a successful and rewarding combination of Internet navigation, print research, and e-mail communication. Mrs. Donna Simon's Special Education fifth grade students each selected a country to research online and in print and also worked with a number of Dr. Connie Van Note's first grade students researching the same countries. They kept logs of information and recommended books and Web sites for each country. As the culminating activity, the fifth graders spent three weeks teaching the first graders how to access and print flags for each country, locate foreign language sites so that the children could print samples of each foreign language spoken in their country, and access and print facts about the countries from resources such as the *CIA World Fact Book.*

In addition, the fifth-graders were the first students to have e-mail accounts and communicated weekly with a 10-year-old girl from South Africa, near Capetown. They learned how to check their messages, print their messages, use an address book feature, and compose and send messages. They were also able to communicate with other keypals and with each other.

The Educational Media Association of New Jersey and Winnebago awarded the 1997 Progressive School Library Media Program Award to Mrs. Simon and me for this program. The project goals were fulfilled in more ways than we could have imagined. They were:

- To encourage understanding of other cultures and of each other through online communication and research.
- To foster self-esteem through successful interaction with technology and others.
- To provide effective communication and research experiences which create lifelong skills necessary for success.
- To sharpen sensory experiences and motor-skill coordination skills through the use of technology.
- To better prepare special education students for inclusion in our multicultural world.
- To provide a working environment for the application of other technology skills such as successful use of CD-ROMs within the classroom.

Some of these recommended keypal/pen pal sites link children with other registered schools, classes, and individuals. Some share successful projects to model. With all projects, teachers should establish e-mail etiquette ('Netiquette) and be actively involved with design and implementation of the telecommunications exchanges.

**All About Education**
http://www.vsns.com/aae/

This free service provides keypal connections. It is divided by categories of pen pals: kindergarten class, elementary teachers, elementary students, elementary parents, middle school teachers, middle school students, middle school class, and middle school parents. (High school, college, home school, and Special Education resources are also included.)

**Classroom Connect's Connected Teacher E-mail Clubs**
http://connectedteacher.classroom.com/listServ/subscribe.asp

This free service connects educators around the world and provides resources for classroom exchanges.

**ePALS Classroom Exchange**
http://www.epals.com/index_en.html

This valuable site, available in English, French, Spanish, German, and Portuguese, is a free international classroom exchange. Established in 1996, ePALS is "committed to offering safe, innovative ways for all learners to make contact with other cultures." It offers Web-mail language translation, monitored e-mail, and profanity filters to maximize students' e-mail experiences.

**Filamentality Online Help Pages**
http://www.kn.pacbell.com/wired/filamentality/topics.html

Pacific Bell's Knowledge Network offers guidelines for picking topics and an idea pool for topics to help teachers design Web-based projects.

**Find a Key Pal**
http://www.kidscom.com/orakc/Friends/newfriends.html
>Teachers can register a class for key pals or individuals may register with a signed parent's permission form.

**Gaggle.Net**
http://www.gaggle.net/
>This is a teacher-controlled free service for e-mail for schools and students ages eight to 18. Special monitoring and filtering capabilities are available.

**How to Design a Pen Pal Program**
http://k-6educators.about.com/education/k-6educators/library/weekly/aa072200a.htm?terms=keypals
>This article discusses the pros and cons of e-mail and snail mail projects and how to find potential pen pals and keypals.

**How to Find Pen Pals**
http://www.siec.k12.in.us/west/online/coll1a.htm
>Tammy Payton, Web editor of this Loogootee Community Schools site in Loogootee, Indiana, discusses pen pal sites, school Web sites, and educational listservs as ways to connect for collaborative projects.

**Intercultural E-Mail Classroom Connections**
http://www.iecc.org/
>This free service, created in 1992, "helps teachers link with partners in other countries and cultures for e-mail classroom pen pal and project exchanges."

**Keypals**
http://www.keypals.com/
>Pitsco Inc. provides Ask an Expert, relevant Web sites, and posts listservs from which to request keypals for collaborative projects or contact with individuals from around the world. Includes e-mail safety tips.

**Kidlink**
http://www.kidlink.org/home-std.html
>This free service allows students to join public mailing lists and participate in chats and other interactive services. It includes Kidcafe (e-mail discussions between youth and kids only), Kidforum (discussions of one topic at a time), and Kidproj (short- and long-term educational projects across language areas).

**Kidworld Keypals**
http://www.bconnex.net/~kidworld/keypals4.htm
>The registration form requires a note of permission from a parent. Children may select keypals by age group (8 or younger, 9–10, 11–12, 13–16). Their first name, country, e-mail address, and interests are listed.

**Mighty Media Keypals Club**
http://www.mightymedia.com/keypals/
> Teachers and students can register online for this service to match classrooms or individual students wishing to communicate electronically. There are attractive privacy features available.

**Penpal Box**
http://www.ks-connection.org/penpal/penpal.html
> Kids' Space Connection offers pen pals by box. Each box is organized by age (aged 6 and younger, 7 and 8, 9 and 10, 11 and 12, and 13 through 16). Guide Bear acts as the tour guide and answers frequently asked questions.

**Penpals Worldwide: International Penfriends**
http://www.oze-mail.com.au/%7Epenpals/
> International Penfriends (IPF), established in 1967, has "over 300,000 members worldwide aged from 8–80 years."

**Safety Tips for Pen Pal Exchanges**
http://www.siec.k12.in.us/west/online/coll1b.htm
> Tammy Payton, Web editor of this Loogootee Community Schools site in Loogootee, Indiana, includes their Acceptable Use Policy with seven safety tips children should practice before e-mailing others.

**Suggested Topics and Activities for Keypals**
http://www.siec.k12.in.us/west/online/coll1c.htm
> Tammy Payton, Web editor of this Loogootee Community Schools site in Loogootee, Indiana, describes activities two or more classrooms can share via the Internet.

**Web66: International School Website Registry**
http://web66.coled.umn.edu/schools.html
> Search this global school registry to establish connections with schools around the world for exchange projects.

**World Kids Network**
http://wkn.org/
> This educational nonprofit site offers original work by volunteers, adults, and children. Children can register for mail lists to communicate with children from around the world. Monitored chat rooms are also available.

# *E-mail*

> Post a call for collaborators for international partners c/o *IECC-projects@stolaf.edu*. For information about the Intercultural E-mail Classroom Connections, see *http://www.stolaf.edu/network/iecc/*.

# *Listservs*

**K12pals**
**listserv@suvm.syr.edu**
>The AskERIC Project sponsors K12Pals, open to K-12 students and teachers seeking pen pals.

**Kidcafe**
**listserv@listserv.nodak.edu**
>KIDLINK sponsors three divisions of Kidcafe. Kidcafe-School is a list for organized school-to-school keypal exchange with thematic dialogue. Kidcafe-Coord is for coordinators to announce for partner classes, plan projects, and discuss Kidcafe activities with other participants. Kidcafe-Individual is for students up to age 15 to announce for keypals, look for keypals, or write messages to keypals. Mail is monitored to ensure 'Netiquette is observed.

# Appendix A: Web Site Title Index

## A

Aaron Shepard's Reader's Theater Page ..... 79
ABC News ..... 94
ABC News.com Country Profiles ..... 83
About.com ..... 83
About Islam and Muslims ..... 104
Adventure Online ..... 83
Al-Islam ..... 104
All About Education ..... 110
Alta Vista: Live! ..... 101
Altapedia Online ..... 83
Amnesty International ..... 104
Ancient World Web ..... 84
AnyDay-in-History ..... 95
Armed Forces of the World ..... 84
The Arts: Web Sites ..... 79-82
ArtsEdNet ..... 79
Atlas of the World ..... 101

## B

Bartleby.com ..... 96
Biographical Dictionary ..... 82
Biographies of Jewish Women ..... 82
Biographies: Web Sites ..... 82-83
Biography.com ..... 82
Bodleian Library Map Room ..... 102
British Museum: Illuminating World Cultures ..... 79
Buddha ..... 104
Buddhist Information Network ..... 104
Buddhist Studies WWW Virtual Library ..... 104

## C

Calendar Zone ..... 95
Capitals of Every Country ..... 84
Catholic Internet Directory ..... 105
CBS News ..... 94
Center for Buddhist Studies Comprehensive
	Online Buddhist Resources ..... 105
Centers for Disease Control & Prevention ..... 84
Chiefs of State and Cabinet Members of Foreign Governments ..... 84
Children's Express ..... 94
The Children's Literature Web Guide ..... 79
Christmas Around the World ..... 98
CIA World Factbook ..... 84
Classroom Connect's Connected Teacher E-mail Clubs ..... 110
CNN CityGuide ..... 84
CNN Interactive News ..... 94
Compton's 3D Atlas Online ..... 102
Confucius ..... 105
Connected Teacher ..... 95
Country Profiles: The Spire Project ..... 84
Country Resources: Web Sites ..... 83-93
Culture Quest World Tour (Internet Public Library) ..... 85
Currency Converter ..... 85
Current Events and News: Web Sites ..... 94-95

## D

Daily Almanacs ..... 95
The Daily Globe: "J" World ..... 95-96
Dates in History: Web Sites ..... 95-96
Dewey Browse ..... 85
Diana's Gourmet Corner ..... 98
Dictionary.com ..... 96

## E

E-Conflict World Encyclopedia ..... 85
ES 2000: Endangered Species of the Next Millennium ..... 108
Elections Around the World ..... 85
Electronic Bodhidharma, International Research
	Institute for Zen Buddhism ..... 105
Electronic Embassy ..... 85
Encarta Learning Zone ..... 96-97
Encyclopedia Britannica ..... 97
Encyclopedia Mythica ..... 80
Encyclopedia Proteus ..... 97
Encyclopedias & Dictionaries: Web Sites ..... 96-98
Endangered Species: An Ongoing SchoolWorld Project ..... 108
ENDANGERED! Exploring a World at Risk ..... 108
ePALS Classroom Exchange ..... 110
Ethnologue: Languages of the World ..... 101
Excite Travel: Countries ..... 85
Exploring Ancient World Cultures ..... 86

## F

Fairrosa Cyber Library of Children's Literature ..... 80
Feasts of the Prophet: Ramadan and Vegetarianism in Islam ..... 105
Festivals & Food: Web Sites ..... 98-99
Filamentality Online Help Pages ..... 110-111
Find a Key Pal ..... 111
Fine Art Resource Directory: Museums and Art History ..... 80
Flags and Anthems ..... 99
Flags and Anthems: Web Sites ..... 99-101
Flags of All Countries ..... 100
Flags of the World ..... 100
Fodor's Travel Guides ..... 86
Foreign Affairs Online ..... 86
Foreign Languages: Web Sites ..... 101
Foreign Language for Travelers ..... 101
4000 Years of Women in Science ..... 82
Frank Rogers' Enchanted Neighborhood ..... 80
The Free Internet Encyclopedia ..... 97
From Past to Present: A Journey Across the World and Through Time ..... 86
Funk and Wagnalls ..... 97

## G

Gaggle.Net ..... 111
Gateway to Art History ..... 80
Gateway to World History ..... 86
Geo Game ..... 102
Geographia ..... 86
Geography ..... 102
Geography and Maps: Web Sites ..... 101-103
Geography of Religion Web Site ..... 105
GeoWorld ..... 102
The Getty Thesaurus of Geographic Names (TGN) ..... 102
The Global Gastronomer: Cuisines of the World ..... 98
Global Grocery List ..... 86
Governments on the WWW ..... 86
The Great Globe Gallery on the World Wide Web (3G on 3W) ..... 102-103
Greenpeace ..... 86

## H

Heritage Map Museum ..........................103
Hindu Kids Universe ..........................105
The Hindu Universe ..........................106
Hinduism for Schools ..........................106
The History Channel ..........................87
The History Net ..........................87
History/Social Studies Web Site for K-12 Teachers ..........87
Holidays on the Net ..........................99
Horus ..........................87
Houghton Mifflin Outline Maps ..........................103
How to Design a Pen Pal Program ..........................111
How to Find Pen Pals ..........................111
The Human Languages Page ..........................101
Human Rights Watch ..........................104
Human Rights: Web Sites ..........................104
HyperHistory Online ..........................87

## I

InfoNation ..........................87
Information Please Almanac (Infoplease.com) ..........97
Intellicast Weather ..........................87
Intercultural E-Mail Classroom Connections ..........111
Interfaith Calendar ..........................106
International Children's Cookbook ..........................99
International Constitutional Law ..........................88
International Database ..........................88
International Monetary Fund ..........................88
Islaam.com ..........................106
IslamiCity ..........................106
Islamic Gateway ..........................106
The Islamic Interlink ..........................106
Islamic Links ..........................107
Islamic Studies, Islam, Arabic, and Religion ..........107
Islamic Voice ..........................106
Islamzine ..........................107

## K

K12pals ..........................113
Keypals ..........................111
Kidcafe ..........................113
Kidlink ..........................111
KidNews ..........................94
Kidworld Keypals ..........................111
Kids' Corner ..........................108
Kids' Space ..........................88
Kids Web ..........................88
Knowledge Adventure's Let's Find Out Encyclopedia ..........97
Koran Online ..........................107

## L

Language Dictionaries and Translators ..........................101
Latitude and Longitude Distance ..........................103
Library of Congress Country Studies ..........................88
Lives, the Biography Resource ..........................82
Lonely Planet: Destination ..........................89
Look in the Mythic Mirror ..........................80
Lycos Zone ..........................98

## M

MSNBC News ..........................94
Medals of the World ..........................100
Merriam-Webster Word Central ..........................98

Metropolitan Museum of Art ..........................80-81
Microsoft's Expedia ..........................89
Mighty Media Keypals Club ..........................112
Mr. Dowling's Electronic Passport ..........................89
Multicultural Holidays ..........................99
Multicultural Recipe Book ..........................99
Museum of World Religions ..........................107
Museums Around the World ..........................81
Muslim Student Association at the University of Buffalo ..........107
Mything Links ..........................81

## N

National Anthems ..........................100
National Anthems of the World ..........................100
National Geographic Society Map Machine ..........................103
National Geographic Society Xpeditions ..........................89
National Standards for History ..........................89
New Countries of the World ..........................89
New York Times Learning Network ..........................94-95
Newsmaker Bios: Names in the News ..........................83

## P

Penpal Box ..........................112
Penpals Worldwide: International Penfriends ..........................112
Political Resources on the Net ..........................89

## Q

The Qur'an and Sunnah Society ..........................107

## R

Refdesk.com ..........................98
Religion and Philosophy: Web Sites ..........................104-108
Resources for the Study of East Asian Language and Thought ..........107
RootsWorld ..........................81
Rulers ..........................83

## S

Safety Tips for Pen Pal Exchanges ..........................112
The Say Hello to the World Project ..........................89
Science and Nature: Web Sites ..........................108
Seven Wonders of the Ancient World ..........................90
Suggested Topics and Activities for Keypals ..........................112

## T

Tales of Wonder ..........................81
Taoism ..........................107
Taoism Information Page ..........................108
Teaching Tolerance ..........................81
ThinkQuest Web Sites ..........................86, 90, 92, 108
This Day in History ..........................96
TIME for Kids ..........................95
Today in History Archive ..........................96
Travel Warnings and Consular Information Sheets ..........90
Travel.org ..........................90
Travlang's Translating Dictionaries ..........................101

## U

UNESCO ..........................90
UNICEF: The Progress of Nations ..........................90
U.S. Census Bureau (World Population Clock Project) ..........90
U.S. Energy Administration Country Analysis Briefs ..........90
U.S. State Department Background Notes ..........................91
U.S. State Department: Regions and Country Information ..........91

USA Today Education Online . . . . . . . . . . . . . . . . . . . . . . . . . . . . .95
United Nations . . . . . . . . . . . . . . . . . . . . . . . . . . . . . . . . . . . . . . .91
United Nations CyberSchoolBus Resource Source . . . . . . . . . . . . .91

## W

The WWW V-L History: Central Catalogue . . . . . . . . . . . . . . . . . .91
The WWW Virtual Library . . . . . . . . . . . . . . . . . . . . . . . . . . . . . .91
WYK's International Food Court . . . . . . . . . . . . . . . . . . . . . . . . . .99
Web66: International School Website Registry . . . . . . . . . . . . . . .112
WebChron: The Web Chronology Project . . . . . . . . . . . . . . . . .91-92
WebMuseum, Paris . . . . . . . . . . . . . . . . . . . . . . . . . . . . . . . . . . . .81
Wonders of the World: From the Pyramids to the St. Louis Arch . . . .92
World Atlas . . . . . . . . . . . . . . . . . . . . . . . . . . . . . . . . . . . . . . . . .103
World Atlas: Maps and Geography of the World . . . . . . . . . . . . . .103
World Bank Countries and Regions . . . . . . . . . . . . . . . . . . . . . . . .92
The World Conservation Monitoring Centre . . . . . . . . . . . . . . . . . .92
World Flag Database . . . . . . . . . . . . . . . . . . . . . . . . . . . . . .100-101
World Health Organization . . . . . . . . . . . . . . . . . . . . . . . . . . . . . .92
World Heritage Centre . . . . . . . . . . . . . . . . . . . . . . . . . . . . . . . . .92
World History Compass . . . . . . . . . . . . . . . . . . . . . . . . . . . . . . . .92
World Kid . . . . . . . . . . . . . . . . . . . . . . . . . . . . . . . . . . . . . . . . . . .92
World Kids Network . . . . . . . . . . . . . . . . . . . . . . . . . . . . . . . . . .112
World Mythology . . . . . . . . . . . . . . . . . . . . . . . . . . . . . . . . . .81-82
The World of KruSader . . . . . . . . . . . . . . . . . . . . . . . . . . . . . .92-93

World Surfari . . . . . . . . . . . . . . . . . . . . . . . . . . . . . . . . . . . . . . . .93
World Travel Guide . . . . . . . . . . . . . . . . . . . . . . . . . . . . . . . . . . . .93
World Travel Guide (Lycos) . . . . . . . . . . . . . . . . . . . . . . . . . . . . . .93
World Wide Holiday and Festival Site . . . . . . . . . . . . . . . . . . . . . .99

## X

Xerox PARC Map Viewer . . . . . . . . . . . . . . . . . . . . . . . . . . . . . .103

## Y

Yahooligans—Around the World: Countries . . . . . . . . . . . . . . . . . .93
Yahooligans—Around the World: Cultures . . . . . . . . . . . . . . . . . . .93
Yahooligans—Around the World: Food and Eating . . . . . . . . . . . .99
Yahooligans! This Day in History . . . . . . . . . . . . . . . . . . . . . . . . .96
Your Nation . . . . . . . . . . . . . . . . . . . . . . . . . . . . . . . . . . . . . . . . .93

## Z

Zárate's Political Collections (ZPC) . . . . . . . . . . . . . . . . . . . . . . . .83
Zen . . . . . . . . . . . . . . . . . . . . . . . . . . . . . . . . . . . . . . . . . . . . . . .108
Zip Codes and Postal Codes of the World . . . . . . . . . . . . . . . . . . .93

# Appendix B: Short Story/Folktale Title Index

## A

The Abbey Bells (Scotland) .................................. .50
Achol and Maper (Sudan) .................................. .42
The Admirable Hare (Ceylon) ................................ .47
The Alchemist (China) ..................................... .47
Alionushka and Ivanushka (Russia) .......................... .42
Anansi and the Pig (Jamaica) ............................... .49
The Armchair Traveler (India) .............................. .46
Aunt Misery (Puerto Rico) .................................. .38

## B

Baba-Yaga (Russia) ........................................ .36
Babushka (Russia) ......................................... .47
The Barber's Wife (India) .................................. .41
The Barking Mouse (Cuba) ................................... .43
Bean Soup (Greece) ........................................ .50
The Beautiful Birds (Japan) ................................ .26
Beauty and the Beast (France) .............................. .51
The Beggar Princess (China) ................................ .46
Beginning with the Ears (Iraq) ............................. .47
Beruriah's Jewels (Israel) ................................. .38
Biggest (Japan) ........................................... .47
The Bird with Golden Feathers (southern Africa) ............ .37
The Birdcage Husband (Kalmuck from Central Asia) ........... .46
The Birth of Krishna (India) ............................... .41
A Birthday Surprise (Caribbean) ............................ .43
The Black Snake (Persia) ................................... .47
The Blind Man and the Hunter (West Africa) ................. .45
Blinded by Greed (Taoist) .................................. .40
The Blood-Drawing Ghost (Ireland) .......................... .49
The Bloody Fangs (Japan) ................................... .47
A Bouquet of Flowers (Aborigines) .......................... .46
The Boy and the Seedpod Canoe (Maori) ...................... .40
The Boy Who Drew Cats (Japan) .............................. .40
The Boy Who Tried to Fool His Father (Zaire) ............... .49
The Bright Blue Jackal (India) ............................. .43

## C

Cam and the Magic Fish (Vietnam) ........................... .40
Can Krishna Die? (India) ................................... .47
Cat v. Rat (Congo) ........................................ .47
Chih-nii The Heavenly Spinner (China) ...................... .46
Chura and Marwe (Africa) ................................... .39
Cinderella (France, Chile, Africa) ..................... .41, 51
Cinderello (Greek) ........................................ .40
Clapping Hands (Russia) .................................... .43
A Clever Old Bride (Korea) ................................. .50
The Clever Old Man (India) ................................. .50
The Corn Maidens (Mexico) .................................. .41
The Crane Wife (Japan) ..................................... .46
The Creation Cat (East India) .............................. .42
Crocodile Hunts for the Monkey (India) ..................... .37
The Crystal Pool (Melanesia) ............................... .46
The Curious Honeybird (Bantu) .............................. .47

## D

The Dance of the Monkey and the Sparrow (Japan) ............ .45
Daughter of the Star (Zaire) ............................... .46
Dear Dog (Japan) .......................................... .47
Deer and Jaguar Share a House (Brazil) ..................... .43
The Dog, the Cat, the Snake, and the Ring:
    A Bichon Frise Tale (Malta) ............................ .42
The Dog Who Married a Princess: A Shar-pei Tale (China) ... .42
The Donkey Egg (Algeria) ................................... .41
The Dumpling (Japan) ....................................... .44

## E

Eat. Coat. Eat! (Turkey) ................................... .49
The Eclipse of the Sun (India) ............................. .36
Empty-Cup Mind (Japan) ..................................... .50
The Enchanted Dog Tales (British Isles, Arabia, Germany) ... .42

## F

Feeding His Clothes (Middle East) .......................... .40
Fish Husband (Africa) ...................................... .48
The Flash of Lightning (Celtic) ............................ .36
The Forty Thieves (Iran) ................................... .38
The Fox and the Crab (China) ............................... .49
The Fox and the Crab Have a Race (China) ................... .43
The Fox and the Tomten (Sweden) ............................ .41
The Frail Old Woman (Bengali) .............................. .50
The Freedom Bird (Thailand) ................................ .43
Fried Plantains (Cuba) ..................................... .50

## G

The Ghostly Weaver: A Retriever Tale (England) ............. .42
The Gift of Fire: A Basenji Tale (Africa) .................. .41
Gifts of Love (Korea) ...................................... .36
The Girl Who Combed Pearls (Portugal) ...................... .48
The Girl Who Couldn't Walk (United States) ................. .39
The Goddess Cat (Ancient Egypt) ............................ .42
The Goddess of Luck (Nepal) ................................ .40
The Gods Down Tools (Sumerian) ............................. .46
Grandmother Death (Mexico) ................................. .38
Grandmother's Basket (Russia) .............................. .47
The Grateful Snake (China) ................................. .37
The Great Day (Namibia) .................................... .26
The Guardian Cat Tales (Southeast Asian, Bahamian, Polynesian) ... .42
Gull-Girl (Siberia) ........................................ .47
Gulnara the Warrior (Mongolia) ............................. .41

## H

Hansel and Gretel (Germany, Syria, Philippines) ........ .42, 51
The Hare and the Rumor (India) ............................. .40
The Haunted Forest (Uzbekistan) ............................ .47
Hiding the Bell (Germany) .................................. .49
Holding Up the Sky (China) ................................. .38
How Brazilian Beetles Got Their Gorgeous Coats (Brazil) .... .41
How Dog Brought Death into the World: A Husky Tale
    (Siberia, North America) ............................... .42

How Hare Drank Boiling Water and Married the Beautiful Princess (Benin) .............43
How the Elephant Was Punished (India) .............44
How the Horse-Head Fiddle Came To Be (Mongolia) .............46
How the Rabbit Lost Its Tail (Haiti) .............43
How the World Was Lit Up by a Bonfire (Aborigines) .............48
How Tigers Got Their Stripes (Vietnam) .............41

## I

Isis and Osiris (Egypt) .............46
Issun Boshi (Japan) .............49
Izinagi and Izanami (Japan) .............44

## J

Juan Bobo's Pig (Puetro Rico) .............43

## K

Kancil and the Crocodile (Indonesia) .............49
King Thrushbeard (Germany) .............38
The Kiss of Evil (Iraq) .............43
Kongjee (Korea) .............40

## L

The Lady and the Unjust Judge (Turkey) .............38
The Lake Lovers (Maori) .............41
Lamia (India) .............47
Lazy Jack (England) .............43
The Legend of the Feathered Serpent (Mexico) .............37
Legend of the Rice Seed (Hmong) .............44
Li Chi and the Serpent (China) .............49
The Lighthouse on the Lake (Japan) .............47
The Lion's Whiskers (Ethiopia) .............38
The Listening Cap (Japan) .............38, 39
The Listening Ear (Japan) .............38
The Little Frog (Chilean) .............39
The Lord of Death (India) .............50
Lump Off, Lump On (Japan) .............50

## M

The Magic Brocade (China) .............38
The Magic Drum (Benin) .............45
The Magic Pot (China) .............39, 43
The Man Who Almost Lived Forever (Sumerian) .............47
Maria and the Stingy Baker (Peru) .............37
The Marvelous Time (Mexico) .............26
Maui-of-a-Thousand Tricks (Polynesian) .............39
The Men in the Moon (Kenya) .............47
The Midwife and the Djinn (Sengalese) .............47
The Mirror (Korea) .............39
Momotaro the Peach Boy (Japan) .............41
Monkey and the Papa God (Haiti) .............45
Monkey Do: The Story of Hanuman (Hindu) .............47
The Monster Cat (Mid-European) .............42
The Monster of Baylock (Ireland) .............49
Moon Cakes (China) .............44
The Mountain Princess (Persia) .............46
Music Charms the Pirates (Japan) .............50

## N

Nail Soup (Switzerland) .............50
Necessity (Romania) .............49

A Nest and a Web (Middle East) .............47
The New Moon (Pakistan) .............26
The Night It Rained Bagels (Russia) .............44
The Noodle (Chinese American) .............50
Nowhere to Hide (Russia) .............47

## O

Odon the Giant (Philippines) .............49
An Old Man's Wisdom (India) .............50
The Old Woman and Tengu (Japan) .............38
The Old Woman and the Fox (India) .............50
The Old Woman and the Rice Cakes (Japan) .............50
The Old Woman Who Was Not Afraid (Japan) .............47
One-inch Boy (Japan) .............49
The Origin of Maize (Mexico) .............44
The Orphan Boy and the Monkeys (Hmong) .............44

## P

The Paradise City (Morocco) .............41
The Peach Boy (Japan) .............36
The Peachling (Japan) .............44
The Pear Tree (China) .............44
People of the Rock (Africa) .............49
The Peri Wife (Persia) .............50
The Pied Piper of Hamelin (Germany) .............38
Prince Ivan and the Frog Princess (Russia) .............38
The Princess and the Music-Maker (Mayan) .............37
The Prodigal Son (Bible) .............39

## Q

Quetzalcoatl (Mexico) .............47

## R

Race to the Top (Maori) .............46
Ragged Emperor (China) .............46
Rapunzel (Germany) .............52
The Red Cow (Armenian) .............42
Rona and the New Moon (New Zealand) .............41
The Ruby (Hindu) .............43
Rumpelstiltskin (Germany) .............51

## S

The Sad Story of Stone Frogs (Australia) .............40
Serpent and the Sea Queen (Japan) .............48
The Seven Baldies and One Shorty (Mongolia) .............41
The Seven Sleepers: A Saluki Tale (Arabia) .............42
A Shepherd Wins His Bride (Turkey) .............45
The Shepherd (Arabia) .............36
The Silken Beard (China) .............36
The Silver-Miners (Bolivia) .............47
The Silver Swindle (China) .............50
Skinning Out (Ethiopia) .............47
The Skull That Spoke (Nigeria) .............49
The Sky-Blue Storybox (Ghana) .............47
Sleeping Beauty (Germany) .............52
The Snake and the Frog (North America) .............43
Spider Flies to the Feast (Liberia) .............36

The Spirits in the Leather Bag (Kampuchea) . . . . . . . . . . . . . . . .50
Stan Bolovan (Romania) . . . . . . . . . . . . . . . . . . . . . . . . . . . . . . .39
The Stolen Wife (Maori) . . . . . . . . . . . . . . . . . . . . . . . . . . . . . . . .50
The Super Dog Tales (England, China) . . . . . . . . . . . . . . . . . . . .42
Sweet and Sour Berries (China) . . . . . . . . . . . . . . . . . . . . . . . . . .43

# T

The Tail of the Linani Beast (Kenya) . . . . . . . . . . . . . . . . . . . . . .43
The Talkative Turtle (Jakata) . . . . . . . . . . . . . . . . . . . . . . . . . . . .40
The Talking Bird (Persia) . . . . . . . . . . . . . . . . . . . . . . . . . . . . . . .46
The Talking Bird and the Singing Tree (Russia) . . . . . . . . . . . . .45
The Talking Skull (West Africa) . . . . . . . . . . . . . . . . . . . . . . . . .40
Three Magic Oranges (Costa Rica) . . . . . . . . . . . . . . . . . . . . . . .48
The Three Sisters (Canada) . . . . . . . . . . . . . . . . . . . . . . . . . . . . .26
Thunder and Smith (China) . . . . . . . . . . . . . . . . . . . . . . . . . . . . .47
The Tiger, the Brahman, and the Jackal (India) . . . . . . . . . . . . . .40
The Tiger Woman (China) . . . . . . . . . . . . . . . . . . . . . . . . . . . . . .48
The Tongue-cut Sparrow (Japan) . . . . . . . . . . . . . . . . . . . . . . . . .38
Trampling the Demons (Japan) . . . . . . . . . . . . . . . . . . . . . . . . . .42
The Tree That Bled Fish (Micronesia) . . . . . . . . . . . . . . . . . . . . .37
The Trickster Cat Tales (Japan, Siberia, North America) . . . . . . .42
Trousers Mehmet and the Sultan's Daughter (Turkey) . . . . . . . . .39
Two Brides for Five Heads (South African Xhosa) . . . . . . . . . . .38
Two Brothers and the Pumpkin Seeds (Korea) . . . . . . . . . . . . . .37

# U

The Unknown Sister (Suriname) . . . . . . . . . . . . . . . . . . . . . . . . .48

# W

Water, Water Will Be Mine (Kenya) . . . . . . . . . . . . . . . . . . . . . .37
Wee Little Boy (China) . . . . . . . . . . . . . . . . . . . . . . . . . . . . . . . .43
What a Bargain! (Arabia) . . . . . . . . . . . . . . . . . . . . . . . . . . . . . .41
The Whistling Monster (Brazil) . . . . . . . . . . . . . . . . . . . . . . . . . .41
The White Rat (France) . . . . . . . . . . . . . . . . . . . . . . . . . . . . . . . .45
Why Ants Are Found Everywhere (Burma) . . . . . . . . . . . . . . . .41
Why Cat Lives with Woman (Africa) . . . . . . . . . . . . . . . . . . . . .38
Why Farmers Have to Work So Hard (Hmong) . . . . . . . . . . . . .44
Why the Beetle Has a Golden Coat (Brazil) . . . . . . . . . . . . . . . .37
Why the Sky Is Separate from the Earth (Botswana) . . . . . . . . .49
Why the Snake Has No Legs (Ashanti) . . . . . . . . . . . . . . . . . . . .48
Why Wisdom Is Everywhere (Ashanti) . . . . . . . . . . . . . . . . . . . .40
Wild Geese Flying (Japan) . . . . . . . . . . . . . . . . . . . . . . . . . . . . . .43
The Wise Judge (Japan) . . . . . . . . . . . . . . . . . . . . . . . . . . . . . . . .43
The Wise Man and the Thief (Sri Lanka) . . . . . . . . . . . . . . . . . .45
Witch of the Sands (Botswana) . . . . . . . . . . . . . . . . . . . . . . . . . .41
Work Shy Rabbit (West Africa) . . . . . . . . . . . . . . . . . . . . . . . . . .47

# Y

Young Buddha (India) . . . . . . . . . . . . . . . . . . . . . . . . . . . . . . . . .46

# Author/Illustrator Index

## A

Aardema, Verna ............................................. 80
Ada, Alma Flor .............................................. 80
Adams, Simon ............................................... 52
Ageorges, Véronique, illus. ............................ 44
Aiyengar, Devi S. ........................................... 65
Ajmera, Maya ........................................... 17, 25
Allison, Anthony ....................................... 58-59
Angell, Carole S. ........................................... 25
Austrian, Guy I. .............................................. 1
Avakian, Monique ......................................... 12
Avi-Yonah, Michael ........................................ 1

## B

Bailey, Sian, illus. .......................................... 47
Baines, John .................................................. 70
Baird, Nicola ................................................. 70
Baker, Beth A., ed. ........................................ 25
Baker, Daniel B. ............................................ 14
Baker, Lawrence W., ed. ................................. 3
Baker, Leslie, illus. ........................................ 42
Balbassi, Haemi ............................................ 80
Bang, Molly ................................................... 70
Barchers, Suzanne I. ................................. 36-37
Barish, Wendy ............................................... 70
Barnett, Russell, illus. ..................................... 4
Barr, Marilynn G., illus. ................................. 28
Baumgartner, Barbara .................................. 37
Bebi, Anna Lisa ............................................. 18
Beecroft, Simon ............................................ 70
Benedict, Kitty .............................................. 12
Bernardin, James, illus. ................................ 49
Bernhard, Durga, illus. ................................. 18
Bernhard, Emery .......................................... 18
Bettmann, Ellen Hofheimer .......................... 63
Bieniek, Denise ....................................... 18, 52
Birdseye, Debbie Holsclaw ........................... 59
Birdseye, Tom ............................................... 59
Blackaby, Susan ............................................ 18
Bode, Janet ................................................... 64
Bonk, Mary Rose, ed. .................................... 18
Bossun, Jo-Ellen, illus. .................................. 49
Boston, David, illus. ..................................... 40
Bowker, John ................................................ 65
Brace, Eric, illus. ........................................... 32
Bradley, Bill .................................................. 25
Bradley, Catherine ........................................ 59
Brenner, Barbara .......................................... 11
Brill, Marlene Targ ........................................ 37
Brown, Mary Ellen, ed. ................................. 37
Brown, Paul .................................................. 71
Brownlie, Alison ........................................... 59
Bryant, Michael, illus. ................................... 26
Bukiet, Suzanne ....................................... 35-36
Bunting, Eve ................................................. 64
Butterfield, Moira ......................................... 71

## C

Caduto, Michael J. ........................................ 37
Campbell, Louise .......................................... 26
Cann, Helen, illus. .......................... 28, 39, 40, 42
Cappelloni, Nancy ........................................ 26
Carpenter, Nancy, illus. ................................ 64
Cassie, Brian ................................................. 71
Chalfonte, Jessica ......................................... 65
Chambers, Catherine .................................... 52
Charney, Israel W., ed. .................................. 59
Chiarelli, A. B. ............................................... 18
Chicola, Nancy A. ......................................... 53
Chrisp, Peter ................................................ 53
Christensen, Karen, ed. ................................ 30
Church, Amanda .......................................... 71
Church, Andrew ........................................... 71
Clarke, Penny ............................................... 61
Climo, Shirley ............................................... 38
Cockcroft, David, illus. ................................. 52
Cole, Trish .................................................... 26
Collard, Sneed B. ........................................... 2
Copolla, Jill, ed. ............................................ 20
Corrick, James A. ........................................... 2
Covington, Karen ......................................... 12
Cranfield, Ingrid ........................................... 71
Creeden, Sharon .......................................... 38
Crespo, George, illus. ................................... 10
Crossley-Holland, Kevin, ed. ................... 38-39

## D

DeRolf, Shane ............................................... 19
DeSpain, Pleasant ........................................ 39
Delafosse, Claude ........................... 53, 55, 70
Delano, Marfe Ferguson ............................... 72
Diaz, David, illus. ......................................... 66
Dineen, Jacqueline ......................................... 2
Doherty, Berlie, ed. ...................................... 39
Doney, Meryl ........................................... 26, 27
Dooley, Norah .............................................. 27
Dudzinski, Kathleen ..................................... 72
Dugan, Karen, illus. ...................................... 29
Dunn, Andrew .............................................. 72
Dunn, Opal ................................................... 27
Duranceau, Suzanne, illus. ........................... 20

## E

Edelman, Marian Wright .............................. 17
English, Eleanor B. ....................................... 53
Erlbach, Arlene ............................................. 28
Evans, Lezlie ................................................. 36
Evetts-Secker, Josephine ......................... 39, 40

## F

Falkenstern, Lisa, illus. ................................. 38
Featherstone, Jane ....................................... 72
Felder, Deborah G. ....................................... 12
Feldman, Eve B. ............................................ 28
Fisher, Leonard Everett, illus. ....................... 30
Ford, Linda M. .............................................. 40
Foreman, Michael, illus. ............................... 48
Forest, Heather ............................................ 40

Fowler, Allan . . . . . . . . . . . . . . . . . . . . . . . . . . . .53, 54, 72, 73
Frank, Vivien . . . . . . . . . . . . . . . . . . . . . . . . . . . . . . . . . . . . . . . .9
Fyson, Nance . . . . . . . . . . . . . . . . . . . . . . . . . . . . . . . . . . . . . .73

## G

Gall, Susan Bevan, ed. . . . . . . . . . . . . . . . . . . . . . . . . . . . . .20
Gall, Timothy, ed. . . . . . . . . . . . . . . . . . . . . . . . . . . . . . . . . .20
Gallant, Roy A. . . . . . . . . . . . . . . . . . . . . . . . . . . . . . . . . . . .73
Gallo, Donald, ed. . . . . . . . . . . . . . . . . . . . . . . . . . . . . . . . .64
Ganeri, Anita . . . . . . . . . . . . . . . . . . . . . . . . . . . . . . . . .65, 66
Garfield, Gary M. . . . . . . . . . . . . . . . . . . . . . . . . . . . . . . . . . .2
Garlake, Teresa . . . . . . . . . . . . . . . . . . . . . . . . . . . . . . . . . .60
Garrity, Linda K. . . . . . . . . . . . . . . . . . . . . . . . . . . . . . . . . . .40
Gavin, Jamila . . . . . . . . . . . . . . . . . . . . . . . . . . . . . . . . .40-41
Gaylord, Susan Kapuscinski . . . . . . . . . . . . . . . . . . . . . . . . .9
George, Lindsay Barrett . . . . . . . . . . . . . . . . . . . . . . . . . . . .19
Gifford, Clive . . . . . . . . . . . . . . . . . . . . . . . . . . . . . . . . . . . .73
Gilchrist, Cherry . . . . . . . . . . . . . . . . . . . . . . . . . . . . . . . .3, 8
Giuliani, Rudolph W. . . . . . . . . . . . . . . . . . . . . . . . . . . . . . .64
Glaser, Linda . . . . . . . . . . . . . . . . . . . . . . . . . . . . . . . . . . . .19
Glass, Henry "Buzz" . . . . . . . . . . . . . . . . . . . . . . . . . . . . . .31
Gold, Susan Dudley . . . . . . . . . . . . . . . . . . . . . . . . . . . . . .73
Gonen, Rivka . . . . . . . . . . . . . . . . . . . . . . . . . . . . . . . . . . . .3
Goodman, Susan E. . . . . . . . . . . . . . . . . . . . . . . . . . . . . . .73
Grant, Donald, ed. . . . . . . . . . . . . . . . . . . . . . . . . . . . .54, 55
Grant, R.G. . . . . . . . . . . . . . . . . . . . . . . . . . . . . . . . . . . . . .60
Green, Jen . . . . . . . . . . . . . . . . . . . . . . . . . . . . . . . . . . .60, 61
Green, Robert . . . . . . . . . . . . . . . . . . . . . . . . . . . . . . . . . . .13
Greenstein, Susan, illus. . . . . . . . . . . . . . . . . . . . . . . . . . . .34
Gresko, Marcia S. . . . . . . . . . . . . . . . . . . . . . . . . . . . . . . . .55
Griffin, Robert H., ed. . . . . . . . . . . . . . . . . . . . . . . . . . . . . .21
Grunsell, Angela . . . . . . . . . . . . . . . . . . . . . . . . . . . . . . . . .61
Gubala, Scott, illus. . . . . . . . . . . . . . . . . . . . . . . . . . . . . . .50
Guevara, Susan, illus. . . . . . . . . . . . . . . . . . . . . . . . . . . . .51
Gulevich, Tanya . . . . . . . . . . . . . . . . . . . . . . . . . . . . . . . . .28
Gust, John . . . . . . . . . . . . . . . . . . . . . . . . . . . . . . . . . . . . . .28

## H

Hall, Amanda, illus. . . . . . . . . . . . . . . . . . . . . . . . . . . . . . .37
Hamanaka, Sheila . . . . . . . . . . . . . . . . . . . . . . . . . . . . . . .20
Hamilton, Martha . . . . . . . . . . . . . . . . . . . . . . . . . . . . . . . .41
Harrison, Michael, ed. . . . . . . . . . . . . . . . . . . . . . . . . . . . .41
Haughton, Emma . . . . . . . . . . . . . . . . . . . . . . . . . . . . . . . .61
Hausman, Gerald . . . . . . . . . . . . . . . . . . . . . . . . . . . . .41, 42
Hausman, Loretta . . . . . . . . . . . . . . . . . . . . . . . . . . . . .41, 42
Haven, Kendall . . . . . . . . . . . . . . . . . . . . . . . . . . . . . . .28-29
Hazell, Rebecca . . . . . . . . . . . . . . . . . . . . . . . . . . . . . . . . .42
Heller, Julek, illus. . . . . . . . . . . . . . . . . . . . . . . . . . . . . .45-46
Henderson, Helene, ed. . . . . . . . . . . . . . . . . . . . . . . . . . . .29
Hénon, Daniel, illus. . . . . . . . . . . . . . . . . . . . . . . . . . . . . . .44
Hewitt, Kathryn, illus. . . . . . . . . . . . . . . . . . . . . . . . . . . . . .13
Hewitt, Sally . . . . . . . . . . . . . . . . . . . . . . . . . . . . . . . . . . . .74
Hirst, Mike . . . . . . . . . . . . . . . . . . . . . . . . . . . . . . . . . . . . .61
Hoehner, Jane, ed. . . . . . . . . . . . . . . . . . . . . . . . . . . . . . . .14
Hoff, Brent . . . . . . . . . . . . . . . . . . . . . . . . . . . . . . . . . . . . .74
Hoffman, Mary . . . . . . . . . . . . . . . . . . . . . . . . . . . . . . .42, 43
Hollyer, Beatrice . . . . . . . . . . . . . . . . . . . . . . . . . . . . . . . . .20
Holm, Sharon Lane, illus. . . . . . . . . . . . . . . . . . . . . . . . . . .28
Holt, David, ed. . . . . . . . . . . . . . . . . . . . . . . . . . . . . . . . . .43
Hook, Sue . . . . . . . . . . . . . . . . . . . . . . . . . . . . . . . . . . . . .55
Hopkins, Lee Bennett . . . . . . . . . . . . . . . . . . . . . . . . . .43-44
Howarth, Sarah . . . . . . . . . . . . . . . . . . . . . . . . . . . . . . . . .55
Howell, Troy, illus. . . . . . . . . . . . . . . . . . . . . . . . . . . . . .47-48

Hyde, Deirdre, illus. . . . . . . . . . . . . . . . . . . . . . . . . . . . . . .45

## I

Ingpen, Robert R., illus. . . . . . . . . . . . . . . . . . . . . . . . . . . .35

## J

Jackson, Carolyn . . . . . . . . . . . . . . . . . . . . . . . . . . . . . . . .74
Jacobs, William Jay . . . . . . . . . . . . . . . . . . . . . . . . . . . . . .66
Jaffe, Deborah . . . . . . . . . . . . . . . . . . . . . . . . . . . . . . . . . . .9
Jeunesse, Gallimard . . . . . . . . . . . . . . . . . . . . . . . .53, 54, 55
Johnson, Sylvia A. . . . . . . . . . . . . . . . . . . . . . . . . . . . . . . .58
Judd, Naomi . . . . . . . . . . . . . . . . . . . . . . . . . . . . . . . . . . .20

## K

Kadodwala, Dilip . . . . . . . . . . . . . . . . . . . . . . . . . . . . . . . .66
Keenan, Sheila . . . . . . . . . . . . . . . . . . . . . . . . . . . . . . . . . .44
Kimber, Kevin, illus. . . . . . . . . . . . . . . . . . . . . . . . . . . . .42-43
Kimmel, Eric A. . . . . . . . . . . . . . . . . . . . . . . . . . . . . . . . . .66
Kindersley, Anabel . . . . . . . . . . . . . . . . . . . . . . . .21, 29, 40-41
Kindersley, Barnabas . . . . . . . . . . . . . . . . . . . . . .21, 29, 40-41
Kirtland, Mark . . . . . . . . . . . . . . . . . . . . . . . . . . . . . . . . . .29
Kleven, Elisa, illus. . . . . . . . . . . . . . . . . . . . . . . . . . . . . . . .19
Knight, Judson . . . . . . . . . . . . . . . . . . . . . . . . . . . . . . . . . . .3
Koenig, Viviane . . . . . . . . . . . . . . . . . . . . . . . . . . . . . . . . .44
Kohl, Mary Ann F. . . . . . . . . . . . . . . . . . . . . . . . . . . . . . . .10
Kottke, Jan . . . . . . . . . . . . . . . . . . . . . . . . . . . . . . . . . . . . .56
Krenina, Katya, illus. . . . . . . . . . . . . . . . . . . . . . . . . . . . . .37
Krull, Kathleen . . . . . . . . . . . . . . . . . . . . . . . . . . . . . . . . . .13
Lakin, Patricia . . . . . . . . . . . . . . . . . . . . . . . . . . . . .10, 21, 29
Lalor, Pauline . . . . . . . . . . . . . . . . . . . . . . . . . . . . . . . . . . .75
Lankford, Mary D. . . . . . . . . . . . . . . . . . . . . . . . . . . . . .29-30
Langley, Andrew . . . . . . . . . . . . . . . . . . . . . . . . . . . . . . . .13
Langley, Myrtle . . . . . . . . . . . . . . . . . . . . . . . . . . . . . . .66-67
Langton, Roger, illus. . . . . . . . . . . . . . . . . . . . . . . . . . .42-43
Laroche, Giles, illus. . . . . . . . . . . . . . . . . . . . . . . . . . . . . .68
Lauber, Patricia . . . . . . . . . . . . . . . . . . . . . . . . . . . . . . . . .30
Lawlor, Veronica . . . . . . . . . . . . . . . . . . . . . . . . . . . . . . . .64
Leedy, Loreen . . . . . . . . . . . . . . . . . . . . . . . . . . . . . . . . . .56
Leeming, David Adams, ed. . . . . . . . . . . . . . . . . . . . . . . . .44
Letzig, Michael, illus. . . . . . . . . . . . . . . . . . . . . . . . . . . . . .19
Levinson, David . . . . . . . . . . . . . . . . . . . . . . . . . . . . . . . . .21
Lewin, Ted . . . . . . . . . . . . . . . . . . . . . . . . . . . . . . . . . . . . .13
Lewis, E. B., illus. . . . . . . . . . . . . . . . . . . . . . . . . . . . . . . . .67
Linn, David, illus. . . . . . . . . . . . . . . . . . . . . . . . . . . . . . . . .47
Liu, Hung, illus. . . . . . . . . . . . . . . . . . . . . . . . . . . . . . . . . .10
Livingston, Myra Cohn . . . . . . . . . . . . . . . . . . . . . . . . . . . .30
Livo, Norma J. . . . . . . . . . . . . . . . . . . . . . . . . . . . .44, 45, 74-75
Llewellyn, Claire . . . . . . . . . . . . . . . . . . . . . . . . . . . . . . . .56
Lowry, Judith, illus. . . . . . . . . . . . . . . . . . . . . . . . . . . . . . .10
Lucas, Steve, illus. . . . . . . . . . . . . . . . . . . . . . . . . . . . . . . .32
Lupton, Hugh . . . . . . . . . . . . . . . . . . . . . . . . . . . . . . . . . .45
Lyon, Carol, illus. . . . . . . . . . . . . . . . . . . . . . . . . . . . . . . . .41

## M

Macdonald, Fiona . . . . . . . . . . . . . . . . . . . . . . . . . . . . . . .21
MacDonald, Margaret R. . . . . . . . . . . . . . . . . . . . . . . . . . .45
Mackey, Stephen, illus. . . . . . . . . . . . . . . . . . . . . . . . . . . .50
Madgwick, Wendy . . . . . . . . . . . . . . . . . . . . . . . . . . . . . . . .4
Maestro, Betsy . . . . . . . . . . . . . . . . . . . . . . . . . . . . . .4, 64, 67
Maestro, Giulio . . . . . . . . . . . . . . . . . . . . . . . . . . . . . . .4, 67
Mama, Raouf . . . . . . . . . . . . . . . . . . . . . . . . . . . . . . . . . . .45
Manders, John, illus. . . . . . . . . . . . . . . . . . . . . . . . . . . . . .30
Marchant, Kerena . . . . . . . . . . . . . . . . . . . . . . . . . . . . . . .67

Markel, Michelle . . . . . . . . . . . . . . . . . . . . . . . . . . . . . .30-31
Markham, Lois . . . . . . . . . . . . . . . . . . . . . . . . . . . . . . . . . .31
Marks, Diana F . . . . . . . . . . . . . . . . . . . . . . . . . . . . . . . . . .31
Mason, Antony . . . . . . . . . . . . . . . . . . . . . . . . . . . . . . . . . . .4
Matthews, Caitlin . . . . . . . . . . . . . . . . . . . . . . . . . . . . . . . .46
Matthews, Mary . . . . . . . . . . . . . . . . . . . . . . . . . . . . . . . . .67
Mayer, Marianna . . . . . . . . . . . . . . . . . . . . . . . . . . . . .45-46
McCarthy, Tara . . . . . . . . . . . . . . . . . . . . . . . . . . . . . . . . . .46
McCaughrean, Geraldine . . . . . . . . . . . . . . . . . . . . . . .46, 47
MccGwire, Scarlett . . . . . . . . . . . . . . . . . . . . . . . . . . . .61-62
McChesney, J. Meghan . . . . . . . . . . . . . . . . . . . . . . . . . . .28
McClure, Judy . . . . . . . . . . . . . . . . . . . . . . . . . . . . . . . . . .14
McConnell, Stacy A., ed. . . . . . . . . . . . . . . . . . . . . . . . . . . .3
McCurdy, Michael, illus. . . . . . . . . . . . . . . . . . . . . . . . . . .10
McDonough, Suzanne . . . . . . . . . . . . . . . . . . . . . . . . . . . .2
Mettler, Rene . . . . . . . . . . . . . . . . . . . . . . . . . . . . . . . . . .70
Milone, Karen, illus. . . . . . . . . . . . . . . . . . . . . . . . . . .29-30
Milord, Susan . . . . . . . . . . . . . . . . . . . . . . . . . . . . . . . . .31
Millard, Anne . . . . . . . . . . . . . . . . . . . . . . . . . . . . . . . . . .4
Millet, Denise, illus. . . . . . . . . . . . . . . . . . . . . . . . . . . . . .53
Mills, Judith Christine, illus. . . . . . . . . . . . . . . . . . . . . . . .46
Mistry, Nilesh, illus. . . . . . . . . . . . . . . . . . . . . . . . . . . . . .48
Moehn, Heather . . . . . . . . . . . . . . . . . . . . . . . . . . . . . . . .31
Moffatt, Judith, illus. . . . . . . . . . . . . . . . . . . . . . . . . . . . .37
Mooney, Bill, ed. . . . . . . . . . . . . . . . . . . . . . . . . . . . . . . .43
Mooney, David, illus. . . . . . . . . . . . . . . . . . . . . . . . . . . . .71
Morgan, Sally . . . . . . . . . . . . . . . . . . . . . . . . . . . . . .75, 76
Morris, Ann . . . . . . . . . . . . . . . . . . . . . . . . . . . . . . . . . . .22
Morris, Jackie, illus. . . . . . . . . . . . . . . . . . . . . . . . . . .65-66
Moser, Barry, illus. . . . . . . . . . . . . . . . . . . . . . . . . . . . . . .41
Muller, Helene, illus. . . . . . . . . . . . . . . . . . . . . . . . . .35-36
Munoz, Claudio, illus. . . . . . . . . . . . . . . . . . . . . . . . . . . .50
Muten, Burleigh . . . . . . . . . . . . . . . . . . . . . . . . . . . . . . .47

## N
Nardo, Don . . . . . . . . . . . . . . . . . . . . . . . . . . . . . . . . .5, 14
Nelson, Wayne E. . . . . . . . . . . . . . . . . . . . . . . . . . . . . . . .31
Nomura, Noriko S. . . . . . . . . . . . . . . . . . . . . . . . . . . . . . .67
Norton, Lindy, illus. . . . . . . . . . . . . . . . . . . . . . . . . . . . . .55
Nye, Naomi Shihab . . . . . . . . . . . . . . . . . . . . . . . . . . . . .10

## O
Oakley, Ruth . . . . . . . . . . . . . . . . . . . . . . . . . . . . . . . . . .32
O'Connor, Maureen . . . . . . . . . . . . . . . . . . . . . . . . . . . . .62
Olson, Arielle North . . . . . . . . . . . . . . . . . . . . . . . . . . . . .47
Ormerod, Jan, illus. . . . . . . . . . . . . . . . . . . . . . . . . . . . . .43
Osborne, Mary Pope . . . . . . . . . . . . . . . . . . . . . . . .47-48, 67

## P
Pancake, Joe, illus. . . . . . . . . . . . . . . . . . . . . . . . . . . . . . .22
Paterson, Diane, illus. . . . . . . . . . . . . . . . . . . . . . . . . . . .22
Paterson, Katherine . . . . . . . . . . . . . . . . . . . . . . . . . . . . .80
Pear, Nancy . . . . . . . . . . . . . . . . . . . . . . . . . . . . . . . . . . .14
Peck, Beth, illus. . . . . . . . . . . . . . . . . . . . . . . . . . . . . . . .64
Penney, Sue . . . . . . . . . . . . . . . . . . . . . . . . . . . . . . . .67-68
Pepper, Dennis . . . . . . . . . . . . . . . . . . . . . . . . . . . . . . . .48
Perols, Sylvaine . . . . . . . . . . . . . . . . . . . . . . . . . . . . . . . .70
Perry, Phyllis J. . . . . . . . . . . . . . . . . . . . . . . . . . . . . . . . . .22
Philip, Neil . . . . . . . . . . . . . . . . . . . . . . . . . . . . . . . . .10, 48
Phuoc, Christian Lai Cong . . . . . . . . . . . . . . . . . . . . . .35-36
Pickering, Mel, illus. . . . . . . . . . . . . . . . . . . . . . . . . . .55, 56
Pilling, Ann . . . . . . . . . . . . . . . . . . . . . . . . . . . . . . . . . . .48
Pollard, Michael . . . . . . . . . . . . . . . . . . . . . . . . . . .14, 15, 76

Pope, Joyce . . . . . . . . . . . . . . . . . . . . . . . . . . . . . . . . . . .57
Potter, Jean . . . . . . . . . . . . . . . . . . . . . . . . . . . . . . . . . . .10
Price-Groff, Claire . . . . . . . . . . . . . . . . . . . . . . . . . . . . . .15
Prior, Katherine . . . . . . . . . . . . . . . . . . . . . . . . . . . . . . . .62

## Q
Quinn, Daniel P. . . . . . . . . . . . . . . . . . . . . . . . . . . . . . . . .68

## R
Raschka, Chris, illus. . . . . . . . . . . . . . . . . . . . . . . . . . . . .51
Ravaglia, Paola, illus. . . . . . . . . . . . . . . . . . . . . . . . . . . . .18
Ray, Jane . . . . . . . . . . . . . . . . . . . . . . . . . . . . . . . . . . . . .68
Rebman, Renee C. . . . . . . . . . . . . . . . . . . . . . . . . . . .64-65
Regan, Michael . . . . . . . . . . . . . . . . . . . . . . . . . . . . . . . .25
Rice, Chris . . . . . . . . . . . . . . . . . . . . . . . . . . . . . . . . . . . . .5
Rice, Earle . . . . . . . . . . . . . . . . . . . . . . . . . . . . . . . . . . . . .5
Rice, Melanie . . . . . . . . . . . . . . . . . . . . . . . . . . . . . . . . . .5
Robins, Deri . . . . . . . . . . . . . . . . . . . . . . . . . . . . . . . . . .32
Robinson, Tony . . . . . . . . . . . . . . . . . . . . . . . . . . . . . . . .20
Roche, Denis . . . . . . . . . . . . . . . . . . . . . . . . . . . . . . .10, 36
Rochford, Dierdre . . . . . . . . . . . . . . . . . . . . . . . . . . . . . .76
Rogers, Jacqueline, illus. . . . . . . . . . . . . . . . . . . . . . . . . .49
Rogers, Linda K. . . . . . . . . . . . . . . . . . . . . . . . . . . . . . . . .57
Rohmer, Harriet . . . . . . . . . . . . . . . . . . . . . . . . . . . . . . .10
Rosenberg, Liz, ed. . . . . . . . . . . . . . . . . . . . . . . . . . . . . . .11
Royston, Angela . . . . . . . . . . . . . . . . . . . . . . . . . .15, 55, 76
Rufus, Anneli S. . . . . . . . . . . . . . . . . . . . . . . . . . . . . . . . .32
Ryan, Susannah, illus. . . . . . . . . . . . . . . . . . . . . . . . . . . .64

## S
Sader, Marion, ed. . . . . . . . . . . . . . . . . . . . . . . . . . . . . . .44
Sammis, Fran . . . . . . . . . . . . . . . . . . . . . . . . . . . . . . . . .57
San Souci, Robert D. . . . . . . . . . . . . . . . . . . . . . . . . . .48, 49
Sanderson, Ruth . . . . . . . . . . . . . . . . . . . . . . . . . . . . . . .68
Sasaki, Ellen, illus. . . . . . . . . . . . . . . . . . . . . . . . . . . . . . .18
Schwartz, Howard . . . . . . . . . . . . . . . . . . . . . . . . . . . . . .47
Sechi-Johnson, Patricia . . . . . . . . . . . . . . . . . . . . . . . . . .22
Sevastiades, Philemon D. . . . . . . . . . . . . . . . . . . . . . . . . .68
Sharkey, Niamh, illus. . . . . . . . . . . . . . . . . . . . . . . . . . . .45
Shaw-Smith, Emma, illus. . . . . . . . . . . . . . . . . . . . . . . . .42
Sherman, Josepha . . . . . . . . . . . . . . . . . . . . . . . . . . . . . .49
Shlichta, Joe, illus. . . . . . . . . . . . . . . . . . . . . . . . . . . . . . .39
Shurgin, Ann H., ed. . . . . . . . . . . . . . . . . . . . . . . . . . . . .21
Sierra, Judy . . . . . . . . . . . . . . . . . . . . . . . . . . . . . . . . . . .49
Simon, Norma . . . . . . . . . . . . . . . . . . . . . . . . . . . . . . . . .22
Sis, Peter . . . . . . . . . . . . . . . . . . . . . . . . . . . . . . . . . . . . .22
Sita, Lisa . . . . . . . . . . . . . . . . . . . . . . . . . . . . . . . . . .32, 68
Skurzynski, Gloria . . . . . . . . . . . . . . . . . . . . . . . . . . . . . . .5
Smith, Carter III . . . . . . . . . . . . . . . . . . . . . . . . . . . . . . .74
Smith, Cat Bowman, illus. . . . . . . . . . . . . . . . . . . . . . . . .33
Smith, Miranda . . . . . . . . . . . . . . . . . . . . . . . . . . . . . . . .22
Solheim, James . . . . . . . . . . . . . . . . . . . . . . . . . . . . . . . .32
Sommerville, Donald . . . . . . . . . . . . . . . . . . . . . . . . . . . .15
Spirn, Michele . . . . . . . . . . . . . . . . . . . . . . . . . . . . . .32, 33
Stavros-Lanning, Mary Ann, illus. . . . . . . . . . . . . . . . . . .28
Stearman, Kaye . . . . . . . . . . . . . . . . . . . . . . . . . . . . .62-63
Steele, Philip . . . . . . . . . . . . . . . . . . . . . . . . . . . .23, 57, 63
Stein, R. Conrad . . . . . . . . . . . . . . . . . . . . . . . . . . . . . . .65
Stern-LaRosa, Caryl . . . . . . . . . . . . . . . . . . . . . . . . . . . . .63
Stowell, Charlotte, illus. . . . . . . . . . . . . . . . . . . . . . . . . . .32
Stryer, Andrea Stenn . . . . . . . . . . . . . . . . . . . . . . . . . . . .49
Stuart-Clark, Christopher, ed. . . . . . . . . . . . . . . . . . . . . .41
Sturges, Philemon . . . . . . . . . . . . . . . . . . . . . . . . . . . . . .68

Swain, Gwenyth .................................... 23, 33
Swain, Ruth Freeman ................................. 33

## T
Thompson, Sue Ellen, ed. ............................ 29
Thornton, Peter J., illus. ........................... 27
Tillery, Angelo, illus. ............................. 38
Tseng, Jean, illus. ................................. 38
Tseng, Mou-sien, illus. ............................. 38
Turner, Stephanie ................................... 76
Tutu, Desmond ..................................... 59-60
Tyrol, Adelaide Murphy, illus. ...................... 37

## V
Van Slyke, Rebecca, illus. .......................... 10
Vaughan, Marcia .................................. 33-34
Versola, Anna Rhesa ................................. 17
Vezza, Diane Simone ................................. 34
Vitale, Stefano, illus. ............................. 49

## W
Walker, Paul Robert ................................. 49
Walker, Richard ..................................... 50
Weatherford, Doris .................................. 63
Webb, Lois Sinako ................................... 34
Weber, Judith Eichler ............................... 50
Weiss, Bernard P. ................................... 68
Weiss, Mitch ........................................ 41

Weiss, Nicki ........................................ 23
Whelan, Olwyn, illus. ............................ 46, 50
Whiting, Shelagh ................................. 76-77
Wiesel, Elie ..................................... 59-60
Wiesenthal, Simon ................................ 59-60
Wijngaard, Juan, illus. ............................. 39
Wilcox, Jane ..................................... 34, 35
Wilkinson, Philip ................................ 35, 77
Willey, Bee, illus. .............................. 46, 47
Winne, Joanne ....................................... 57
Winter, Susan, illus. ............................... 27
Wong, Jeanyee, illus. ............................... 58
Wood, Gerald ........................................ 21
Wood, Tim ............................................ 6
Woods, Mary B. .................................... 6, 7
Woods, Michael .................................... 6, 7
Wukovits, John ...................................... 35

## Y
Yolen, Jane ................................. 11, 50, 51
Yorinks, Adrienne, illus. ........................... 58
Yorinks, Arthur ..................................... 58
Young, Ed ........................................... 80

## Z
Zaslavsky, Claudia .................................. 35
Zeitlin, Steve ...................................... 51

# Title Index

## A

*Acid Rain* .......... 75
*Acka Backa Boo! : Playground Games from Around the World* ..... 27
*All About Maps* .......... 52
*All Kinds of Children* .......... 22
*All the Colors of the Earth* .......... 20
*The Alphabet Atlas* .......... 58
*Altapedia* .......... 97
*Amazing Animals* .......... 77
*American Heritage Book of English Usage* .......... 96
*American Heritage Dictionary* .......... 96
*Ancient Agriculture: From Foraging to Farming* .......... 6
*Ancient Civilizations* .......... 1, 4
*Ancient Civilizations Almanac* .......... 3
*Ancient Machines: From Wedges to Waterwheels* .......... 6
*Ancient Medicine: From Sorcery to Surgery* .......... 7
*Ancient Times: A Watts Guide for Children* .......... 1
*Ancient Transportation: From Camels to Canals* .......... 7
*Ancient Wonders* .......... 6
*The Animal Kingdom* .......... 77
*Animals* .......... 74
*Animal Rescue: The Best Job There Is* .......... 73
*Animal Safari: Tree Frogs* .......... 72
*Animals in Hot Places* .......... 71
*Animals in Trees* .......... 71
*The Anti-Defamation League's Hate Hurts: How Children Learn and Unlearn Prejudice* .......... 63
*Around the World: Who's Been Here?* .......... 19
*Art: A World History* .......... 9
*Art Around the World: Loo-Loo, Boo, and More Art You Can Do* ..... 10
*Artcyclopedia* .......... 97
*Ask the Bones: Scary Stories from Around the World* .......... 47
*The Assyrian Empire* .......... 5
*The Atlas of Ancient Worlds* .......... 4
*Atlas of Animals* .......... 70
*Atlas of Countries* .......... 55
*Atlas of Islands* .......... 54-55
*Atlas of People* .......... 53
*Atlas of the Earth* .......... 52
*The Atlas of World Cultures* .......... 18

## B

*The Barefoot Book of Brother and Sister Tales* .......... 42
*The Barefoot Book of Father and Son Tales* .......... 39
*The Barefoot Book of Heroic Children* .......... 42
*The Barefoot Book of Mother and Son Tales* .......... 39-40
*The Barefoot Book of Pirates* .......... 50
*The Barefoot Book of Princesses* .......... 46
*The Barefoot Book of Trickster Tales* .......... 50
*The Barefoot Book of Tropical Tales* .......... 45
*Bartlett's Familiar Quotations* .......... 96
*Be Not Far From Me: The Oldest Love Story, Legends From the Bible* ..66
*Bedtime!* .......... 33
*Being Human: The Human Race* .......... 23
*Biomes of the World* .......... 52
*Birth* .......... 32-33
*Birthdays!: Celebrating Life Around the World* .......... 27
*Blame It On El Niño* .......... 73

*Blue Planet* .......... 77
*The Bronze Cauldron: Myths and Legends of the World* .......... 46
*Buddhism* .......... 67
*The Byzantine Empire* .......... 2

## C

*A Calendar of Festivals* .......... 27
*Can You Count Ten Toes? Count to 10 in 10 Different Languages* .... 36
*Carrying* .......... 33
*Cats of Myth: Tales from Around the World* .......... 42
*Celebrating* .......... 33
*Celebrating the Earth: Stories, Experiences, and Activities* ..... 74-75
*A Celebration of Customs & Rituals of the World* .......... 35
*Celebrations Around the World: A Multicultural Handbook* .......... 25
*The Celestial River: Creation Tales of the Milky Way* .......... 49
*Censorship: Changing Attitudes 1900-2000* .......... 61-62
*Changing Climate* .......... 75
*Charge! Weapons and Warfare in Ancient Times* .......... 3
*Children from Australia to Zimbabwe: A Photographic Journey Around the World* .......... 17
*Children Just Like Me* .......... 21
*Children Just Like Me: Celebrations!* .......... 29
*Children Just Like Me: Our Favorite Stories From Around the World* .......... 40-41
*The Children's Atlas of Civilizations: Trace the Rise and Fall of the World's Great Civilizations* .......... 4
*The Children's Atlas of Natural Wonders* .......... 57
*The Children's Atlas of Scientific Discoveries & Inventions* .......... 72
*The Children's Atlas of the Twentieth Century* .......... 55
*The Children's Atlas of the World* .......... 57
*The Children's Dictionary of Mythology* .......... 44
*Chinese New Year* .......... 69
*Christianity* .......... 67-68
*Chronicle Encyclopedia of History* .......... 7
*Chronicle of the 20th Century* .......... 7
*CIA World Factbook* .......... 88, 97
*Circling the Globe: A Guide to Countries and Cultures of the World* ...19
*Coasts* .......... 70
*The Colors of Freedom: Immigrant Stories* .......... 64
*Columbia Encyclopedia* .......... 96, 97
*Coming of Age* .......... 32
*Coming to America: The Story of Immigration* .......... 64
*Common Ground: The Water, Earth, and Air We Share* .......... 70
*Communities* .......... 76
*The Complete National Geographic: 108 years of National Geographic Magazine on CD-ROM* .......... 7
*Compton's Encyclopedia* .......... 97
*Cornhusk, Silk, and Wishbones: A Book of Dolls From Around the World* .......... 30-31
*The Crayon Box That Talked* .......... 19
*Creation: Read-Aloud Stories from Many Lands* .......... 48
*Creators: Artists, Designers, Craftswomen* .......... 12
*Creativity: Around the World* .......... 10
*Crime and Punishment: Changing Attitudes 1900-2000* .......... 59
*Crocodile! Crocodile! Stories Told Around the World* .......... 37
*The Crystal Pool: Myths and Legends of the World* .......... 46
*Culturgrams: The Nations Around Us* .......... 19
*Current Leaders: Rulers of Nations in the 1990s* .......... 15

## D

The DK Geography of the World . . . . . . . . . . . . . . . . . . . . . . . . . . . .53
DK Student Atlas . . . . . . . . . . . . . . . . . . . . . . . . . . . . . . . . . . . . . . . .53
Dance of the Continents . . . . . . . . . . . . . . . . . . . . . . . . . . . . . . . . . .73
Dazzling! : Jewelry of the Ancient World . . . . . . . . . . . . . . . . . . . . . .2
Dealing with Racism . . . . . . . . . . . . . . . . . . . . . . . . . . . . . . . . . .60-61
Desserts Around the World . . . . . . . . . . . . . . . . . . . . . . . . . . . . . . .26
Dictators . . . . . . . . . . . . . . . . . . . . . . . . . . . . . . . . . . . . . . . . . . . . . .13
Dig That Site: Exploring Archaeology, History, and
    Civilization on the Internet . . . . . . . . . . . . . . . . . . . . . . . . . . .2
Discovering Endangered Wildlife: A Multimedia Expedition
    in Fun and Learning . . . . . . . . . . . . . . . . . . . . . . . . . . . . . . .77
Discovering World Geography with Books Kids Love . . . . . . . . . .53
Dog Myths from Around the World . . . . . . . . . . . . . . . . . . . . .41-42
Dominoes Around the World . . . . . . . . . . . . . . . . . . . . . . . . . . . .29

## E

Earth Tales from Around the World . . . . . . . . . . . . . . . . . . . . . . . .37
Eating . . . . . . . . . . . . . . . . . . . . . . . . . . . . . . . . . . . . . . . . . . . . . . .33
Ellis Island . . . . . . . . . . . . . . . . . . . . . . . . . . . . . . . . . . . . . . . . . . .65
Encarta Online Encyclopedia . . . . . . . . . . . . . . . . . . . . . . . . . .96-97
Encarta World English Dictionary . . . . . . . . . . . . . . . . . . . . . .96-97
Encyclopedia Britannica Online . . . . . . . . . . . . . . . . . . . . . . . . . .97
The Encyclopedia of Animals . . . . . . . . . . . . . . . . . . . . . . . . . . . .97
Encyclopedia of Christmas . . . . . . . . . . . . . . . . . . . . . . . . . . . . . .27
Encyclopedia of Folklore and Literature . . . . . . . . . . . . . . . . . . .37
Encyclopedia of Genocide . . . . . . . . . . . . . . . . . . . . . . . . . . . .59-60
The Encyclopedia of the Environment . . . . . . . . . . . . . . . . . . . . .72
The Encyclopedia of World Sport: From Ancient Times to the Present . . .30
The Encyclopedia of World Sports . . . . . . . . . . . . . . . . . . . . . . . .35
Encyclopedia.com . . . . . . . . . . . . . . . . . . . . . . . . . . . . . . . . . . . . .97
Encyclopedia Smithsonian . . . . . . . . . . . . . . . . . . . . . . . . . . . . . .97
Endangered Animals . . . . . . . . . . . . . . . . . . . . . . . . . . . . . . .70, 77
Energy . . . . . . . . . . . . . . . . . . . . . . . . . . . . . . . . . . . . . . . . . . . . . .72
Energy and Resources . . . . . . . . . . . . . . . . . . . . . . . . . . . . . . . . .71
Equal Rights . . . . . . . . . . . . . . . . . . . . . . . . . . . . . . . . . . . . . . . . .62
Ethics and values . . . . . . . . . . . . . . . . . . . . . . . . . . . . . . . . . . . . .60
Ethnic Cooking the Microwave Way . . . . . . . . . . . . . . . . . . . . . .26
Ethnic Groups Worldwide: A Ready Reference Handbook . . . . . . . .21
Even More Short and Shivery: Thirty Spine-tingling Stories . . . . . . .49
Everybody Bakes Bread . . . . . . . . . . . . . . . . . . . . . . . . . . . . . . . .27
Everybody Cooks Rice . . . . . . . . . . . . . . . . . . . . . . . . . . . . . . . . .27
Everybody Serves Soup . . . . . . . . . . . . . . . . . . . . . . . . . . . . . . . .27
EXEGY: Current Country Profiles . . . . . . . . . . . . . . . . . . . . . . . .23
Explore the World: Social Studies Projects and Activities . . . . . . . .18
The Explorers: A Century of Discovery . . . . . . . . . . . . . . . . . . . . .7
Explorers & Discoverers: From Alexander the Great to Sally Ride . . .14
Exploring the World . . . . . . . . . . . . . . . . . . . . . . . . . . . . . . . . . . .21
Eyewitness Children's Encyclopedia . . . . . . . . . . . . . . . . . . . . . . .8
Eyewitness Encyclopedia of Nature . . . . . . . . . . . . . . . . . . . . . . .78
Eyewitness History of the World . . . . . . . . . . . . . . . . . . . . . . . . . .8
Eyewitness Living Earth . . . . . . . . . . . . . . . . . . . . . . . . . . . . . . . .22

## F

The Fairies' Ring: A Book of Fairy Stories and Poems . . . . . . . .50
Fairy Tales from Around the World: Beauty and the Beast and
    Other Animated Fables . . . . . . . . . . . . . . . . . . . . . . . . . . . .50
Fairy Tale Encyclopedia . . . . . . . . . . . . . . . . . . . . . . . . . . . . . . . .97
Fairy Tales from Around the World: Cinderella and Other
    Animated Fables . . . . . . . . . . . . . . . . . . . . . . . . . . . . . . . . .51
Fairy Tales from Around the World: Sleeping Beauty and
    Other Animated Fables . . . . . . . . . . . . . . . . . . . . . . . . . . . .52
Families . . . . . . . . . . . . . . . . . . . . . . . . . . . . . . . . . . . . . . . . . . . . .22

Family: Around the World . . . . . . . . . . . . . . . . . . . . . . . . . . . . . .21
A Family Treasury of Myths from Around the World . . . . . . . . . . .44
Farming . . . . . . . . . . . . . . . . . . . . . . . . . . . . . . . . . . . . . . . . . . . . .72
Festivals . . . . . . . . . . . . . . . . . . . . . . . . . . . . . . . . . . . . . . . . .26, 30
Fired Up! : Making Pottery in Ancient Times . . . . . . . . . . . . . . . . .3
A First Atlas . . . . . . . . . . . . . . . . . . . . . . . . . . . . . . . . . . . . . . . . .55
A First Book of Myths: Myths and Legends for the Very Young
    from Around the World . . . . . . . . . . . . . . . . . . . . . . . . .42-43
Flags of the World . . . . . . . . . . . . . . . . . . . . . . . . . . . . . . . . . . . .36
Founding Leaders: Shapers of Modern Nations . . . . . . . . . . . . .16
The Four Corners of the Sky: Creation Stories and Cosmologies
    from Around the World . . . . . . . . . . . . . . . . . . . . . . . . . . . .51
Freedom of Belief . . . . . . . . . . . . . . . . . . . . . . . . . . . . . . . . . . . . .61
Freedom of Movement . . . . . . . . . . . . . . . . . . . . . . . . . . . . . . . . .59
Freedom of Speech . . . . . . . . . . . . . . . . . . . . . . . . . . . . . . . . . . . .63
Funk & Wagnalls Multimedia Encyclopedia . . . . . . . . . . . . . .97, 98

## G

Games . . . . . . . . . . . . . . . . . . . . . . . . . . . . . . . . . . . . . . . . . . . . . .26
Games with Rope and String . . . . . . . . . . . . . . . . . . . . . . . . . . . .32
Gardner's Art Through the Ages . . . . . . . . . . . . . . . . . . . . . . . . . .80
Geographic Literacy Through Children's Literature . . . . . . . . . . .57
GeoHistory Maps: Europe to Eurasia . . . . . . . . . . . . . . . . . . . . .58
Global Art: Activities, Projects, and Inventions from
    Around the World . . . . . . . . . . . . . . . . . . . . . . . . . . . . . . . .10
Gods, Goddesses, and Monsters: An Encyclopedia of
    World Mythology . . . . . . . . . . . . . . . . . . . . . . . . . . . . . . . . .44
Going to Grandma's Around the World . . . . . . . . . . . . . . . . .23, 36
The Golden Hoard: Myths and Legends of the World . . . . . . . . . .47
Good as Gold: Stories of Values from Around the World . . . . . . . .37
Grandmothers' Stories: Wise Woman Tales from Many Cultures . . . . .47
Gray Heroes: Elder Tales from Around the World . . . . . . . . . . . .50
Great Conquerors . . . . . . . . . . . . . . . . . . . . . . . . . . . . . . . . . . . . .15
A Green World? . . . . . . . . . . . . . . . . . . . . . . . . . . . . . . . . . . . . . .70
Grolier Student Library of Explorers and Exploration . . . . . . . . . .3
Growing Up: Around the World . . . . . . . . . . . . . . . . . . . . . . . . . .21
Growing Up: From Child to Adult . . . . . . . . . . . . . . . . . . . . .65-66

## H

Hands Around the World: 365 Creative Ways to Build Cultural
    Awareness & Global Respect . . . . . . . . . . . . . . . . . . . . . . .31
Harvest . . . . . . . . . . . . . . . . . . . . . . . . . . . . . . . . . . . . . . . . . . . . .31
Healers and Researchers: Physicians, Biologists, Social Scientists . . .14
Hear These Voices: Youth at the Edge of the Millennium . . . . . .58-59
Hinduism . . . . . . . . . . . . . . . . . . . . . . . . . . . . . . . . . . . . . . . . . . .68
Holi . . . . . . . . . . . . . . . . . . . . . . . . . . . . . . . . . . . . . . . . . . . . . . . .66
Holidays and Anniversaries of the World: A Comprehensive
    Catalogue Containing Detailed Information on Every
    Month and Day of the Year . . . . . . . . . . . . . . . . . . . . . . . . .25
Holidays, Festivals, and Celebrations of the World Dictionary . . . . .29
Holidays of the World Cookbook for Students . . . . . . . . . . . . . . . .34
Homes and Cities . . . . . . . . . . . . . . . . . . . . . . . . . . . . . . . . . . . . .75
Honoring Our Ancestors: Stories and Pictures by Fourteen Artists . . .10
Hopscotch Around the World . . . . . . . . . . . . . . . . . . . . . . . . .29-30
How & Why Stories: World Tales Kids Can Read and Tell . . . . .41
How Children Lived: A First Book of History . . . . . . . . . . . . . . . . .5
How Many Days to America?: A Thanksgiving Story . . . . . . . . .64
How the Future Began: Everyday Life . . . . . . . . . . . . . . . . . . . . .73
How to Cook Gooseberry Fool: Unusual Recipes from
    Around the World . . . . . . . . . . . . . . . . . . . . . . . . . . . . . .33-34

## I

I Am Buddhist . . . . . . . . . . . . . . . . . . . . . . . . . . . . . . . . . . . . . . .68

*I Am Eastern Orthodox* .................................68
*I Am Hindu* ........................................65
*I Am Jewish* .......................................69
*I Am Muslim* .......................................65
*I Am Protestant* ....................................68
*I Am Roman Catholic* ................................68
*I Am Shinto* .......................................67
*I Was Dreaming to Come to America: Memories from the
    Ellis Island Oral History Project* .....................64
*Id-ul-Fitr* .........................................67
*The Illustrated Book of Fairy Tales* ....................48
*In Full Bloom: Tales of Women in Their Prime* .........38
*Infoplease* .........................................97
*International Playtime: Classroom Games
    and Dances from Around the World* ...............31
*Islam* .............................................68
*It Could Still Be Endangered* ......................72-73
*It's a Woman's World: a Century of Women's Voices in Poetry* .......10
*It's Disgusting-And We Ate It! : True Food Facts from Around the
    World — And Throughout History!* ................32

## J

*Jacks Around the World* ............................30
*Join In: Multiethnic Short Stories by Outstanding Writers
    for Young Adults* ...............................64
*Judaism* ...........................................68
*Junior Worldmark Encyclopedia of Cities* ...............20
*Junior Worldmark Encyclopedia of World Cultures* .....20-21
*Junior Worldmark Encyclopedia of World Holidays* ......21

## K

*Keeping the Traditions: A Multicultural Resource* ........22
*Kids' Almanac* .................................97, 98
*Kids Around-the-World Cookbook* .....................32
*Kids Culture: The Great Explorers* .....................8
*The Kingfisher Facts and Records Book* .................3
*The Kingfisher Young People's Atlas of the World* .......57

## L

*Learning About Cultures: Literature, Celebrations, Games
    and Art Activities* ..............................27
*Let the Games Begin!* ..............................25
*Let There Be Light: Bible Stories* ....................68
*Letsfindout* ........................................97
*Let's Celebrate Today: Calendars, Events, and Holidays* ...31
*Let's Visit Some Islands* .............................53
*Library of Congress Country Studies* ..................97
*Life During the Crusades* .............................5
*Life on Ellis Island* ..............................64-65
*Light-Gathering Poems* ..............................11
*The Literary Crowd: Writers, Critics, Scholars, Wits* .....12
*Little Folk: Stories From Around the World* ............49
*Lives of Extraordinary Women: Rulers, Rebels (and What
    the Neighbors Thought)* .........................13
*Living in a Desert* .........................53-54, 56
*Living in a Rain Forest* .............................54
*Living in the Mountains* ............................54
*Living Near a River* ................................54
*Living Near the Sea* ................................54
*Living on an Island* ................................57
*Living on Farms* ...................................54
*Living on the Plains* ................................54
*Love Can Build a Bridge* ............................20

## M

*Madlenka* .........................................22
*Magid Fasts for Ramadan* ...........................67
*Make a Book: Six Different Books to Make, Write, and Illustrate* .....9
*Mapping Epidemics: A Historical Atlas of Disease* .......74
*Mapping Penny's World* .............................56
*Mapping the World* .................................55
*Maps and Mapmaking* ...............................57
*Math Games & Activities from Around the World* .......35
*Meeting Dolphins: My Adventures in the Sea* ...........72
*Melting Pots: Family Stories and Recipes* ..............50
*Mermaid Tales from Around the World* ..............47-48
*Moon Cakes to Maize: Delicious World Folktales* .......44
*More Ready-to-Tell Tales from Around the World* .......43
*Mother Goose Around the World* ..................43-44
*Multicultural Books To Make and Share: Easy-to-make,
    Authentic, Cross-curricular* ........................9
*Multicultural Cookbook of Life-Cycle Celebrations* .......34
*Multicultural Folktales For the Feltboard and Readers' Theater* .....49
*Multicultural Folktales: Readers Theatre for
    Elementary Students* .........................36-37
*Multicultural Myths and Legends: Stories
    and Activities to Promote Cultural Awareness* ......46
*Musings: Tales of Truth & Wisdom* ...................40
*My First Amazing World Explorer* ....................24
*Myths and Legends* .................................48

## N

*National Geographic Beginner's World Atlas* ............56
*The New Book of El Niño* ...........................70
*New Year* .........................................33
*New Year's to Kwanzaa: Original Stories of Celebration* ....28-29
*The New York Times on the Web* .....................94
*Noodlehead Stories: World Tales Kids Can Read and Tell* ....41
*Not One Damsel in Distress: World Folktales for Strong Girls* ....51
*Nursery Tales Around the World* .....................49

## O

*On Time: From Seasons to Split Seconds* ................5
*Once upon a Forest* ................................78
*100 Greatest Archaeological Discoveries* .................2
*100 Greatest Disasters* ..............................76
*100 Greatest Explorers* ..............................14
*100 Greatest Inventions* .............................77
*100 Greatest Manmade Wonders* ......................22
*100 Greatest Medical Discoveries* .....................76
*100 Greatest Men* ..................................15
*100 Greatest Natural Wonders* .......................71
*100 Greatest Sports Champions* ......................15
*100 Greatest Tyrants* ...............................13
*100 Greatest Women* ...............................15
*The 100 Most Influential Women of All Time* ...........12
*1000 Makers of the Millennium* ......................11
*1,000 Years Ago on Planet Earth* ......................2
*One World, Many Religions: The Ways We Worship* .....67
*One World: Multicultural Projects & Activities* ..........18
*Our Big Home: An Earth Poem* ......................19
*Our Planet Earth* ...................................56
*Our World: A Child's First Picture Atlas* ...............56
*The Oxford Book of Animal Stories* ...................48
*Oxford Shakespeare* ................................96
*The Oxford Treasury of World Stories* .................41
*The Ozone Hole* ....................................75

## P

*Papercraft* .................................................27
*Passport on a Plate: A Round-the-World Cookbook for Children* ....34
*A Picnic in October* ........................................64
*Picture Reference Atlas* ....................................56
*Piece by Piece! : Mosaics of the Ancient World* ..............1
*Play: Around the World* .....................................29
*Poverty: Changing Attitudes 1900-2000* ......................60
*A Pride of Princesses: Princess Tales From Around the World* ......38

## R

*Racism* .....................................................61
*Racism: Changing Attitudes 1900-2000* .......................60
*Ramadan* ....................................................69
*Random House Webster's College Dictionary* ...............97, 98
*Reader's Digest Book of Amazing Facts: A Children's Guide to the World* ........................................4
*Ready-to-Tell Tales: Sure-fire Stories from America's Favorite Storytellers* .................................43
*Reformers: Activists, Educators, Religious Leaders* .........12
*Religion* ...............................................66-67
*Religions Explained: A Beginner's Guide to World Faiths* ....66
*ResourceLink: 17th-Century World History* ...................8
*ResourceLink: 18th-Century World History* .................8-9
*ResourceLink: 19th-Century World History* ...................9
*ResourceLink: 20th-Century World History* ...................9
*A Ride on Mother's Back: A Day of Baby Carrying Around the World* ...18
*Rights for Animals?* ........................................76
*Rights in the Home* .........................................61
*Rivers* .....................................................76
*Roget's II: The New Thesaurus* ..............................96
*Roget's Thesaurus* ..........................................96
*Roget's 21st Century Thesaurus* .............................97

## S

*Sacred Places* ..............................................69
*Save the Rain Forests* ......................................73
*Saving the Rain Forests* ....................................76
*Say It Again* ...............................................71
*Scrawl! : Writing in Ancient Times* ..........................5
*Scripts of the World* ....................................35-36
*The Search for a Northern Route* ............................53
*A Serenade of Mermaids: Mermaid Tales From Around the World* ....38
*Sesame Street Celebrates Around the World* ..................24
*Shake-It-Up Tales! : Stories to Sing, Dance, Drum, and Act Out* .....45
*Sidewalk Games Around the World* ............................28
*Sikhism* ....................................................68
*The Silver Treasure: Myths and Legends of the World* ........47
*Simpson's Contemporary Quotations* ..........................96
*Slavery Today* ..............................................62
*Sleep Rhymes Around the World* ..............................11
*Smiling* ....................................................23
*Sold! : The Origins of Money and Trade* ......................6
*The Story of Clocks and Calendars: Marking a Millennium* .....4
*The Story of Religion* ......................................67
*Storytelling Encyclopedia: Historical, Cultural, and Multiethnic Approaches to Oral Traditions Around the World* .....44
*Street Rhymes Around the World* .............................11
*Street Smart! : Cities of the Ancient World* .................6
*Sun-Day, Moon-Day: How the Week Was Made* ....................3

## T

*The Tale Spinner: Folktales, Themes, and Activities* ........40
*Tales of Wisdoms and Wonder* ................................45
*Tales of Wonder and Magic* ..................................39
*Talking About Racism* .......................................61
*Tapestries: Stories of Women in the Bible* ..................68
*A Terrifying Taste of Short & Shivery: Thirty Creepy Tales* ......48
*Thirty-Three Multicultural Tales to Tell* ...................39
*This Same Sky: A Collection of Poems from Around the World* ......10
*3D Talking Globe: The "See and Hear" Atlas Gazetteer* .......58
*Time* .......................................................74
*Time Magazine* ..............................................95
*Told Tales: Nine Folktales from Around the World* ...........49
*Tooth Tales from Around the World* ..........................37
*Touch and Go: Travels of a Children's Book Illustrator* .....13
*Transportation* .............................................71
*Travel the World with Timmy Deluxe* .........................24
*A Treasury of Mermaids: Mermaid Tales From Around the World* ....38
*Troubadour's Storybag: Musical Folktales of the World* ......45
*Twentieth (20th) Century Video Almanac* ......................9
*A Twist in the Tail: Animal Stories from Around the World* ..43

## U

*Under Our Skin: Kids Talk About Race* .......................59
*USA Today* ..................................................95

## V

*Vegetarian Cooking Around the World* ........................34
*Voices: Poetry and Art from Around the World* ...............11

## W

*Wake Up, World! : A Day in the Life of Children Around the World* ...20
*War and the Pity of War* ....................................10
*Washington Post* ............................................97
*Weather* ....................................................74
*What Do We Know About Buddhism?* ............................66
*What Do We Know About Hinduism?* ............................66
*What You Never Knew About Fingers, Forks, & Chopsticks* .....30
*Where in the World is Carmen Sandiego?* .....................24
*Where on Earth is Carmen Sandiego?* .........................25
*While the Bear Sleeps: Winter Tales and Traditions* .........46
*Why Do We Celebrate That?* ...............................34-35
*Why Do We Do That?* .........................................29
*Why Do We Use That?* ........................................35
*Why Do We Wear That?* .......................................26
*Wide World of Animals* ......................................78
*Wisdom Tales from Around the World* .........................40
*Women Leaders of Nations* ...................................14
*Women Leaders: Rulers Throughout History* ...................16
*Women Warriors: Myths and Legends of Heroic Women* .......45-46
*Women's Almanac 2000* .......................................63
*Women's Rights: Changing Attitudes 1900-2000* ............62-63
*Wonder Tales from Around the World* .........................40
*Workers' Rights* ............................................62
*The World Around Us: Geography Projects and Activities* .....52
*World Food* .................................................75
*World Geography Online* .....................................23
*The World Holiday Book: Celebrations for Every Day of the Year* ....32
*World Holiday, Festival, and Calendar Books* ................27
*World Holidays: A Watts Guide for Children* .................31
*World Military Leaders* .....................................16
*A World of Communities* .....................................55
*A World of Holidays!* .......................................26
*World Political Leaders* ....................................17
*World Population* ...........................................73

*World Religions: Great Lives* . . . . . . . . . . . . . . . . . . . . . . . . . . . . .66
*World Religions: The Great Faiths Explored & Explained* . . . . . . . . .65
*World Social Leaders* . . . . . . . . . . . . . . . . . . . . . . . . . . . . . . . . .17
*World Statistics Pocketbook and Statistical Yearbook* . . . . . . . . . . . .87
*The World Turns Round and Round* . . . . . . . . . . . . . . . . . . . . . . . .23
*Worlds of Belief: Religion and Spirituality* . . . . . . . . . . . . . . . . . . . .69
*Worldmark Encyclopedia of the Nations* . . . . . . . . . . . . . . . . . . . . .18
*Worldmark Yearbook 2000* . . . . . . . . . . . . . . . . . . . . . . . . . . . . . .18

# Y

*Year 2000 Grolier Multimedia Encyclopedia School Edition* . . . . . . .25
*The Young Oxford Book of Folk Tales* . . . . . . . . . . . . . . . . . . . . . . .38

# Subject Index

## A

Aardema, Verna .44
Abigail (Biblical character) .68
Aborigines
    mythology .80
Abortion .9
Abraham (Biblical character) .1, 66
Abraham's God .69
Abuse of the elderly .61
Achebe, Chinua .17
Acid rain .23, 72, 75, 76
Acquired immune deficiency syndrome (AIDS) .74, 76
Adams, Abigail .8
Adams, John .8
Adana massacre of Armenians .59-60
    See also Human Rights.
Adults' Day .31
Afghanistan
    rhymes .11
    Taliban .62-63
Africa
    apartheid .9, 60, 61-62
    art .9, 79
    Botswana .13
    Cameroon .21, 33
    civilization .4
    Colonial Africa .89
    cookery .32, 34, 85
    culture .79, 85
    Eastern Africa .19
    Ethiopia .22, 29, 37, 47, 61-62
    female genital mutilation .62-63
    folktales .38, 39, 41, 45, 46, 47-48, 49, 81
        See also Folktales under country names.
    games .35
    geography .86
    Ghana .20, 26, 41, 46, 47
    Great Zimbabwe .11
    Guinea, Equatorial .33-34
    holidays .85
    Ibn Battuta (Ibn Batuta) .12, 14
    Johannesburg, South Africa .20, 55
    Kalahari Desert .13
    Kenya .23, 24, 29, 34, 37, 43, 47
    language .89, 101
    Mali .5, 8
    Mansa Musa, King of Africa .12
    Morocco .21, 41, 50
    music .81
    mythology .44, 46, 51, 80
    Nairobi .20
    Namib Desert .71
    Namibia .26
    Nigeria .11, 28-29, 30, 43, 49
    North Africa .90, 91
    Northern Africa .19
    Nzingha, Queen of Africa .13, 16
    Rwanda .59, 104
    Songhai (Songhay) .12
    South Africa .6, 20, 55, 62
    Southern Africa .18, 92
    spirit religions .66
    Sub-Saharan Africa .90, 91
    Sudan .23, 42
    Suleyman the Merchant (Suleiman I) .12, 14, 82
    Sundiata, African warrior .42
    Tanzania .20
    Togo .10
    Uganda .11
    Victoria Falls .71
    Western Africa .19
    women .63
    Zambia .29
    Zimbabwe .17, 30
African American
    art .79
    authors .18
    culture .93
    games .28
Agenda 21 of the Earth Summit .71, 73, 75
Agriculture .75
    See also Farming; Food.
AIDS (Acquired immune deficiency syndrome) .74, 76
Akayesu, Jean-Paul .59
Akbar, Mogul emperor of India .8
Akihito, Emperor (Japan) .16
Akkadians .4
Al-Hegira .67
Albright, Madeleine .9
Alexander the Great .15
Alexandria, Egypt .6, 90
Allah .65
Almanacs .88, 95, 97, 98
Alternate fuels .90-91
    See also Fuel.
Amazon .57
    mythology .81-82
    rainforest .71
American Association of School Librarians (AASL)
    Information Literacy Standards .vii
Americas .19, 90
    art .79
    Aztec .5, 6, 80, 81-82
    civilization .4
    culture .79
    Maya .4, 6, 80, 81-82
    music .81
    Olmec .6
    religion .69
Amin, Idi .13, 16
Amnesty International .104
Amritsar massacre (India) .60
Amundsen, Roald .14
An-yang, China .6
Anansi tales .41, 43
Ancient art .79, 80
Ancient China .4, 5, 6, 7, 8, 86, 89
Ancient Civilizations .1-9, 84, 86, 92, 93
    Africa .89
    agriculture .6
    Akkadians .4
    Americas .2, 6, 8

An-yang (China) .6
Angkor Wat (Cambodia) .22
archaeology .84
art .79, 80, 84
Asia .2, 84
Assyrians .5
Aztec .5, 6, 80, 81-82
Babylonians .5
Byzantine Empire .2
Byzantium .92
Changan (China) .6
China .4, 5, 6, 7, 8, 86, 89
    culture .93
    currency .6
Egypt .4, 5, 6, 7, 86, 89, 92
Europe .2, 86
Great Zimbabwe (Africa) .6
Greece .1, 5, 6, 7, 86
Harappa (Indus Valley) .6
history .84, 87
Incas .8, 51, 80
India .7, 86
Indus Valley .4, 6
Islam .86
jewelry .2
language and literature .84
machinery .6-7
Mali, Africa .5, 8
Maya .4, 6, 80, 81-82
medicine .7
Mediterranean .6, 91
Mesoamerica .7
Mesopotamia .5
Middle East .1, 2, 6, 7
Mohenjo-Daro (Indus Valley) .6
mosaics .1
mythology .84
Near East .79, 86, 91
Olmec .6
People of the Totem .8
pottery .3
religion .84
Roman Empire .1, 4, 5, 6, 7
science .84
Seven Wonders of the World .6, 18, 22, 90, 92
Songhai, Africa .12
Sumerians .4, 6, 46, 47, 48, 81-82
Tell al-Amarna (Egypt) .6
Tigris and Euphrates River valleys .5
transportation .7
warfare .5
weapons .5
writing .5
Zhengzhou, China .6
Ancient Egypt .4, 5, 6, 7, 86, 89, 92
Ancient Greece .1, 5, 6, 7, 86
Andromeda (mythological character) .42
Angelou, Maya .12
Angkor Wat (Cambodia) .22
Animal
    abuse .76
    deserts .71
    endangered species .70, 73
    experimentation .76

    habitats .70, 71
    protection .76
    rescue .73
    rights .76
    stories .41, 42, 43, 48
    world .70, 74, 77, 78
Anna (Biblical character) .68
Annan, Kofi .59
Antarctica .2, 92
    culture .85
    cuisine .85
    food .33
Anthems .83, 85, 97, 99, 103
Anti-Semitism .60
Apartheid .9, 60, 61-62
Aquino, Corazon .15, 16
Arabia
    desert .53-54
    exploration .3
    games .28
    language .23, 36, 89
Arable farming
    *See* Farming.
Arafat, Yasir (Yasser) .16, 59
Argentina (South America) .24, 49, 51
Armed forces .84
Armenia
    human rights .59-60
    rhymes .11
Armstrong, Neil .14
Arranged marriages
    *See* Marriages.
Art .9-11, 79-82
    Africa .9
    African American .79
    ancient .79, 80
    Ancient Near East .79, 80
    Asian .9, 79
    Brazil .10
    Buddhism .66, 105
    censorship .63
    Central America .9
    China .10
    Egypt .10, 79, 80
    Europe .9
    France .10
    Greco, El .8
    Greece .1
    Hindu .106
    history .9, 80
    India .10, 79
    Iran .10
    Israel .10
    Italy .10
    Java .10
    Mexican American .10, 79
    Middle East .79, 80
    Near East .79
    North America .9
    Norway .10
    Pacific .79
    Peru .10
    Rome .1
    Thailand .9

Togo . . . . . . . . . . . . . . . . . . . . . . . . . . . . . . . . . . . .10
Aruba (Caribbean)
    games . . . . . . . . . . . . . . . . . . . . . . . . . . . . . . . . . .30
Artists
    Bourke-White, Margaret . . . . . . . . . . . . . . . . . . . . . . .12
    Cezanne, Paul . . . . . . . . . . . . . . . . . . . . . . . . . . . . . . .9
    Greco, El . . . . . . . . . . . . . . . . . . . . . . . . . . . . . . . . . . .8
    Kahlo, Frida . . . . . . . . . . . . . . . . . . . . . . . . . . . . . . . .11
    Lange, Dorothea . . . . . . . . . . . . . . . . . . . . . . . . . . . .12
    Rembrandt van Rijn . . . . . . . . . . . . . . . . . . . . . . . . . . .8
    Ringgold, Faith . . . . . . . . . . . . . . . . . . . . . . . . . . . . .12
    Rossi, Prosperzia de' . . . . . . . . . . . . . . . . . . . . . . . . .12
    Tao-sheng, Kuan . . . . . . . . . . . . . . . . . . . . . . . . . . . .12
Asia
    ancient . . . . . . . . . . . . . . . . . . . . . . . . . . . . . . . . .2, 84
    art . . . . . . . . . . . . . . . . . . . . . . . . . . . . . . . . . . . .9, 79
    Central Asia . . . . . . . . . . . . . . . . . . . . . . . . . . . . .81, 90
    civilization . . . . . . . . . . . . . . . . . . . . . . . . . . . . . . . . .4
    cuisine . . . . . . . . . . . . . . . . . . . . . . . . . . . . . . . . . . .85
    culture . . . . . . . . . . . . . . . . . . . . . . . . . . . . . . . .79, 85
    East Asia . . . . . . . . . . . . . . . . . . . . . . . . . . . . . . . . . .4
    Eastern Asia . . . . . . . . . . . . . . . . . . . . . . . . . . . . . . .19
    Far East . . . . . . . . . . . . . . . . . . . . . . . . . . . . . . . . . .85
    folktales . . . . . . . . . . . . . . . . . . . . . . . . . . . . . . .37, 81
    games . . . . . . . . . . . . . . . . . . . . . . . . . . . . . . . . . . .31
    geography . . . . . . . . . . . . . . . . . . . . . . . . . . . . . . . .86
    music . . . . . . . . . . . . . . . . . . . . . . . . . . . . . . . . . . .81
    Near East . . . . . . . . . . . . . . . . . . . . . . . . . . . . . .79, 91
    religion . . . . . . . . . . . . . . . . . . . . . . . . . . . . . . .69, 107
    South Asia . . . . . . . . . . . . . . . . . . . . . . . . . . . . . . .4, 91
    Southeast Asia . . . . . . . . . . . . . . . . . . . . . . . . . . . . .89
    Southern Asia . . . . . . . . . . . . . . . . . . . . . . . . . . . .19, 91
    West Asia . . . . . . . . . . . . . . . . . . . . . . . . . . . . . .4, 91-92
    Western Asia . . . . . . . . . . . . . . . . . . . . . . . . . . . . . .19
Asian American
    authors . . . . . . . . . . . . . . . . . . . . . . . . . . . . . . . . . .18
    culture . . . . . . . . . . . . . . . . . . . . . . . . . . . . . . . . . . .93
Assyrians . . . . . . . . . . . . . . . . . . . . . . . . . . . . . . . . . . . . . .5
Atalanta the Huntress (Greece) . . . . . . . . . . . . . . . . . . .16, 51
Atlases . . . . . . . . . . . . . . . . . . . . . . . . . . . .52-58, 72, 101-103
Attila the Hun . . . . . . . . . . . . . . . . . . . . . . . . . . . . . . . . .15
Augustus the Great . . . . . . . . . . . . . . . . . . . . . . . . . . . . .15
Aung San . . . . . . . . . . . . . . . . . . . . . . . . . . . . . . . . . . . .16
Aung San Suu Kyi . . . . . . . . . . . . . . . . . . . . . . . . . . .13, 62
Australia . . . . . . . . . . . . . . . . . . . . . . . . . . . . . .17, 19, 92-93
    Ayers Rock . . . . . . . . . . . . . . . . . . . . . . . . . . . . . . . .71
    children . . . . . . . . . . . . . . . . . . . . . . . . . . . . . . . .20, 23
    cookery . . . . . . . . . . . . . . . . . . . . . . . . . . . . . .32, 34, 85
    culture . . . . . . . . . . . . . . . . . . . . . . . . . . . . . . . .85, 93
    desert . . . . . . . . . . . . . . . . . . . . . . . . . . . . . . . . . . . . .5
    Falklands War . . . . . . . . . . . . . . . . . . . . . . . . . . . .61-62
    folktales . . . . . . . . . . . . . . . . . . . . . . . . . . . . .39, 40, 43
    games . . . . . . . . . . . . . . . . . . . . . . . . . . . . . . . . . . .35
    Great Barrier Reef . . . . . . . . . . . . . . . . . . . . . . . . .57, 71
    holidays . . . . . . . . . . . . . . . . . . . . . . . . . . . . . . . . . .85
    mythology . . . . . . . . . . . . . . . . . . . . . . . . . . . . . .44, 48
    religion . . . . . . . . . . . . . . . . . . . . . . . . . . . . . . . . . . .66
    Sydney . . . . . . . . . . . . . . . . . . . . . . . . . . . . . . . . . . .22
Authors
    Achebe, Chinua . . . . . . . . . . . . . . . . . . . . . . . . . . . . .17
    African American . . . . . . . . . . . . . . . . . . . . . . . . . . .18
    Angelou, Maya . . . . . . . . . . . . . . . . . . . . . . . . . . . . .12
    Asian American . . . . . . . . . . . . . . . . . . . . . . . . . . . .18
    Basho, Matsuo . . . . . . . . . . . . . . . . . . . . . . . . . . . .8, 12

    Blake, William . . . . . . . . . . . . . . . . . . . . . . . . . . . . . . .8
    Chiyo, Uno . . . . . . . . . . . . . . . . . . . . . . . . . . . . . . . .12
    Desai, Anita . . . . . . . . . . . . . . . . . . . . . . . . . . . . . . .12
    Dickens, Charles . . . . . . . . . . . . . . . . . . . . . . . . . . . . .9
    Dickinson, Emily . . . . . . . . . . . . . . . . . . . . . . . . . . . .12
    Ding Ling . . . . . . . . . . . . . . . . . . . . . . . . . . . . . . . . .12
    Dostoevsky, Fyodor . . . . . . . . . . . . . . . . . . . . . . . . . .12
    Frank, Anne . . . . . . . . . . . . . . . . . . . . . . . . . . . . .12, 42
    Hispanic American . . . . . . . . . . . . . . . . . . . . . . . . . .18
    Khayyam, Omar . . . . . . . . . . . . . . . . . . . . . . . . . . . .12
    Kiyotsugu, playwright . . . . . . . . . . . . . . . . . . . . . . . .12
    Moliere (Jean Baptiste Poquelin) . . . . . . . . . . . . . . . . . .8
    Native American . . . . . . . . . . . . . . . . . . . . . . . . . . . .18
    Potter, Beatrix . . . . . . . . . . . . . . . . . . . . . . . . . . . . . .12
    Ringgold, Faith . . . . . . . . . . . . . . . . . . . . . . . . . . . . .12
    Shakespeare, William . . . . . . . . . . . . . . . . . . . . . . . . .8
    Shikibu, Murasaki . . . . . . . . . . . . . . . . . . . . . . . . .13, 15
    Solzhenitsyn, Alexander . . . . . . . . . . . . . . . . . . . .61-62
    Tolstoy, Leo . . . . . . . . . . . . . . . . . . . . . . . . . . . . . . . .12
    Wilder, Laura Ingalls . . . . . . . . . . . . . . . . . . . . . . . . .12
Ayers Rock (Australia) . . . . . . . . . . . . . . . . . . . . . . . . . . .71
Aztecs . . . . . . . . . . . . . . . . . . . . . . . . . . . . . . . .5, 6, 80, 81-82
    calendar . . . . . . . . . . . . . . . . . . . . . . . . . . . . . . . . . . .5
    mythology . . . . . . . . . . . . . . . . . . . . . . . . . . . .80, 81-82

# B

Babylonians . . . . . . . . . . . . . . . . . . . . . . . . . . . . . . . . . . . .5
Bach, Johann Sebastian . . . . . . . . . . . . . . . . . . . . . . . . . . .8
Bacon's Rebellion . . . . . . . . . . . . . . . . . . . . . . . . . . . . . . .8
Baha'i . . . . . . . . . . . . . . . . . . . . . . . . . . . . . . . . . . . .66, 106
Bali, Indonesia . . . . . . . . . . . . . . . . . . . . . . . . . . . . . .10, 18
Bandaranaike, Sirimavo . . . . . . . . . . . . . . . . . . . . . . . . . .15
Bangkok, Thailand . . . . . . . . . . . . . . . . . . . . . . . . . . .20, 84
Bangladesh
    censorship . . . . . . . . . . . . . . . . . . . . . . . . . . . . . . . .63
    cyclones . . . . . . . . . . . . . . . . . . . . . . . . . . . . . . . . . .76
Bar Mitzvah . . . . . . . . . . . . . . . . . . . . . . . . . . . . . . . . . . .69
Barbados (Caribbean)
    cookery . . . . . . . . . . . . . . . . . . . . . . . . . . . . . . . .27, 34
Basho, Matsuo . . . . . . . . . . . . . . . . . . . . . . . . . . . . . . .8, 12
Bathsheba (Biblical character) . . . . . . . . . . . . . . . . . . . . .68
Beijing, China . . . . . . . . . . . . . . . . . . . . . . . . . . . . . .20, 84
Beirut, Lebanon . . . . . . . . . . . . . . . . . . . . . . . . . . . . . . . .2
Ben-Gurion, David . . . . . . . . . . . . . . . . . . . . . . . . . . . . .16
Bethune, Mary McLeod . . . . . . . . . . . . . . . . . . . . . . . . .17
Bhagavad Gita . . . . . . . . . . . . . . . . . . . . . . . . . . . . . . . . .65
Bhopal chemical leak (India) . . . . . . . . . . . . . . . . . . . . . .76
Bhutto, Benazir . . . . . . . . . . . . . . . . . . . . . . . . . . . . .14, 16
Bias *See* Prejudice: Racism.
Bible . . . . . . . . . . . . . . . . . . . . . . . . . . . . . . . . . . . . . . . .67
    stories . . . . . . . . . . . . . . . . . . . . . . . . . . . . . .39, 67, 68
Big Kite Flying Day . . . . . . . . . . . . . . . . . . . . . . . . . . . . .32
Biko, Stephen . . . . . . . . . . . . . . . . . . . . . . . . . . . . . . .61, 62
Biodiversity . . . . . . . . . . . . . . . . . . . . . . . . . . . . . . . .92, 102
Biographical resources . . . . . . . . . . . . . . . . . . . . . . . .82-83
Biomes . . . . . . . . . . . . . . . . . . . . . . . . . . . . . . . . . . . . . .52
Birds . . . . . . . . . . . . . . . . . . . . . . . . . . . . . . . . . . . . . . .108
Birth celebrations . . . . . . . . . . . . . . . . . . . . . . . . . . . .32, 35
Bismarck, Otto von . . . . . . . . . . . . . . . . . . . . . . . . . . . . .17
Blackwell, Elizabeth . . . . . . . . . . . . . . . . . . . . . . . . . . . .14
Blake, William . . . . . . . . . . . . . . . . . . . . . . . . . . . . . . . . .8
Bolívar, Simón . . . . . . . . . . . . . . . . . . . . . . . . . . . . . . .9, 17
Bolivia, South America
    children . . . . . . . . . . . . . . . . . . . . . . . . . . . . . . . . . .21

| | |
|---|---|
| games | .30 |
| mythology | .47 |
| Bombay, India | .20 |
| Bonaparte, Napoleon | 15, 16 |
| Bosnia | |
| ethnic cleansing | .62 |
| human rights | .62 |
| Botswana (Africa) | |
| folktales | 41, 49 |
| Bourke-White, Margaret | .12 |
| Brazil (South America) | |
| adventure | .13 |
| children | 18, 20, 22 |
| cookery | .26 |
| folktales | 37, 41, 43 |
| games | 29-30 |
| holidays | 29, 31 |
| Pantanal | .71 |
| rhymes | .11 |
| Buddha, Siddhartha Gautama | 67, 104, 105 |
| *See also* Buddhism. | |
| Buddha Day | .68 |
| Buddha's Birthday | 21 |
| Buddhism | 65, 66, 67, 68, 69, 91-92, 104, 105, 106, 107 |
| art | 66, 104 |
| Eightfold Path | .67 |
| festivals | .66 |
| lifestyle | .66 |
| literature | .66 |
| origin | .66 |
| philosophers | .67 |
| Tibetan | 66, 105, 107 |
| traditions | .28 |
| worship | 66, 67 |
| Burmese and Indian Founder's Day | .26 |
| Byzantine Empire | .2 |
| Byzantium | .92 |

## C

| | |
|---|---|
| Cabinet members | .84 |
| Cairo, Egypt | .20 |
| Calendars | |
| Aztec | .5 |
| China | 4, 5, 31 |
| Egypt | 3, 5 |
| Greece | .3 |
| Gregorian | .4 |
| Hebrew | 4, 31 |
| Hindu | .31 |
| Islam | .31 |
| Julian | .31 |
| Rome | 3, 5, 31 |
| Viking | .3 |
| world | 25, 95 |
| Cambodia | |
| Angkor Wat | .22 |
| human rights | .59 |
| Kampuchea | 22, 50 |
| Cameroon (Africa) | |
| children | 21, 33 |
| Canada | |
| children | 8, 22 |
| culture | 26, 93 |

| | |
|---|---|
| Caribbean | |
| Aruba | .30 |
| Barbados | 27, 34 |
| cookery | 27, 34 |
| games | .31 |
| geography | .86 |
| Tobago | .30 |
| traditions | .28 |
| treasure | .83 |
| Trinidad | .30 |
| Carson, Rachel | .17 |
| Caste system (India) | .60 |
| Castro, Fidel | 13, 59 |
| Cat myths | .42 |
| Cathay (China) | .53 |
| Catherine the Great, Tzarina of Russia | 12, 13, 14, 16 |
| Catholicism | 66, 68, 105, 107 |
| customs | .68 |
| history | .68 |
| holy days | .68 |
| rituals | .68 |
| Caves of the Thousand Buddhas | .2 |
| Celebrations | 25-35 |
| Celtic | |
| culture | .93 |
| language | .36 |
| mythology | .44 |
| traditions | .28 |
| Censorship | |
| art | 61-62, 63 |
| censors | 61-62 |
| dissidents | 61-62 |
| history | 61-62 |
| literature | .63 |
| media | .63 |
| propaganda | .63 |
| victims | 61-62 |
| Census | .90 |
| Central America | 18, 89 |
| chronology | 91-92 |
| cookery | .85 |
| culture | .85 |
| El Salvador | .27 |
| games | .34 |
| Guatemala | .18 |
| holidays | .85 |
| Central Asia | 81, 90 |
| folktales | 46, 81 |
| Central Intelligence Agency | .84 |
| Cezanne, Paul | .9 |
| Changan, China | .6 |
| Chanukah (Hanukkah) | 46, 68, 98, 99 |
| Charlemagne | .15 |
| Chat rooms | .109 |
| Chavez, Cesar | .17 |
| Chernobyl nuclear accident | .76 |
| Cherry Blossom Festival | .30 |
| Chichen Itza, Mexico | .6 |
| Child | |
| Convention of the Rights of the Child | .90 |
| labor | .62 |
| rights | .61 |
| survivorship | .88 |
| Children's and young adult literature | 5, 79, 80 |

*Subject Index* 133

China
- ancient ... 4, 5, 6, 7, 8, 86, 89
- An-yang ... 6
- art ... 10
- Beijing ... 20, 84
- calendar ... 4, 5, 31
- Cathay ... 53
- Changan ... 6
- children ... 21, 23
- Chinese New Year ... 26, 28-29, 30, 33, 69
- Communism ... 71, 63
- cookery ... 26
- culture ... 93
- folktales ... 38, 39, 43, 44, 46, 48, 49, 50, 51, 81
- footbinding ... 62-63
- games ... 28, 29, 30, 35
- Guangzhou ... 55
- history ... 89
- Hong Kong ... 84
- Huang He flood ... 76
- human rights ... 62-63
- language ... 36, 89-90
- mythology ... 44, 46, 47, 48, 51, 80, 81-82
- Peking ... 69
- religions ... 65
- terra cotta warriors ... 2
- Tiananmen Square ... 61-62
- Yangzi Gorges ... 71
- Zhengzhou ... 6
- zodiac ... 69

Chiyo, Uno ... 12
Chou En-lai (Zhou Enlai) ... 16
Christianity ... 28, 65, 66, 67, 69, 91-92, 105, 106
- Catholicism ... 66, 68, 105, 107
- Eastern Orthodox ... 66, 68, 107
- Orthodox ... 105
- Protestantism ... 68, 105, 107
- Roman Catholicism ... 66, 68, 105, 107
- Traditions ... 28

Christmas ... 16, 18, 32, 98
Churchill, Winston ... 17
Cinderella theme ... 40
City councils ... 86
City profiles ... 84
Cleopatra, Queen of Egypt ... 13, 14, 15, 16
Climate ... 52, 53, 56, 75, 92, 93, 102
Clocks ... 4, 5
Clothing ... 26
Coal ... 90-91
   See also Fuel.
Coasts
- endangered species ... 70
- lifestyle ... 70
- resources ... 70

Cochise (Native American) ... 16
Collaborative projects ... 109-113
Colonial Africa ... 89
Coming of Age ceremonies ... 32, 35
Communism ... 61, 63
Confucianism ... 67, 105, 107
Confucius ... 15, 66
Conservation
   See also Ecology; Environment.
- Greenpeace ... 86-87
- literature ... 74-75
- monitoring ... 92
- rain forest ... 73, 76
- resources ... 70

Convention of the Rights of the Child ... 90
Cookery
- Africa ... 32, 34
- Australia ... 32, 34
- Barbados ... 27, 34
- Brazil ... 26
- Caribbean ... 27, 34
- children ... 99
- China ... 26
- El Salvador ... 27
- England ... 34
- Equatorial Guinea ... 34
- Ghana ... 26
- Greece ... 27, 34
- Haiti ... 27
- India ... 27, 32, 34
- Indonesia ... 32
- international ... 98-99
- Israel ... 27
- Japan ... 26, 27, 34
- Kenya ... 34
- Lebanon ... 26
- Mexico ... 26, 32, 34
- Middle East ... 27, 32, 85
- Morocco ... 33
- Puerto Rico ... 27
- Russia ... 32, 34
- Sri Lanka ... 26
- Thailand ... 32
- Turkey ... 32
- United States ... 34
- Vietnam ... 27
- world ... 64, 98-99

Country resources ... 17-25
Creation stories ... 44, 51
Crime ... 59
Criminals ... 59
Crusades ... 5
Cultures ... 23-35
Current events ... 94-95, 102, 103
Currency ... 18, 85
Current Leaders
- Akihito, Emperor ... 16
- Annan, Kofi ... 59
- Aquino, Corazon ... 15-16
- Arafat, Yasir ... 16, 59
- Deng Xiaoping ... 9
- Hussein, King ... 16
- Milosevic, Slobodan ... 16
- Mandela, Nelson ... 15, 16, 82
- Peres, Shimon ... 16
- Thatcher, Margaret ... 14, 16
- Yeltsin, Boris ... 16

Customs ... 25-35
Cyclones
- Bangladesh ... 76

# D

Dalai Lama ... 15, 17
Dashiki ... 23

Day of the Dead . . . . . . . . . . . . . . . . . . . . . . . . .21, 28-29, 30, 99
de Beauvoir, Simone . . . . . . . . . . . . . . . . . . . . . . . . . . . . . . .17
Dead Sea Scrolls . . . . . . . . . . . . . . . . . . . . . . . . . . . . . . . .2, 57
Deborah (Biblical character) . . . . . . . . . . . . . . . . . . . . . .66, 68
Debt bondage . . . . . . . . . . . . . . . . . . . . . . . . . . . . . . . . . . . .62
Deng Xiaoping . . . . . . . . . . . . . . . . . . . . . . . . . . . . . . . . . . . .9
Dep 23
Desai, Anita . . . . . . . . . . . . . . . . . . . . . . . . . . . . . . . . . . . . .12
Descartes, Rene . . . . . . . . . . . . . . . . . . . . . . . . . . . . . . . . . . .8
Desert
    Arabian . . . . . . . . . . . . . . . . . . . . . . . . . . . . . . . . .53-54
    Gobi . . . . . . . . . . . . . . . . . . . . . . . . . . . . . . . . .53-54, 56
    irrigation . . . . . . . . . . . . . . . . . . . . . . . . . . . . . . .53-54
    Kalahari Desert . . . . . . . . . . . . . . . . . . . . . . . . . . . . .13
    lifestyle . . . . . . . . . . . . . . . . . . . . . . . . . . . . . . . . .53-54
    Namib Desert . . . . . . . . . . . . . . . . . . . . . . . . . . . . . . .71
    North America . . . . . . . . . . . . . . . . . . . . . . . . . . .53-54
    Sahara . . . . . . . . . . . . . . . . . . . . . . . . . . . .53-54, 56, 57
    Syrian . . . . . . . . . . . . . . . . . . . . . . . . . . . . . . . . . . . . .56
Dewey decimal classifications . . . . . . . . . . . . . . . . . . . . . .85
Dharma . . . . . . . . . . . . . . . . . . . . . . . . . . . . . . . . . . . . . . . .68
Diana, Princess of Wales . . . . . . . . . . . . . . . . . . . . . . . . . .17
Dickens, Charles . . . . . . . . . . . . . . . . . . . . . . . . . . . . . . . . . .9
Dickinson, Emily . . . . . . . . . . . . . . . . . . . . . . . . . . . . . . . .12
Dictators
    Castro, Fidel . . . . . . . . . . . . . . . . . . . . . . . . . . . . .13, 59
    Franco, Francisco . . . . . . . . . . . . . . . . . . . . . . . . . . .13
    Hitler, Adolf . . . . . . . . . . . . . . . . . . . . . . . . . . . . . . . .13
    Hussein, Saddam . . . . . . . . . . . . . . . . . . . . .13, 16, 61-62
    Mao Zedong . . . . . . . . . . . . . . . . . . . . . .13, 17, 59, 61-62
    Stalin, Joseph . . . . . . . . . . . . . . . . . . . . . . . . . . . .13, 82
Dictionaries . . . . . . . . . . . . . . . . . . . . . . . . . . . . . . .96-98, 101
Diderot, Denis . . . . . . . . . . . . . . . . . . . . . . . . . . . . . . . . . . . .9
Ding Ling . . . . . . . . . . . . . . . . . . . . . . . . . . . . . . . . . . . . . .12
Disasters . . . . . . . . . . . . . . . . . . . . . . . . . . . . . . . . . . . . . . .76
Disease . . . . . . . . . . . . . . . . . . . . . . . . . . . . . . . . . .74, 84, 92
    control . . . . . . . . . . . . . . . . . . . . . . . . . . . . . . . . .74, 84
    epidemics . . . . . . . . . . . . . . . . . . . . . . . . . . . . . . . . . .74
    Lyme . . . . . . . . . . . . . . . . . . . . . . . . . . . . . . . . . . . . . .74
    West Nile virus . . . . . . . . . . . . . . . . . . . . . . . . . . . . .74
Dissidents . . . . . . . . . . . . . . . . . . . . . . . . . . . . . . . . . . . . . .63
Diversity . . . . . . . . . . . . . . . . . . . . . . . . . . . . . . . . .19, 20, 22
Diwali (Divali) . . . . . . . . . . . . . . . . . . . . . . . . . .29, 30, 33, 65
Dog myths . . . . . . . . . . . . . . . . . . . . . . . . . . . . . . . . . . .41-42
Dolls 30-31
Dostoevsky, Fyodor . . . . . . . . . . . . . . . . . . . . . . . . . . . . . .12
Dracula, Vlad . . . . . . . . . . . . . . . . . . . . . . . . . . . . . . . . . . .13
Drought
Dulles, John Foster . . . . . . . . . . . . . . . . . . . . . . . . . . . . . . .17
Dussehra . . . . . . . . . . . . . . . . . . . . . . . . . . . . . . . . . . . . . . .65

# E

Earhart, Amelia . . . . . . . . . . . . . . . . . . . . . . . . . . . . . . . . . . .9
Earle, Sylvia Alice . . . . . . . . . . . . . . . . . . . . . . . . . . . . . . .14
Earth
    awareness . . . . . . . . . . . . . . . . . . . . . . . . . . . . . .74-75, 77
    stories . . . . . . . . . . . . . . . . . . . . . . . . . . . . .37, 48, 49, 51
Earthquakes . . . . . . . . . . . . . . . . . . . . . . . . . . . . . . . . . . . .76
East Asia . . . . . . . . . . . . . . . . . . . . . . . . . . . . . . . . . . . . . . . .4
East Timor, Indonesia
    human rights . . . . . . . . . . . . . . . . . . . . . . . . . . . . . . .62
Easter Island, Pacific . . . . . . . . . . . . . . . . . . . . . . . . . . . . . . .6
Eastern Africa . . . . . . . . . . . . . . . . . . . . . . . . . . . . . . . . . . .19
Eastern Asia . . . . . . . . . . . . . . . . . . . . . . . . . . . . . . . . . . . .19

Eastern European immigration . . . . . . . . . . . . . . . . . . . . . .64
    See also Immigration.
Eastern Orthodox Christianity . . . . . . . . . . . . . . . .66, 68, 107
    customs . . . . . . . . . . . . . . . . . . . . . . . . . . . . . . . . . . .68
    history . . . . . . . . . . . . . . . . . . . . . . . . . . . . . . . . . . . .68
    holy days . . . . . . . . . . . . . . . . . . . . . . . . . . . . . . . . . .68
    rituals . . . . . . . . . . . . . . . . . . . . . . . . . . . . . . . . . . . . .68
Ecology . . . . . . . . . . . . . . . . . . . . . . . . . . . . . . . . . . . . .83-93
    See also Conservation; Environment.
    global warming . . . . . . . . . . . . . . . . . . . . . . . . . . . . .70
    pollution . . . . . . . . . . . . . . . . . . . . . . . . . . . . . . . . . .70
    rain forest . . . . . . . . . . . . . . . . . . . . . . . . . . . . . . .73, 76
    recycling . . . . . . . . . . . . . . . . . . . . . . . . . . . . . . . . . .70
    resources . . . . . . . . . . . . . . . . . . . . . . . . . . . . . .70, 74-75
Economy . . . . . . . . . . . . . . . . . . . . . . . . . . . . . .23, 83-93, 100
Education . . . . . . . . . . . . . . . . . . . . . . . . . . . . . . . . . . . . . .90
Egypt
    Alexandria . . . . . . . . . . . . . . . . . . . . . . . . . . . . . . .6, 90
    ancient . . . . . . . . . . . . . . . . . . . . . . . .4, 5, 6, 7, 86, 89, 92
    art . . . . . . . . . . . . . . . . . . . . . . . . . . . . . . . . . .10, 79, 80
    Cairo . . . . . . . . . . . . . . . . . . . . . . . . . . . . . . . . . . . . .20
    calendar . . . . . . . . . . . . . . . . . . . . . . . . . . . . . . . . . . .35
    children . . . . . . . . . . . . . . . . . . . . . . . . . . . . . . . . .21, 23
    Cleopatra, Queen of
     . . . . . . . . . . . . . . . . . . . . . . . . . . . . . . . . . . . . . .Egypt
    13, 14, 15, 16
    folktales . . . . . . . . . . . . . . . . . . . . . . . . . . . . . . . . . . .42
    mythology . . . . . . . . . . . . . . . . . . . .44, 46-47, 48, 80, 81-82
    Pyramids . . . . . . . . . . . . . . . . . . . . . . . . . . . . . .6, 90, 92
    Sphinx . . . . . . . . . . . . . . . . . . . . . . . . . . . . . . . . . . . . .6
    Tell al-Amarna . . . . . . . . . . . . . . . . . . . . . . . . . . . . . . .6
    tombs . . . . . . . . . . . . . . . . . . . . . . . . . . . . . . . . . . . .2, 6
    Tutankhamen . . . . . . . . . . . . . . . . . . . . . . . . . . . . . .2, 6
Eid Festivals . . . . . . . . . . . . . . . . . . . . . . . . . . . . . . . . . . . .26
Eid-ul-Fitr . . . . . . . . . . . . . . . . . . . . . . . . . . . . . . . . . . .26, 29
    See also Id-ul-Fitr.
Eightfold Path . . . . . . . . . . . . . . . . . . . . . . . . . . . . . . . . . . .67
Elderly abuse . . . . . . . . . . . . . . . . . . . . . . . . . . . . . . . . . . . .61

Electricity . . . . . . . . . . . . . . . . . . . . . . . . . . . . . . . . . .90-91, 93
    See also Energy.
El Greco . . . . . . . . . . . . . . . . . . . . . . . . . . . . . . . . . . . . . . . .8
Elijah (Biblical character) . . . . . . . . . . . . . . . . . . . . . . . . . .66
Elizabeth (Biblical character) . . . . . . . . . . . . . . . . . . . . . . .68
Elizabeth I, Queen of England . . . . . . . . . . . . . . . . . . . . . .14
Ellis Island, New York . . . . . . . . . . . . . . . . . . . . . . . . .64, 64
    See also Immigration.
El Niño . . . . . . . . . . . . . . . . . . . . . . . . . . . . . . . . . . . . .70, 73
El Salvador, Central America
    cookery . . . . . . . . . . . . . . . . . . . . . . . . . . . . . . . . . . .27
Elections . . . . . . . . . . . . . . . . . . . . . . . . . . . . . . . . . . . .85, 89
Electronic field trips . . . . . . . . . . . . . . . . . . . . . . . . . . . . .109
E-mail (email) . . . . . . . . . . . . . . . . . . . . . . . . . . . . . .109-113
Embassies . . . . . . . . . . . . . . . . . . . . . . . . . . . . . . . . . . .85, 86
Employment . . . . . . . . . . . . . . . . . . . . . . . . . . . . . . . . . . . .88
En Hedu'Anna . . . . . . . . . . . . . . . . . . . . . . . . . . . . . . . . . .82
Encyclopedias . . . . . . . . . . . . . . . . . . . . . . . . . . . . . . . .96-98
Endangered species
    animals on list . . . . . . . . . . . . . . . . . . . . . . . . . . . .73, 77
    coasts . . . . . . . . . . . . . . . . . . . . . . . . . . . . . . . . . . . . .70
    meaning . . . . . . . . . . . . . . . . . . . . . . . . . . . . . . . . . . .73
    monitoring . . . . . . . . . . . . . . . . . . . . . . . . . . . . . . . . .92
    rain forest . . . . . . . . . . . . . . . . . . . . . . . . . . . . . . . . . .73
    wildlife preservation . . . . . . . . . . . . . . . . . . . . . . .70, 77

Energy
- Agenda 21 of the Earth Summit . . . . . . . . . . . . . . . . . . . 71, 73, 75
- analysis . . . . . . . . . . . . . . . . . . . . . . . . . . . . . . . . . . . . . 90-91
- effects on environment . . . . . . . . . . . . . . . . . . . . . . . . . . . . 72
- electricity . . . . . . . . . . . . . . . . . . . . . . . . . . . . . . . . . 90-91, 93
- fuel . . . . . . . . . . . . . . . . . . . . . . . . . . . . . . . . . . . . . . . . 90-91
- geothermal power . . . . . . . . . . . . . . . . . . . . . . . . . . . . . . . 72
- natural gas . . . . . . . . . . . . . . . . . . . . . . . . . . . . . . . . . . 90-91
- nuclear . . . . . . . . . . . . . . . . . . . . . . . . . . . . . . . . . . . . . 90-91
- resources . . . . . . . . . . . . . . . . . . . . . . . . . . . . 71, 72, 90-91, 92
- renewable resources . . . . . . . . . . . . . . . . . . . . . . . . . 72, 90-91
- solar power . . . . . . . . . . . . . . . . . . . . . . . . . . . . . . . . . . . . 72
- wind power . . . . . . . . . . . . . . . . . . . . . . . . . . . . . . . . . . . . 72

Engels, Friedrich . . . . . . . . . . . . . . . . . . . . . . . . . . . . . . . . . . . . 17
England
- cookery . . . . . . . . . . . . . . . . . . . . . . . . . . . . . . . . . . . . . . . 34
- folktales . . . . . . . . . . . . . . . . . . . . . . . . . . . . . . . . . . . . . . . 43
- London . . . . . . . . . . . . . . . . . . . . . . . . . . . . . . . . . . . . . . . 55

Environment
*See also* Conservation; Ecology.
- disasters . . . . . . . . . . . . . . . . . . . . . . . . . . . . . . . . . . . . . . 76
- encyclopedia . . . . . . . . . . . . . . . . . . . . . . . . . . . . . . . . . . . 72
- protection . . . . . . . . . . . . . . . . . . . . . . . . . . . . . . . . 86-87, 92
- rain forest . . . . . . . . . . . . . . . . . . . . . . . . . . . . . . . . . . 73, 76
- resources . . . . . . . . . . . . . . . . . . . . . . . . . . . . . . . . . . . 74-75

Epidemics . . . . . . . . . . . . . . . . . . . . . . . . . . . . . . . . . . . . . . . . . 74
Equatorial Guinea . . . . . . . . . . . . . . . . . . . . . . . . . . . . . . . . . . 64
Equal pay . . . . . . . . . . . . . . . . . . . . . . . . . . . . . . . . . . . . . . 62, 63
Equal rights . . . . . . . . . . . . . . . . . . . . . . . . . . . . . . . . . . . . 62, 63
Erik the Red . . . . . . . . . . . . . . . . . . . . . . . . . . . . . . . . . . . . . . . 14

Ethiopia, Africa
- children . . . . . . . . . . . . . . . . . . . . . . . . . . . . . . . . . . . . . . . 22
- famine . . . . . . . . . . . . . . . . . . . . . . . . . . . . . . . . . . . . . 61-62
- folktales . . . . . . . . . . . . . . . . . . . . . . . . . . . . . . . . . . . . . . . 37
- holidays . . . . . . . . . . . . . . . . . . . . . . . . . . . . . . . . . . . . . . . 29
- mythology . . . . . . . . . . . . . . . . . . . . . . . . . . . . . . . . . . . . . 47

Ethnic cleansing . . . . . . . . . . . . . . . . . . . . . . . . . . . . . . . . . . . . 62
Ethnicity . . . . . . . . . . . . . . . . . . . . . . . . . . . . . . . . . . . . . . . 21, 88
Europe . . . . . . . . . . . . . . . . . . . . . . . . . . . . . . . . . . . 19, 90, 91, 93
- ancient . . . . . . . . . . . . . . . . . . . . . . . . . . . . . . . . . . . . . 2, 86
- art . . . . . . . . . . . . . . . . . . . . . . . . . . . . . . . . . . . . . . . . . . . . 9
- civilization . . . . . . . . . . . . . . . . . . . . . . . . . . . . . . . . . . . . . . 4
- cuisine . . . . . . . . . . . . . . . . . . . . . . . . . . . . . . . . . . . . . . . . 85
- culture . . . . . . . . . . . . . . . . . . . . . . . . . . . . . . . . . . . . . . . . 85
- European Community . . . . . . . . . . . . . . . . . . . . . . . . . . . . 91
- geography . . . . . . . . . . . . . . . . . . . . . . . . . . . . . . . . . . . . . 86
- folktales . . . . . . . . . . . . . . . . . . . . . . . . . . . . . . . . . . . . 37, 39
- holidays . . . . . . . . . . . . . . . . . . . . . . . . . . . . . . . . . . . . . . . 85
- Medieval . . . . . . . . . . . . . . . . . . . . . . . . . . . . . . . . . . . . . . . 8
- music . . . . . . . . . . . . . . . . . . . . . . . . . . . . . . . . . . . . . . . . 81
- Northern Europe . . . . . . . . . . . . . . . . . . . . . . . . . . . . . . . . 19
- Northeastern Europe . . . . . . . . . . . . . . . . . . . . . . . . . . . . . 19

Eve (Biblical character) . . . . . . . . . . . . . . . . . . . . . . . . . . . . . . . 68
Everest, Mount . . . . . . . . . . . . . . . . . . . . . . . . . . . . . . . . . . . . . 71
Exploration
- Northern Route . . . . . . . . . . . . . . . . . . . . . . . . . . . . . . . . . 53
- world . . . . . . . . . . . . . . . . . . . . . . . . . . . . . . . . . . . 3, 7-8, 24

Explorers
- Amundsen, Roald . . . . . . . . . . . . . . . . . . . . . . . . . . . . . . . 14
- Armstrong, Neil . . . . . . . . . . . . . . . . . . . . . . . . . . . . . . . . . 14
- Earhart, Amelia . . . . . . . . . . . . . . . . . . . . . . . . . . . . . . . . . . 9
- Erik the Red . . . . . . . . . . . . . . . . . . . . . . . . . . . . . . . . . . . 14
- Finch, Linda . . . . . . . . . . . . . . . . . . . . . . . . . . . . . . . . . . . 14
- Gagarin, Yuri . . . . . . . . . . . . . . . . . . . . . . . . . . . . . . . . . . 14
- Heyerdahl, Thor . . . . . . . . . . . . . . . . . . . . . . . . . . . . . . . . 14
- Ibn Battuta . . . . . . . . . . . . . . . . . . . . . . . . . . . . . . . . . 12, 14
- Kingsley, Mary . . . . . . . . . . . . . . . . . . . . . . . . . . . . . . . . . 14
- Livingstone, David . . . . . . . . . . . . . . . . . . . . . . . . . . . . . . 14
- Magellan, Ferdinand . . . . . . . . . . . . . . . . . . . . . . . . . . . . . 14
- Nunez de Balboa, Vasco . . . . . . . . . . . . . . . . . . . . . . . . . . 14
- Suleyman the Merchant . . . . . . . . . . . . . . . . . . . . . 12, 14, 82
- Uemura, Naomi . . . . . . . . . . . . . . . . . . . . . . . . . . . . . . . . 14
- Xuan Zang . . . . . . . . . . . . . . . . . . . . . . . . . . . . . . . . . . . . 14
- world . . . . . . . . . . . . . . . . . . . . . . . . . . . . . . . . . . . 3, 7-8, 24
- Zhang Qian . . . . . . . . . . . . . . . . . . . . . . . . . . . . . . . . . . . 14

# F

Fairies . . . . . . . . . . . . . . . . . . . . . . . . . . . . . . . . . . . . . . . . . 49, 50
Fairy tales . . . . . . . . . . . . . . . . . . . . . . . . . . . . . . . . . . . . . . . . . 48
*See also* Folktales.
Falklands War, Australia . . . . . . . . . . . . . . . . . . . . . . . . . . . 61-62
Family
- planning . . . . . . . . . . . . . . . . . . . . . . . . . . . . . . . . . . . . . . 88
- size controls . . . . . . . . . . . . . . . . . . . . . . . . . . . . . . . . . . . 61

Far East (Asia) . . . . . . . . . . . . . . . . . . . . . . . . . . . . . . . . . . . . . 85
Farms and farming
*See also* Agriculture; Food.
- arable . . . . . . . . . . . . . . . . . . . . . . . . . . . . . . . . . . . . . . . . 72
- lifestyle . . . . . . . . . . . . . . . . . . . . . . . . . . . . . . . . . . . . . . . 54
- livestock . . . . . . . . . . . . . . . . . . . . . . . . . . . . . . . . . . . . . . 72
- specialized . . . . . . . . . . . . . . . . . . . . . . . . . . . . . . . . . . . . 54
- sustainable . . . . . . . . . . . . . . . . . . . . . . . . . . . . . . . . . . . . 72
- traditional . . . . . . . . . . . . . . . . . . . . . . . . . . . . . . . . . . . . . 54

Female genital mutilation in Africa . . . . . . . . . . . . . . . . . . . 62-63
Fertility . . . . . . . . . . . . . . . . . . . . . . . . . . . . . . . . . . . . . . . . . . . 88
Festivals . . . . . . . . . . . . . . . . . . . . . . . . . . . . 25-35, 65-69, 98-99
*See also* Holidays; Holidays, Religious.
- Al-Hegira . . . . . . . . . . . . . . . . . . . . . . . . . . . . . . . . . . . . . 67
- Cherry Blossom Festival . . . . . . . . . . . . . . . . . . . . . . . . . . 30
- Eid Festivals . . . . . . . . . . . . . . . . . . . . . . . . . . . . . . . . . . . 26
- Festival of Color . . . . . . . . . . . . . . . . . . . . . . . . . . . . . . . . 66
- Festival of Lights . . . . . . . . . . . . . . . . . . . . . . . . . . . . . . . . 26
- Festival of the Grapes . . . . . . . . . . . . . . . . . . . . . . . . . . . . 31
- Hindu . . . . . . . . . . . . . . . . . . . . . . . . . . . 33, 65, 66, 67, 68, 106
- Hina Matsuri . . . . . . . . . . . . . . . . . . . . . . . . . . . . . . . . . . . 67
- Kwanzaa . . . . . . . . . . . . . . . . . . . . . . . . . . . . . . . 27, 28-29, 46
- Lantern Festival . . . . . . . . . . . . . . . . . . . . . . . . . . . . . . . . . 33
- Mid-Autumn Festival . . . . . . . . . . . . . . . . . . . . . . . . . . . . 31
- New Yam Festival . . . . . . . . . . . . . . . . . . . . . . . . . . . . . . . 31
- Now-Ruz Festivals . . . . . . . . . . . . . . . . . . . . . . . . . . . . . . 30
- 7-5-3 Festival . . . . . . . . . . . . . . . . . . . . . . . . . . . . . . . . . . 67
- Spring Festival . . . . . . . . . . . . . . . . . . . . . . . . . . . . . . . . . 26
- Tanabata (Star Festival) . . . . . . . . . . . . . . . . . . . . . . . . 28, 29
- Tet Nguyen-Dan (Lunar New Year Festival) . . . . . . . . . 29, 30
- Trung Thu . . . . . . . . . . . . . . . . . . . . . . . . . . . . . . . . . . . . . 29

Finch, Linda . . . . . . . . . . . . . . . . . . . . . . . . . . . . . . . . . . . . . . . 14
Flags . . . . . . . . . . . . . . . . . . . . . . . . . . . . . 36, 57, 83, 97, 99-101, 103
Floods . . . . . . . . . . . . . . . . . . . . . . . . . . . . . . . . . . . . . . . . . . . 76
Folktales
*See also* Mythology.
- Aborigines . . . . . . . . . . . . . . . . . . . . . . . . . . . . . . . . . . 48, 49
- Africa . . . . . . . . . . . . . . . . . . . . . . . . 38, 39, 41, 45, 46, 47-48,
  49, 51, 81
- Algeria . . . . . . . . . . . . . . . . . . . . . . . . . . . . . . . . . . . . . . . . 41
- Anansi tales . . . . . . . . . . . . . . . . . . . . . . . . . . . . . . . . . 41, 43
- Arabia . . . . . . . . . . . . . . . . . . . . . . . . . . . . . . . . . . . . . . . . 41
- Argentina . . . . . . . . . . . . . . . . . . . . . . . . . . . . . . . . . . . . . 49

Armenia . . . . . . . . . . . . . . . . . . . . . . . . . . . . . . . . . . . . . . . . . . . . .42
Ashanti . . . . . . . . . . . . . . . . . . . . . . . . . . . . . . . . . . . . . . . . .40, 48
Asia . . . . . . . . . . . . . . . . . . . . . . . . . . . . . . . . . . . . . . . . . . . . . .37
Australia . . . . . . . . . . . . . . . . . . . . . . . . . . . . . . . . . . .39, 40, 43
Bangladesh . . . . . . . . . . . . . . . . . . . . . . . . . . . . . . . . . . . . . . .52
Bengal . . . . . . . . . . . . . . . . . . . . . . . . . . . . . . . . . . . . . . . . . . .50
Benin . . . . . . . . . . . . . . . . . . . . . . . . . . . . . . . . . . . . . . . .43, 45
Botswana . . . . . . . . . . . . . . . . . . . . . . . . . . . . . . . . . . . . .41, 49
Brazil . . . . . . . . . . . . . . . . . . . . . . . . . . . . . . . . . . . .37, 41, 43
Burma . . . . . . . . . . . . . . . . . . . . . . . . . . . . . . . . . . . . . . . . . . .41
Cape Verde . . . . . . . . . . . . . . . . . . . . . . . . . . . . . . . . . . . . . . .43
Caribbean . . . . . . . . . . . . . . . . . . . . . . . . . . . . . . . . . . . . . . . .43
Central America . . . . . . . . . . . . . . . . . . . . . . . . . . . . . . . . . . .38
Central Asia . . . . . . . . . . . . . . . . . . . . . . . . . . . . . . . . . . .46, 81
Chile . . . . . . . . . . . . . . . . . . . . . . . . . . . . . . . . . . . . . . . . .39, 51
China . . . . . . . . . . . . . . . . . . . . . . . . .38, 39, 43, 44, 46, 48,
. . . . . . . . . . . . . . . . . . . . . . . . . . . . . . . . . . . . . . . . . . . . . . . .
49, 50, 51, 81
Costa Rica . . . . . . . . . . . . . . . . . . . . . . . . . . . . . . . . . . . . . . . .48
Cuba . . . . . . . . . . . . . . . . . . . . . . . . . . . . . . . . . . . . . . . . .43, 50
Egypt . . . . . . . . . . . . . . . . . . . . . . . . . . . . . . . . . . . . . . . . . . . .42
England . . . . . . . . . . . . . . . . . . . . . . . . . . . . . . . . . . . . . . . . . .43
Ethiopia . . . . . . . . . . . . . . . . . . . . . . . . . . . . . . . . . . . . . . . . . .37
Europe . . . . . . . . . . . . . . . . . . . . . . . . . . . . . . . . . . . . . . . .37, 39
Fiji . . . . . . . . . . . . . . . . . . . . . . . . . . . . . . . . . . . . . . . . . . . . . .39
France . . . . . . . . . . . . . . . . . . . . . . . . . . . . . . .39, 45, 49, 51, 52
Germany . . . . . . . . . . . . . . . . . . . . . . . .37, 39, 42, 49, 50, 51, 52
Ghana . . . . . . . . . . . . . . . . . . . . . . . . . . . . . . . . . . . . . . . . . . .41
Greece . . . . . . . . . . . . . . . . . . . . . . . . . . . . . . .38, 39, 40, 49, 50
Guatemala . . . . . . . . . . . . . . . . . . . . . . . . . . . . . . . . . . . . . . . .39
Haiti . . . . . . . . . . . . . . . . . . . . . . . . . . . . . . . . . . . . . . . . .43, 45
Hmong . . . . . . . . . . . . . . . . . . . . . . . . . . . . . . . . . . . . . . . . . . .44
Holland . . . . . . . . . . . . . . . . . . . . . . . . . . . . . . . . . . . . . . . . . .39
Iceland . . . . . . . . . . . . . . . . . . . . . . . . . . . . . . . . . . .38, 41, 49
India . . . . . . . . . . . . . . . . . . . . . . . . . . . . . .37, 38, 40, 41, 42, 43,
. . . . . . . . . . . . . . . . . . . . . . . . . . . . . . . . . . . . . . . . . . . . . . . .
46, 47-48, 50, 81
Indonesia . . . . . . . . . . . . . . . . . . . . . . . . . . . . . . . . . . . . . .41, 49
Iran . . . . . . . . . . . . . . . . . . . . . . . . . . . . . . . . . . . . . . . .37, 47-48
Iraq . . . . . . . . . . . . . . . . . . . . . . . . . . . . . . . . . . . . . . . . . . . . .43
Ireland . . . . . . . . . . . . . . . . . . . . . . . . . . . . . . . . . . . . . . . .38, 49
Israel . . . . . . . . . . . . . . . . . . . . . . . . . . . . . . . . . . . . . .38, 51, 52
Italy . . . . . . . . . . . . . . . . . . . . . . . . . . . . . . . . . . . . . . . . . . . . .52
Jakata tales . . . . . . . . . . . . . . . . . . . . . . . . . . . . . . . . . . . . . . .40
Jamaica . . . . . . . . . . . . . . . . . . . . . . . . . . . . . . . . . . . . . . . . . .49
Japan . . . . . . . . . . . . . . . . . . . . . . .36, 38, 39, 40, 41, 42, 44,
. . . . . . . . . . . . . . . . . . . . . . . . . . . . . . . . . . . . . . . . . . . . . . . .
45, 46, 47, 48, 49, 50, 81
Kalmuck (Central Asia) . . . . . . . . . . . . . . . . . . . . . . . . . . . . .46
Kampuchea . . . . . . . . . . . . . . . . . . . . . . . . . . . . . . . . . . . . . . .50
Kenya . . . . . . . . . . . . . . . . . . . . . . . . . . . . . . . . . . . . . . . .37, 43
Korea . . . . . . . . . . . . . . . . . . . . . . . . . . . . . . . .36, 37, 39, 40, 50
Lebanon . . . . . . . . . . . . . . . . . . . . . . . . . . . . . . . . . . . . . . . . .41
Liberia . . . . . . . . . . . . . . . . . . . . . . . . . . . . . . . . . . . . . . . . . . .37
Malaysia . . . . . . . . . . . . . . . . . . . . . . . . . . . . . . . . . . . . . . . . .43
Malta . . . . . . . . . . . . . . . . . . . . . . . . . . . . . . . . . . . . . . . . . . . .52
Maori . . . . . . . . . . . . . . . . . . . . . . . . . . . . . . . . .40, 41, 49, 50
Martinique . . . . . . . . . . . . . . . . . . . . . . . . . . . . . . . . . . . . . . .49
Mexico . . . . . . . . . . . . . . . . . . . . . . . . . . . .37, 39, 41, 45, 49, 81
Micronesia . . . . . . . . . . . . . . . . . . . . . . . . . . . . . . . . . . . . . . .31
Middle East . . . . . . . . . . . . . . . . . . . . . . . . . . . . . . . .37, 40, 81
Mongolia . . . . . . . . . . . . . . . . . . . . . . . . . . . . . . . . . . . . .41, 46
Morocco . . . . . . . . . . . . . . . . . . . . . . . . . . . . . . . . . . . . . .41, 50
Native America . . . . . . . . . . . . . . . . . . . . . . . . . . . . . . . . .39, 49
Navajo . . . . . . . . . . . . . . . . . . . . . . . . . . . . . . . . . . . . . . . . . . .49
Near East . . . . . . . . . . . . . . . . . . . . . . . . . . . . . . . . . . . . . . . .37
Nepal . . . . . . . . . . . . . . . . . . . . . . . . . . . . . . . . . . . . . . . . . . .40
New Zealand . . . . . . . . . . . . . . . . . . . . . . . . . . . . . . . . . .38, 41
Nigeria . . . . . . . . . . . . . . . . . . . . . . . . . . . . . . . . . . . . . . .43, 49
North America . . . . . . . . . . . . . . . . . . . . . . . . . . . . . .37, 39, 43
Norway . . . . . . . . . . . . . . . . . . . . . . . . . . . . . . . . . . . . . . . . . .51
Pacific . . . . . . . . . . . . . . . . . . . . . . . . . . . . . . . . . . . . . . . . . . .38
Persia . . . . . . . . . . . . . . . . . . . . . . . . . . . . . . . . . . . .46, 47, 50
Peru . . . . . . . . . . . . . . . . . . . . . . . . . . . . . . . . . . . . . . . . . . . .37
Philippines . . . . . . . . . . . . . . . . . . . . . . . . . . . . . . . . . . . .49, 51
Poland . . . . . . . . . . . . . . . . . . . . . . . . . . . . . . . . . . . . . . . . . .49
Polynesia . . . . . . . . . . . . . . . . . . . . . . . . . . . . . . . . . . . . . . . .39
Portugal . . . . . . . . . . . . . . . . . . . . . . . . . . . . . . . . . . . . . . . . .48
Puerto Rico . . . . . . . . . . . . . . . . . . . . . . . . . . . . . . . . . . .38, 43
Romania . . . . . . . . . . . . . . . . . . . . . . . . . . . . . . . . . . . . .39, 49
Russia . . . . . . . . . . . . . . . . . . . . . . . . . .36, 39, 42, 43, 44,
. . . . . . . . . . . . . . . . . . . . . . . . . . . . . . . . . . . . . . . . . . . . . . . .
45, 47, 50, 81
Scotland . . . . . . . . . . . . . . . . . . . . . . . . . . . . . . . . . . . . . . . . .38
Senegal . . . . . . . . . . . . . . . . . . . . . . . . . . . . . . . . . . . . . . . . .47
Siberia . . . . . . . . . . . . . . . . . . . . . . . . . . . . . . . . . . . . . . . . . .81
South America . . . . . . . . . . . . . . . . . . . . . . . . . . . . . . . . . . . .37
Southeast Asia . . . . . . . . . . . . . . . . . . . . . . . . . . . . . . . . . . . .42
southern Africa . . . . . . . . . . . . . . . . . . . . . . . . . . . . . . . . . . .38
Sri Lanka . . . . . . . . . . . . . . . . . . . . . . . . . . . . . . . . . . . . . . . .45
Sudan . . . . . . . . . . . . . . . . . . . . . . . . . . . . . . . . . . . . . . . . . . .42
Suriname . . . . . . . . . . . . . . . . . . . . . . . . . . . . . . . . . . . . . . . .48
Sweden . . . . . . . . . . . . . . . . . . . . . . . . . . . . . . . . . . . . . . . . . .41
Switzerland . . . . . . . . . . . . . . . . . . . . . . . . . . . . . . . . . . .38, 50
Syria . . . . . . . . . . . . . . . . . . . . . . . . . . . . . . . . . . . . . . . . . . . .51
Taoist . . . . . . . . . . . . . . . . . . . . . . . . . . . . . . . . . . . . . . . . . . .40
Thailand . . . . . . . . . . . . . . . . . . . . . . . . . . . . . . . . . . . . . . . . .43
Turkey . . . . . . . . . . . . . . . . . . . . . . . . . . . . .38, 39, 43, 45, 49
Ukraine . . . . . . . . . . . . . . . . . . . . . . . . . . . . . . . . . . . . . . .47-48
United States . . . . . . . . . . . . . . . . . . . . . . . . . . . . .37, 39, 41, 49
Uruguay . . . . . . . . . . . . . . . . . . . . . . . . . . . . . . . . . . . . . . . . .41
Uzbekistan . . . . . . . . . . . . . . . . . . . . . . . . . . . . . . . . . . . . . . .47
Venezuela . . . . . . . . . . . . . . . . . . . . . . . . . . . . . . . . . . . . . . . .43
Vietnam . . . . . . . . . . . . . . . . . . . . . . . . . . . . . . . . . . . . . .40, 41
West Africa . . . . . . . . . . . . . . . . . . . . . . . . . . . . . . . . . . . .40, 45
women . . . . . . . . . . . . . . . . . . . . . . . . . . . . . . . . . . . . . . . . . .51
Zaire . . . . . . . . . . . . . . . . . . . . . . . . . . . . . . . . . . . . . . . . . . . .43
Fon
    mythology . . . . . . . . . . . . . . . . . . . . . . . . . . . . . . . . . . .81-82
Food 18, 25-35, 98-99
    organic . . . . . . . . . . . . . . . . . . . . . . . . . . . . . . . . . . . . . . . .70
    prices . . . . . . . . . . . . . . . . . . . . . . . . . . . . . . . . . . . . . . . . .86
    stories . . . . . . . . . . . . . . . . . . . . . . . . . . . . . . . . . . .44-45, 50
    world . . . . . . . . . . . . . . . . . . . . . . . . . . . . . . . . . . . . . . . . .75
Footbinding (China) . . . . . . . . . . . . . . . . . . . . . . . . . . . . . .62-63
Foreign languages
    *See* Languages.
Foreign states . . . . . . . . . . . . . . . . . . . . . . . . . . . . . . . . . . . . . . .86
Forests . . . . . . . . . . . . . . . . . . . . . . . . . . . . . . . . . . . . . . . . . . . .92
Founding Leaders
    Aung San . . . . . . . . . . . . . . . . . . . . . . . . . . . . . . . . . . . . . .16
    Ben-Gurion, David . . . . . . . . . . . . . . . . . . . . . . . . . . . . . . .16
    Chou En-lai (Zhou En-lai) . . . . . . . . . . . . . . . . . . . . . . . . .16
    Gandhi, Indira . . . . . . . . . . . . . . . . . . . . . . . . . .12, 13, 15, 16
    Gorbachev, Mikhail . . . . . . . . . . . . . . . . . . . . . . . . . . . .15, 16
    Hussein, Saddam . . . . . . . . . . . . . . . . . . . . . . . .13, 16, 61-62
    Mandela, Nelson . . . . . . . . . . . . . . . . . . . . . . . . . . . .15, 16, 82

France
- culture . . . . . . . . . . . . . . . . . . . . . . . . . . . . . . . . . . . . . . . . . . . .24
- folktales . . . . . . . . . . . . . . . . . . . . . . . . . . . . .39, 45, 49, 51, 52
- pre-Revolution . . . . . . . . . . . . . . . . . . . . . . . . . . . . . . . . . . . . .5

Franco, Francisco . . . . . . . . . . . . . . . . . . . . . . . . . . . . . . . . . .13, 16
Frank, Anne . . . . . . . . . . . . . . . . . . . . . . . . . . . . . . . . . . . . . .12, 62
Freedom . . . . . . . . . . . . . . . . . . . . . . . . . . . . . . . . . . . . . . . . .58-65
- belief . . . . . . . . . . . . . . . . . . . . . . . . . . . . . . . . . . . . . . . . . . .61
- movement . . . . . . . . . . . . . . . . . . . . . . . . . . . . . . . . . . . . . . .59
- press . . . . . . . . . . . . . . . . . . . . . . . . . . . . . . . . . . .60, 61-2, 63
- speech . . . . . . . . . . . . . . . . . . . . . . . . . . . . . . . . . .60, 61-62, 63
- thought . . . . . . . . . . . . . . . . . . . . . . . . . . . . . . . . . . . . . .61-62
- women's rights . . . . . . . . . . . . . . . . . . . . . . . . . . . . . . . . .62-63

Fuel *See also* Energy.
- alternate . . . . . . . . . . . . . . . . . . . . . . . . . . . . . . . . . . . . . .90-91
- coal . . . . . . . . . . . . . . . . . . . . . . . . . . . . . . . . . . . . . . . . .90-91
- petroleum . . . . . . . . . . . . . . . . . . . . . . . . . . . . . . . . . . . .90-91

Fuji, Mount . . . . . . . . . . . . . . . . . . . . . . . . . . . . . . . . . . . . . . . . . .71
Future . . . . . . . . . . . . . . . . . . . . . . . . . . . . . . . . . . . . . . . . . . . . .73

# G

Gagarin, Yuri . . . . . . . . . . . . . . . . . . . . . . . . . . . . . . . . . . . . . . . .14
Galilei, Galileo . . . . . . . . . . . . . . . . . . . . . . . . . . . . . . . . . . . . . . . .8
Games . . . . . . . . . . . . . . . . . . . . . . . . . . . . . . . . . . . . . . . . . .25-35
- African-American . . . . . . . . . . . . . . . . . . . . . . . . . . . . . . . . .28
- Arabic . . . . . . . . . . . . . . . . . . . . . . . . . . . . . . . . . . . . . . . . . .28
- Aruba . . . . . . . . . . . . . . . . . . . . . . . . . . . . . . . . . . . . . . . . . .30
- Asia . . . . . . . . . . . . . . . . . . . . . . . . . . . . . . . . . . . . . . . . . . . .31
- Australia . . . . . . . . . . . . . . . . . . . . . . . . . . . . . . . . . . . . . . . .35
- Bolivia . . . . . . . . . . . . . . . . . . . . . . . . . . . . . . . . . . . . . . . . . .30
- Brazil . . . . . . . . . . . . . . . . . . . . . . . . . . . . . . . . . . . . . . . .29, 30
- Caribbean . . . . . . . . . . . . . . . . . . . . . . . . . . . . . . . . . . . . . . .31
- Central America . . . . . . . . . . . . . . . . . . . . . . . . . . . . . . . . . .31
- China . . . . . . . . . . . . . . . . . . . . . . . . . . . . . . . . . .28, 29, 30, 35
- Egypt . . . . . . . . . . . . . . . . . . . . . . . . . . . . . . . . . . . . . . . . . . .29
- Israel . . . . . . . . . . . . . . . . . . . . . . . . . . . . . . . . . . . . . .28, 29, 30
- Japan . . . . . . . . . . . . . . . . . . . . . . . . . . . . . . . . . . . . . . . .28, 35
- Java . . . . . . . . . . . . . . . . . . . . . . . . . . . . . . . . . . . . . . . . . . . .31
- Jewish . . . . . . . . . . . . . . . . . . . . . . . . . . . . . . . . . . . . . . . . . .28
- Kenya . . . . . . . . . . . . . . . . . . . . . . . . . . . . . . . . . . . . . . . . . .29
- Korea . . . . . . . . . . . . . . . . . . . . . . . . . . . . . . . . . . . . . . . . . . .28
- Malta . . . . . . . . . . . . . . . . . . . . . . . . . . . . . . . . . . . . . . . . . . .29
- Mexico . . . . . . . . . . . . . . . . . . . . . . . . . . . . . . . . . . . . . . .28, 29
- Native American . . . . . . . . . . . . . . . . . . . . . . . . . . . . . . . . . .28
- New Zealand . . . . . . . . . . . . . . . . . . . . . . . . . . . . . . . . . . . . .30
- Nigeria . . . . . . . . . . . . . . . . . . . . . . . . . . . . . . . . . . . . . . . . . .30
- Pacific . . . . . . . . . . . . . . . . . . . . . . . . . . . . . . . . . . . . . . . . . .31
- Pakistan . . . . . . . . . . . . . . . . . . . . . . . . . . . . . . . . . . . . . . . . .29
- Russia . . . . . . . . . . . . . . . . . . . . . . . . . . . . . . . . . . . . . . . . . .29
- Somalia . . . . . . . . . . . . . . . . . . . . . . . . . . . . . . . . . . . . . . . . .30
- South America . . . . . . . . . . . . . . . . . . . . . . . . . . . . . . . . . . .31
- Trinidad . . . . . . . . . . . . . . . . . . . . . . . . . . . . . . . . . . . . . . . . .30
- Tobago . . . . . . . . . . . . . . . . . . . . . . . . . . . . . . . . . . . . . . . . .30
- Ukraine . . . . . . . . . . . . . . . . . . . . . . . . . . . . . . . . . . . . . . . . .29
- Vietnam . . . . . . . . . . . . . . . . . . . . . . . . . . . . . . . . . . . . . . . . .29
- Zimbabwe . . . . . . . . . . . . . . . . . . . . . . . . . . . . . . . . . . . . . .30

Gandhi, Indira . . . . . . . . . . . . . . . . . . . . . . . . . . . . . . . . .12, 13, 16
Gandhi, Mahatma . . . . . . . . . . . . . . . . . . . . . . . . . . . . . . .15, 66, 82
Ganesha (Hindu god) . . . . . . . . . . . . . . . . . . . . . . . . . . . . . . . . . .65
Gautama, Siddhartha . . . . . . . . . . . . . . . . . . . . . . . . . . . .66, 67, 104
*See also* Buddhism.
Gay marriages
*See* Marriages.
Gazetteer . . . . . . . . . . . . . . . . . . . . . . . . . . . . . . . . . . . . . . . . . . .58

Genocide
- Adana massacre of Armenians . . . . . . . . . . . . . . . . . . . . .59-60
- Rwanda . . . . . . . . . . . . . . . . . . . . . . . . . . . . . . . . . . . . . .59-60
- Yugoslavia . . . . . . . . . . . . . . . . . . . . . . . . . . . . . . . . . . . .59-60

Geography . . . . . . . . . . . . . . . . . . . . . . . . . . . . . . . . .52-58, 83-93
- names . . . . . . . . . . . . . . . . . . . . . . . . . . . . . . . . . . . . . . . . .102
- standards . . . . . . . . . . . . . . . . . . . . . . . . . .viii, 52, 53, 57, 74, 89

Geology . . . . . . . . . . . . . . . . . . . . . . . . . . . . . . . . . . . . . . . . . . . .73
Geothermal power . . . . . . . . . . . . . . . . . . . . . . . . . . . . . . . . . . . .72
*See also* Energy.
Germany
- Berlin Wall . . . . . . . . . . . . . . . . . . . . . . . . . . . . . . . . . . . . . . .9
- folktales . . . . . . . . . . . . . . . . . . . . . . . . . .37, 39, 42, 49, 50, 51, 52

Ghana (Africa)
- children . . . . . . . . . . . . . . . . . . . . . . . . . . . . . . . . . . . . . . . . .20
- cookery . . . . . . . . . . . . . . . . . . . . . . . . . . . . . . . . . . . . . . . . .26
- folktales . . . . . . . . . . . . . . . . . . . . . . . . . . . . . . . . . . . . . . . . .41
- mythology . . . . . . . . . . . . . . . . . . . . . . . . . . . . . . . . . . . .46-47

Global
- obligations . . . . . . . . . . . . . . . . . . . . . . . . . . . . . . . . . . . . . . .60
- registry . . . . . . . . . . . . . . . . . . . . . . . . . . . . . . . . . . . . . . . .112
- responsibility . . . . . . . . . . . . . . . . . . . . . . . . . . . . . . . . . . . . .70
- trends . . . . . . . . . . . . . . . . . . . . . . . . . . . . . . . . . . . . . . . . . .90
- warming . . . . . . . . . . . . . . . . . . . . . . . . . . . . . . . . . . . . .23, 70

Gods and goddesses . . . . . . . . . . . . . . . . . . . . . . . . . . . . . . . . . . .44
Gorbachev, Mikhal . . . . . . . . . . . . . . . . . . . . . . . . . . . . . . . . .15, 16
Governmental
- institutions . . . . . . . . . . . . . . . . . . . . . . . . . . . . . . . . . . . . . . .86
- organizations . . . . . . . . . . . . . . . . . . . . . . . . . . . . . . . . . . . . .86

Great Barrier Reef (Australia) . . . . . . . . . . . . . . . . . . . . . . . . .57, 71
Great Zimbabwe . . . . . . . . . . . . . . . . . . . . . . . . . . . . . . . . . . . . . . .6
Greco, El . . . . . . . . . . . . . . . . . . . . . . . . . . . . . . . . . . . . . . . . . . . .8
Greece
- ancient . . . . . . . . . . . . . . . . . . . . . . . . . . . . . . . . .1, 5, 6, 7, 86
- calendar . . . . . . . . . . . . . . . . . . . . . . . . . . . . . . . . . . . . . . . . .3
- cookery . . . . . . . . . . . . . . . . . . . . . . . . . . . . . . . . . . . . . .27, 34
- folktales . . . . . . . . . . . . . . . . . . . . . . . . . . . . . . .38, 39, 40, 49, 50
- mythology . . . . . . . . . . . . . . . . . . . . . . . . . . . . . . . . .44, 48, 51

Greenpeace . . . . . . . . . . . . . . . . . . . . . . . . . . . . . . . . . . . . . . . . .86
Gregorian calendar . . . . . . . . . . . . . . . . . . . . . . . . . . . . . . . . . . . .4
Guatemala (Central America)
- babies . . . . . . . . . . . . . . . . . . . . . . . . . . . . . . . . . . . . . . . . . .18
- folktales . . . . . . . . . . . . . . . . . . . . . . . . . . . . . . . . . . . . . . . . .39

Guevara, Che . . . . . . . . . . . . . . . . . . . . . . . . . . . . . . . . . . . . . . . .16
Guinea, Equatorial (Africa)
- cookery . . . . . . . . . . . . . . . . . . . . . . . . . . . . . . . . . . . . . . . . .34

Gulf War (Persian Gulf War) . . . . . . . . . . . . . . . . . . . . . . . . .55, 61-62

# H

Hagia Sophia . . . . . . . . . . . . . . . . . . . . . . . . . . . . . . . . . . . . . . . . .6
Haiti (West Indies)
- children . . . . . . . . . . . . . . . . . . . . . . . . . . . . . . . . . . . . . . . . .23
- cookery . . . . . . . . . . . . . . . . . . . . . . . . . . . . . . . . . . . . . . . . .27
- folktales . . . . . . . . . . . . . . . . . . . . . . . . . . . . . . . . . . . . . .43, 45
- mythology . . . . . . . . . . . . . . . . . . . . . . . . . . . . . . . . . . . .51, 80

Hajj . . . . . . . . . . . . . . . . . . . . . . . . . . . . . . . . . . . . . . . . . . . . . . .65
Halloween . . . . . . . . . . . . . . . . . . . . . . . . . . . . . . . . . . . . . . . . . .28
Hammurabi . . . . . . . . . . . . . . . . . . . . . . . . . . . . . . . . . . . . . . . . .15
Hanging Gardens of Babylon . . . . . . . . . . . . . . . . . . . . . . . . . .6, 90
Hannah (Biblical character) . . . . . . . . . . . . . . . . . . . . . . . . . . . . .68
Hanukkah (Chanukah) . . . . . . . . . . . . . . . . . . . . . . . . .46, 68, 98, 99
Hanuman (mythological character) . . . . . . . . . . . . . . . . . . . . . . .42
Harappa (Indus Valley) . . . . . . . . . . . . . . . . . . . . . . . . . . . . . . . . . .6
Hare Krishna . . . . . . . . . . . . . . . . . . . . . . . . . . . . . . . . . . . . . . . .66

Harvest celebrations . . . . . . . . . . . . . . . . . . . . . . . . . . . . . . .35
Hate
    combating . . . . . . . . . . . . . . . . . . . . . . . . . . . . . . . . . . .63
    crimes . . . . . . . . . . . . . . . . . . . . . . . . . . . . . . . . . . . . . . .63
    Internet . . . . . . . . . . . . . . . . . . . . . . . . . . . . . . . . . . . . . .63
    media . . . . . . . . . . . . . . . . . . . . . . . . . . . . . . . . . . . . . . .63
Hatshepsut . . . . . . . . . . . . . . . . . . . . . . . . . . . . . . . . . . . . . . . .16
Health
    organizations . . . . . . . . . . . . . . . . . . . . . . . . . . . . . . . .92
    personal . . . . . . . . . . . . . . . . . . . . . . . . . . . . . . . . . . . . .92
    world . . . . . . . . . . . . . . . . . . . . . . . . . . . . . . . . .90, 92, 93
Hebrew
    bible . . . . . . . . . . . . . . . . . . . . . . . . . . . . . . . . . . . . . . . .69
    calendar . . . . . . . . . . . . . . . . . . . . . . . . . . . . . . . . . . .4, 31
    language . . . . . . . . . . . . . . . . . . . . . . . . . . . . .23, 36, 89-90
    Midrash (scriptures) . . . . . . . . . . . . . . . . . . . . . . . . . . . .66
Herbs and spices . . . . . . . . . . . . . . . . . . . . . . . . . . . . . . . . . .98
Herod (Biblical character) . . . . . . . . . . . . . . . . . . . . . . . . . .13
Heyerdahl, Thor . . . . . . . . . . . . . . . . . . . . . . . . . . . . . . . . . . .14
Hiera, Amazon queen . . . . . . . . . . . . . . . . . . . . . . . . . . .16, 46
High Holy Days . . . . . . . . . . . . . . . . . . . . . . . . . . . . . . . . . . .69
Hijab . . . . . . . . . . . . . . . . . . . . . . . . . . . . . . . . . . . . . . . . . . .107
Hina Matsuri . . . . . . . . . . . . . . . . . . . . . . . . . . . . . . . . . .29, 67
Hinduism . . . . . . . . . . . . . . . . . . .65, 66, 67, 69, 105, 106, 107
    arts . . . . . . . . . . . . . . . . . . . . . . . . . . . . . . . . . . . . .106, 107
    beliefs . . . . . . . . . . . . . . . . . . . . . . . . . . . . . . . . . . . . . . .66
    customs . . . . . . . . . . . . . . . . . . . . . . . . . . . . . . . . . .65, 68
    Dharma . . . . . . . . . . . . . . . . . . . . . . . . . . . . . . . . . . . . .68
    festivals . . . . . . . . . . . . . . . . . . . .33, 65, 66, 67, 68, 106
    gods and goddesses . . . . . . . . . . . . . . . . . . . . . . . .66, 67
    history . . . . . . . . . . . . . . . . . . . . . . . . . . . . . . . . . . .66, 68
    Karma . . . . . . . . . . . . . . . . . . . . . . . . . . . . . . . . . . . . . .67
    language . . . . . . . . . . . . . . . . . . . . . . . . . . . . . . . . . . . .89
    marriage . . . . . . . . . . . . . . . . . . . . . . . . . . . . . . . . . . . .65
    mythology . . . . . . . . . . . . . . . . . . . . . . .46-47, 51, 80, 81-82
    rituals . . . . . . . . . . . . . . . . . . . . . . . . . . . . . . . . . . . . . . .65
    Sangha . . . . . . . . . . . . . . . . . . . . . . . . . . . . . . . . . . . . . .68
    sutras . . . . . . . . . . . . . . . . . . . . . . . . . . . . . . . . . . . . . . .68
    traditions . . . . . . . . . . . . . . . . . . . . . . . . . . . . . . . . . . . .28
    Vedas . . . . . . . . . . . . . . . . . . . . . . . . . . . . . . . . . . . . . . .68
    women . . . . . . . . . . . . . . . . . . . . . . . . . . . . . . . . .62-63, 107
Hirohito, Emperor ( Japan) . . . . . . . . . . . . . . . . . . . . . . . . .12
Hiroshima, Japan . . . . . . . . . . . . . . . . . . . . . . . . . . . . . . . . . .9
Hispanic American authors . . . . . . . . . . . . . . . . . . . . . . . .18
History
    world . . . . . . . . . . . . . . . . . . . . . . . . . . . . . . . . . . . .83-96
Hitler, Adolf . . . . . . . . . . . . . . . . . . . . . . . . . . . . . . . . . .13, 16
Hmong
    folktales . . . . . . . . . . . . . . . . . . . . . . . . . . . . . . . . . . . . .44
Ho Chi Minh . . . . . . . . . . . . . . . . . . . . . . . . . . . . . . . . . . . . .16
Holi 28, 29, 66
Holidays . . . . . . . . . . . . . . . . . . . . . . . . . . . . . . . . . . . . .93, 95-96
    See also Festivals; Holidays, Religious.
    Adults' Day . . . . . . . . . . . . . . . . . . . . . . . . . . . . . . . . . .31
    Big Kite Flying Day . . . . . . . . . . . . . . . . . . . . . . . . . . .32
    Burmese and Indian Founder's Day . . . . . . . . . . . . . .26
    Chinese New Year . . . . . . . . . . . . . . . . . .26, 28-29, 30, 33, 69
    Halloween . . . . . . . . . . . . . . . . . . . . . . . . . . . . . . . . . . .28
    Hina Matsuri . . . . . . . . . . . . . . . . . . . . . . . . . . . . . .29, 67
    Independence days . . . . . . . . . . . . . . . . . . . . . . . . . . . .21
    Ladies' Day . . . . . . . . . . . . . . . . . . . . . . . . . . . . . . . . . .32
    New Year's celebrations . . . . . . . . .23, 28-29, 32, 33, 46, 67, 69
    Kwanzaa . . . . . . . . . . . . . . . . . . . . . . . . . . . . . . . . . .28, 46
    Multicultural . . . . . . . . . . . . . . . . . . . . . . . . . . . . . . . . .99
    Seyin-no-Hi . . . . . . . . . . . . . . . . . . . . . . . . . . . . . . . . . .67
    Tet Nguyen-Dan (Lunar New Year Festival) . . . . . . . . . . . . . . .30
    Trung Thu . . . . . . . . . . . . . . . . . . . . . . . . . . . . . . . . . . .29
    Warriors' Memorial Day . . . . . . . . . . . . . . . . . . . . . . . .30
    Winter Solstice . . . . . . . . . . . . . . . . . . . . . . . . . . . . . . .46
Holidays, Religious
    See also Festivals; Holidays.
    Al-Hegira . . . . . . . . . . . . . . . . . . . . . . . . . . . . . . . . . . . .67
    Buddha Day . . . . . . . . . . . . . . . . . . . . . . . . . . . . . . . . .68
    Buddha's Birthday . . . . . . . . . . . . . . . . . . . . . . . . . . . .21
    Chanukah (Hanukkah) . . . . . . . . . . . . . . . . . .46, 68, 98, 99
    Christmas . . . . . . . . . . . . . . . . . . . . . . . . . . . . . .26, 28, 32
    Day of the Dead . . . . . . . . . . . . . . . . . . . .21, 28-29, 30, 99
    Diwali . . . . . . . . . . . . . . . . . . . . . . . . . . . . . . .29, 30, 33, 65
    Dussehra . . . . . . . . . . . . . . . . . . . . . . . . . . . . . . . . . . . .65
    Easter . . . . . . . . . . . . . . . . . . . . . . . . . . . . . . . . . . . .26, 29
    Eid Festivals . . . . . . . . . . . . . . . . . . . . . . . . . . . . . . . . .26
    Eid-ul-Fitr . . . . . . . . . . . . . . . . . . . . . . . . . . . . . . . . .26, 29
        See also Id-ul-Fitr.
    Hajj . . . . . . . . . . . . . . . . . . . . . . . . . . . . . . . . . . . . . . . . .65
    Hanukkah (Chanukah) . . . . . . . . . . . . . . . . . .46, 68, 98, 99
    High Holy Days . . . . . . . . . . . . . . . . . . . . . . . . . . . .69, 99
    Holi . . . . . . . . . . . . . . . . . . . . . . . . . . . . . . . . . .28, 29, 66
    Id-ul-Fitr . . . . . . . . . . . . . . . . . . . . . . . . . . . . . . . . . .30, 67
        See also Eid-ul-Fitr.
    Krishna's birthday . . . . . . . . . . . . . . . . . . . . . . . . . . . . .65
    Las Posadas . . . . . . . . . . . . . . . . . . . . . . . . . . . . . . .26, 30
    Meelad-ul-Nabal . . . . . . . . . . . . . . . . . . . . . . . . . . . . . .67
    Passover . . . . . . . . . . . . . . . . . . . . . . . . . . . . . . . . . . . . .99
    Pongal . . . . . . . . . . . . . . . . . . . . . . . . . . . . . . . . . . . . . .31
    Purim . . . . . . . . . . . . . . . . . . . . . . . . . . . . . . . . .28, 30, 99
    Ramadan . . . . . . . . . . . . . . . .21, 26, 30, 65, 67, 69, 99, 105
    Rosh Hashanah . . . . . . . . . . . . . . . . . . . . . . . . . . . .33, 99
    Shavuot . . . . . . . . . . . . . . . . . . . . . . . . . . . . . . . . . . . . .99
    Sukkot . . . . . . . . . . . . . . . . . . . . . . . . . . . . . . . . . . . .31, 99
    Twelfth Night . . . . . . . . . . . . . . . . . . . . . . . . . . . . . . . .46
    Vesak . . . . . . . . . . . . . . . . . . . . . . . . . . . . . . . . . . . . . . .28
    world . . . . . . . . . . . . . . . . . . . . . . . . . . . . . . . . . . . . . . .99
    Yom Kippur . . . . . . . . . . . . . . . . . . . . . . . . . . . . . . .31, 99
Holocaust . . . . . . . . . . . . . . . . . . . . . . . . . . . . . . . . . . . . .59, 60
Hong Kong . . . . . . . . . . . . . . . . . . . . . . . . . . . . . . . . . . . . . .84
Hortensia . . . . . . . . . . . . . . . . . . . . . . . . . . . . . . . . . . . . . . . .12
Households . . . . . . . . . . . . . . . . . . . . . . . . . . . . . . . . . . . . . .88
Huang He flood (China) . . . . . . . . . . . . . . . . . . . . . . . . . . . .76
Human Rights
    See also Freedom.
    abuses . . . . . . . . . . . . . . . . . . . . . . . . . . . . . . . . . . . . .104
    Armenia . . . . . . . . . . . . . . . . . . . . . . . . . . . . . . . . . .59-60
    Bosnia . . . . . . . . . . . . . . . . . . . . . . . . . . . . . . . . . . . . . .62
    Cambodia . . . . . . . . . . . . . . . . . . . . . . . . . . . . . . . . . . .59
    China . . . . . . . . . . . . . . . . . . . . . . . . . . . . . . . . . . . .62-63
    East Timor, Indonesia . . . . . . . . . . . . . . . . . . . . . . . . .62
    Nigeria . . . . . . . . . . . . . . . . . . . . . . . . . . . . . . . . . . .61-62
    political prisoners . . . . . . . . . . . . . . . . . . . . . . . . . . . .104
    Rwanda . . . . . . . . . . . . . . . . . . . . . . . . . . . . . . . . . . . . .59
    Universal Declaration of Human Rights . . . . . . . .61, 62, 63, 104
    Yugoslavia . . . . . . . . . . . . . . . . . . . . . . . . . . . . . . . .59-60
Hussein I, King (Jordan) . . . . . . . . . . . . . . . . . . . . . . . . . . . .16
Hussein, Saddam . . . . . . . . . . . . . . . . . . . . . . . . . . .13, 16, 61-62

# I

Ibn Battuta (Ibn Batuta) . . . . . . . . . . . . . . . . . . . . . . . . .12, 14
Icarus (mythological character) . . . . . . . . . . . . . . . . . . . . . .42

Id-Ul-Fitr . . . . . . . . . . . . . . . . . . . . . . . . . . . . . . . . . . . .30, 67
   *See also* Eid-ul-Fitr.
Immigrants
   Africa . . . . . . . . . . . . . . . . . . . . . . . . . . . . . . . . . . . . . . .64
   Americas . . . . . . . . . . . . . . . . . . . . . . . . . . . . . . . . . . . .64
   assimilation . . . . . . . . . . . . . . . . . . . . . . . . . . . . . . . . .64
   Caribbean . . . . . . . . . . . . . . . . . . . . . . . . . . . . . . . . . . .64
   contributions . . . . . . . . . . . . . . . . . . . . . . . . . . . . . .22, 64
   Eastern European . . . . . . . . . . . . . . . . . . . . . . . . . . . . .64
   Ellis Island, New York . . . . . . . . . . . . . . . .30, 64, 65, 67
   history . . . . . . . . . . . . . . . . . . . . . . . . . . . . . . . . . . . . . .64
   Mexico . . . . . . . . . . . . . . . . . . . . . . . . . . . . . . . . . . . . .64
   Middle East . . . . . . . . . . . . . . . . . . . . . . . . . . . . . . . . .64
   present-day . . . . . . . . . . . . . . . . . . . . . . . . . . . . . . .64-65
   stories . . . . . . . . . . . . . . . . . . . . . . . . . . . . . . . . . . . . . .64
   Subcontinent . . . . . . . . . . . . . . . . . . . . . . . . . . . . . . . .64
Incas
   civilization . . . . . . . . . . . . . . . . . . . . . . . . . . . . . . . . . . .8
   mythology . . . . . . . . . . . . . . . . . . . . . . . . . . . . . . .51, 80
Income . . . . . . . . . . . . . . . . . . . . . . . . . . . . . . . . . . . . . . . .88
Independence days . . . . . . . . . . . . . . . . . . . . . . . . . . . . .21
India
   Amritsar massacre . . . . . . . . . . . . . . . . . . . . . . . . . . . .61
   ancient . . . . . . . . . . . . . . . . . . . . . . . . . . . . . . . . . . .7, 86
   art . . . . . . . . . . . . . . . . . . . . . . . . . . . . . . . . .10, 79, 106
   Bhopal chemical leak . . . . . . . . . . . . . . . . . . . . . . . . . .76
   Bombay . . . . . . . . . . . . . . . . . . . . . . . . . . . . . . . . .20, 55
   caste system . . . . . . . . . . . . . . . . . . . . . . . . . . . . . . . . .60
   cookery . . . . . . . . . . . . . . . . . . . . . . . . . . . . . .27, 32, 34
   holidays . . . . . . . . . . . . . . . . . . . . . . . . . . .29, 31, 33, 98
   folktales . . . . . . . . . . .37, 38, 40, 41, 42, 43, 46, 47-48, 50, 81
   Moghul India . . . . . . . . . . . . . . . . . . . . . . . . . . . . . . . . .5
   mythology . . . . . . . . . . . . . . . . . . . . . . . . . .44, 46, 47, 48
   purdah . . . . . . . . . . . . . . . . . . . . . . . . . . . . . . . . . . .62-63
   rhymes . . . . . . . . . . . . . . . . . . . . . . . . . . . . . . . . . . . . .11
   sati . . . . . . . . . . . . . . . . . . . . . . . . . . . . . . . . . . . . . .62-63
   women . . . . . . . . . . . . . . . . . . . . . . . . . . . . . . . .62-63, 106
Indonesia
   Bali . . . . . . . . . . . . . . . . . . . . . . . . . . . . . . . . . . . . .10, 18
   cookery . . . . . . . . . . . . . . . . . . . . . . . . . . . . . . . . . . . .32
   East Timor . . . . . . . . . . . . . . . . . . . . . . . . . . . . . . . . . .62
   folktales . . . . . . . . . . . . . . . . . . . . . . . . . . . . . . . . .41, 49
   Java . . . . . . . . . . . . . . . . . . . . . . . . . . . . . . . . . . . . . . .31
   Krakatoa . . . . . . . . . . . . . . . . . . . . . . . . . . . . . . . . . . .76
   language . . . . . . . . . . . . . . . . . . . . . . . . . . . . . . . . . . .89
Indus Valley . . . . . . . . . . . . . . . . . . . . . . . . . . . . . . . . . .4, 6
   Harappa . . . . . . . . . . . . . . . . . . . . . . . . . . . . . . . . . . . . .6
   Mohenjo-Daro . . . . . . . . . . . . . . . . . . . . . . . . . . . . . . . .6
Infant mortality . . . . . . . . . . . . . . . . . . . . . . . . . . . . . . . .88
Information Literacy Standards (AASL) . . . . . . . . . . . .vii
International law . . . . . . . . . . . . . . . . . . . . . . . . . . . .86, 91
International organizations . . . . . . . . . . . . . . . . .90-91, 100
Inventions . . . . . . . . . . . . . . . . . . . . . . . . . . . . . . . . . .35, 77
Iran
   ancient . . . . . . . . . . . . . . . . . . . . . . . . . . . . . . . . . . . . .92
   art . . . . . . . . . . . . . . . . . . . . . . . . . . . . . . . . . . . . . . . . .10
   folktales . . . . . . . . . . . . . . . . . . . . . . . . . . . . . . . .37, 47-48
   Kurds . . . . . . . . . . . . . . . . . . . . . . . . . . . . . . . . . . . . . .62
   punishment . . . . . . . . . . . . . . . . . . . . . . . . . . . . . . . . .59
   rhymes . . . . . . . . . . . . . . . . . . . . . . . . . . . . . . . . . . . . .11
Iraq
   children . . . . . . . . . . . . . . . . . . . . . . . . . . . . . . . . . . . .21
   folktales . . . . . . . . . . . . . . . . . . . . . . . . . . . . . . . . . . . .43
Isabella I, Queen of Spain . . . . . . . . . . . . . . . . . . . . .13, 16

Islam . . . . . . . . . . . . . . . . . . .65, 66, 67, 91-92, 104, 105, 106, 107
   *See also* Muslims.
   Allah . . . . . . . . . . . . . . . . . . . . . . . . . . . . . . . . . . . . . .65
   calendar . . . . . . . . . . . . . . . . . . . . . . . . . . . . . . . . . . . .31
   culture . . . . . . . . . . . . . . . . . . . . . . . . . . . . . . . . . . . . .65
   five pillars . . . . . . . . . . . . . . . . . . . . . . . . . . . . . . . . . .69
   hijab . . . . . . . . . . . . . . . . . . . . . . . . . . . . . . . . . . . . . .107
   history . . . . . . . . . . . . . . . . . . . . . . . . . . . . . . . . . .65, 106
   holy days . . . . . . . . . . . . . . . . . . . . . . . . . . . . . . . .65, 104
   Jihad . . . . . . . . . . . . . . . . . . . . . . . . . . . . . . . . . . . . .104
   law . . . . . . . . . . . . . . . . . . . . . . . . . . . . . . . . . . . .65, 104
   mosques . . . . . . . . . . . . . . . . . . . . . . . . . . . . . . . .65, 106
   Muhammed (Mohammed), prophet . . . . . . . . . .65, 66, 69, 106
   Quran (Koran, Qu'ran) . . . . . . . . . . . . . . . . . .65, 69, 104
   rituals . . . . . . . . . . . . . . . . . . . . . . . . . . . . . . . . . . . . . .65
   Sunnah . . . . . . . . . . . . . . . . . . . . . . . . . . . . . . . . . . .104
   women . . . . . . . . . . . . . . . . . . . . . . . . . . . . . . . .104, 107
Islands
   famous . . . . . . . . . . . . . . . . . . . . . . . . . . . . . . . . . .54, 57
   formation . . . . . . . . . . . . . . . . . . . . . . . . . . . . . . . . . .53
   lifestyle . . . . . . . . . . . . . . . . . . . . . . . . . . . . . . .53, 54, 57
   vegetation . . . . . . . . . . . . . . . . . . . . . . . . . . . . . . .53, 54
Israel
   art . . . . . . . . . . . . . . . . . . . . . . . . . . . . . . . . . . . . . . . . .10
   children . . . . . . . . . . . . . . . . . . . . . . . . . . . . . . . . . . . .21
   cookery . . . . . . . . . . . . . . . . . . . . . . . . . . . . . . . . . . . .27
   games . . . . . . . . . . . . . . . . . . . . . . . . . . . . . . . . . . .29, 30
   holidays . . . . . . . . . . . . . . . . . . . . . . . . . . . . . . . . .31, 33
   Jerusalem . . . . . . . . . . . . . . . . . . . . . . . . . . . . . . . . . .55
   Judaism . . . . . . . . . . . . . . . . . . . . . . . . .65, 66, 67, 69, 105, 107
   rhymes . . . . . . . . . . . . . . . . . . . . . . . . . . . . . . . . . . . . .11
Italy
   folktales . . . . . . . . . . . . . . . . . . . . . . . . . . . . . . . . . . . .52
   language . . . . . . . . . . . . . . . . . . . . . . . . . . . . .23, 36, 101
Ivan the Terrible . . . . . . . . . . . . . . . . . . . . . . . . . . . .12, 13
Ivanova, Anna . . . . . . . . . . . . . . . . . . . . . . . . . . . . . . . . . .8

# J

Jael (Biblical character) . . . . . . . . . . . . . . . . . . . . . . . . .68
Jainism . . . . . . . . . . . . . . . . . . . . . . . . . . .65, 66, 67, 105, 106
Japan
   art . . . . . . . . . . . . . . . . . . . . . . . . . . . . . . . . . . . . . . .9, 79
   cookery . . . . . . . . . . . . . . . . . . . . . . . . . . . . . . .26, 27, 34
   culture . . . . . . . . . . . . . . . . . . . . . . . . . . . . . . . .24, 79, 93
   folktales . . . . .36, 38, 39, 40, 41, 42, 44, 45, 46, 47, 48, 49, 50, 81
   games . . . . . . . . . . . . . . . . . . . . . . . . . . . . . . . . . . .28, 35
   Hiroshima . . . . . . . . . . . . . . . . . . . . . . . . . . . . . . . . . . .9
   holidays . . . . . . . . . . . . . . . . . . . . . . . . . . . . . . . . . . . .98
   Kabuki theater . . . . . . . . . . . . . . . . . . . . . . . . . . . . . . . .9
   Kobe . . . . . . . . . . . . . . . . . . . . . . . . . . . . . . . . . . . . . .76
   language . . . . . . . . . . . . . . . . . . . . . . . . . . . . .23, 36, 89-90
   mythology . . . . . . . . . . . . . . . . . . . . . .44, 46, 47, 48, 80, 81-82
   religions . . . . . . . . . . . . . . . . . . . . . . . . . . . . . . . . . . . .65
   rhymes . . . . . . . . . . . . . . . . . . . . . . . . . . . . . . . . . . . . .11
   Tokugawa Japan . . . . . . . . . . . . . . . . . . . . . . . . . . . . . .5
   Tokyo . . . . . . . . . . . . . . . . . . . . . . . . . . . . . . . . . . . . . .84
   traditions . . . . . . . . . . . . . . . . . . . . . . . . . . . . . . . . . . .28
Java, Indonesia
   games . . . . . . . . . . . . . . . . . . . . . . . . . . . . . . . . . . . . .31
Jemison, Mae . . . . . . . . . . . . . . . . . . . . . . . . . . . . . . . . . .14
Jerusalem . . . . . . . . . . . . . . . . . . . . . . . . . . . . . . . . . . . . .69
Jesus (Biblical character) . . . . . . . . . . . . . . . . . . .66, 67, 68
Jewelry . . . . . . . . . . . . . . . . . . . . . . . . . . . . . . . . . . . . . . . .2

Johannesburg, South Africa . . . . . . . . . . . . . . . . . . . . . . . . . . . . .20
Jordan
    games . . . . . . . . . . . . . . . . . . . . . . . . . . . . . . . . . . . . . . . . .28
    holidays . . . . . . . . . . . . . . . . . . . . . . . . . . . . . . . . . . . . . . .29
    Petra . . . . . . . . . . . . . . . . . . . . . . . . . . . . . . . . . . . . . . . .6, 22
Judaism . . . . . . . . . . . . . . . . . . . . . . . . . . .65, 66, 67, 69, 105, 107
    Bar Mitzvah . . . . . . . . . . . . . . . . . . . . . . . . . . . . . . . . . . . .69
    customs . . . . . . . . . . . . . . . . . . . . . . . . . . . . . . . . . . . . . . .69
    Hebrew bible . . . . . . . . . . . . . . . . . . . . . . . . . . . . . . . . . .69
    High holy days . . . . . . . . . . . . . . . . . . . . . . . . . . . . . . . .69
    Jerusalem . . . . . . . . . . . . . . . . . . . . . . . . . . . . . . . . . . . . .69
    mythology . . . . . . . . . . . . . . . . . . . . . . . . . . . . . . . . . . . .80
    rituals . . . . . . . . . . . . . . . . . . . . . . . . . . . . . . . . . . . . . . . .69
    Sabbath . . . . . . . . . . . . . . . . . . . . . . . . . . . . . . . . . . . . . . .69
    traditions . . . . . . . . . . . . . . . . . . . . . . . . . . . . . . . . . . . . .28
    women . . . . . . . . . . . . . . . . . . . . . . . . . . . . . . . . . . . . . . .82
Jung, Carl . . . . . . . . . . . . . . . . . . . . . . . . . . . . . . . . . . . . . . . . . . .17

# K

Kabuki theater, Japan . . . . . . . . . . . . . . . . . . . . . . . . . . . . . . . . .9
Kaffiyeh . . . . . . . . . . . . . . . . . . . . . . . . . . . . . . . . . . . . . . . . . . . .23
Kahlo, Frida . . . . . . . . . . . . . . . . . . . . . . . . . . . . . . . . .11, 12, 13
Kalahari Desert (Africa) . . . . . . . . . . . . . . . . . . . . . . . . . . . . .13
Kami 67
Kampuchea, Cambodia
    Angkor Wat . . . . . . . . . . . . . . . . . . . . . . . . . . . . . . . . . . .22
    folktales . . . . . . . . . . . . . . . . . . . . . . . . . . . . . . . . . . . . . . .50
Karma . . . . . . . . . . . . . . . . . . . . . . . . . . . . . . . . . . . . . . . . . . . . .67
Keller, Helen . . . . . . . . . . . . . . . . . . . . . . . . . . . . . . . . . . . . . . .42
Kenya (Africa )
    cookery . . . . . . . . . . . . . . . . . . . . . . . . . . . . . . . . . . . . . . .34
    culture . . . . . . . . . . . . . . . . . . . . . . . . . . . . . . . . . . . . .23, 24
    games . . . . . . . . . . . . . . . . . . . . . . . . . . . . . . . . . . . . . . . .29
    folktales . . . . . . . . . . . . . . . . . . . . . . . . . . . . . . . . . . . .37, 43
    mythology . . . . . . . . . . . . . . . . . . . . . . . . . . . . . . . . . . . .47
Keypals (key pals) . . . . . . . . . . . . . . . . . . . . . . . . . . . . . .109-112
Khan, Genghis . . . . . . . . . . . . . . . . . . . . . . . . . . . . . . .12, 13, 15
Khan, Kublai, Mongol emperor of China . . . . . . . . . . . . . . .15
Khayyam, Omar . . . . . . . . . . . . . . . . . . . . . . . . . . . . . . . . . . . .12
Khomeini, Ayatollah . . . . . . . . . . . . . . . . . . . . . . . . . . .12, 61-62
Kim Il-Sung . . . . . . . . . . . . . . . . . . . . . . . . . . . . . . . . . . . . . . .13
King, Martin Luther Jr. . . . . . . . . . . . . . . . . . . . . . . . . . . .17, 63
Kingsley, Mary . . . . . . . . . . . . . . . . . . . . . . . . . . . . . . . . . . . . .14
Kiyotsugu, Japanese playwright . . . . . . . . . . . . . . . . . . . . . . .12
Kobe, Japan . . . . . . . . . . . . . . . . . . . . . . . . . . . . . . . . . . . . . . .76
Koran (Qu'ran, Quran) . . . . . . . . . . . . . . . . . . . . . . .65, 69, 104
Korea
    games . . . . . . . . . . . . . . . . . . . . . . . . . . . . . . . . . . . . . . . .28
    folktales . . . . . . . . . . . . . . . . . . . . . . . . . . . . . .36, 37, 39, 40, 50
Korean War . . . . . . . . . . . . . . . . . . . . . . . . . . . . . . . . . . . . . . . .9
    language . . . . . . . . . . . . . . . . . . . . . . . . . . . . . . . . . . . . . .89
    mythology . . . . . . . . . . . . . . . . . . . . . . . . . . . . . . . . . . . .80
Krakatoa (Indonesia) . . . . . . . . . . . . . . . . . . . . . . . . . . . . . . . .76
Krishna's birthday . . . . . . . . . . . . . . . . . . . . . . . . . . . . . . . . . .65
Kubler-Ross, Elisabeth . . . . . . . . . . . . . . . . . . . . . . . . . . . . . .14
Kwanzaa . . . . . . . . . . . . . . . . . . . . . . . . . . . . . . . . . .27, 28-29, 46

# L

Labor . . . . . . . . . . . . . . . . . . . . . . . . . . . . . . . . . . . . . .23, 62, 88
    child . . . . . . . . . . . . . . . . . . . . . . . . . . . . . . . . . . . . . . . . . .62
    forced . . . . . . . . . . . . . . . . . . . . . . . . . . . . . . . . . . . . . .62, 88
    unfair practices . . . . . . . . . . . . . . . . . . . . . . . . . . . . . . . . . .2
Ladies' Day . . . . . . . . . . . . . . . . . . . . . . . . . . . . . . . . . . . . . . . .32
Lange, Dorothea . . . . . . . . . . . . . . . . . . . . . . . . . . . . . . . . . . .36

Languages
    Africaans . . . . . . . . . . . . . . . . . . . . . . . . . . . . . . . . . . . . .101
    Arabic . . . . . . . . . . . . . . . . . . . . . . . . . . . . . . . .23, 36, 89-90
    Celtic . . . . . . . . . . . . . . . . . . . . . . . . . . . . . . . . . . . . . . . . .36
    Chinese . . . . . . . . . . . . . . . . . . . . . . . . . . . . . . . . . . .36, 89-90
    Czech . . . . . . . . . . . . . . . . . . . . . . . . . . . . . . . . . . . . . . . .101
    Dutch . . . . . . . . . . . . . . . . . . . . . . . . . . . . . . . . . . . . . . . .101
    English . . . . . . . . . . . . . . . . . . . . . . . . . . . . . . . . . . . . . . .101
    Finnish . . . . . . . . . . . . . . . . . . . . . . . . . . . . . . . . . . . . . . .101
    foreign . . . . . . . . . . . . . . . . . . . . . . . . . . . . . . . . . . . .18, 101
    French . . . . . . . . . . . . . . . . . . . . . . . . . . . . . . . . . .23, 36, 101
    German . . . . . . . . . . . . . . . . . . . . . . . . . . . . . . . . . . . . . . .101
    Hebrew . . . . . . . . . . . . . . . . . . . . . . . . . . . . . . .23, 36, 89-90
    Hindi . . . . . . . . . . . . . . . . . . . . . . . . . . . . . . . . . . . . . .89-90
    Hungarian . . . . . . . . . . . . . . . . . . . . . . . . . . . . . . . . . .23, 36
    India . . . . . . . . . . . . . . . . . . . . . . . . . . . . . . . . . . . . . . . . .36
    Indonesian . . . . . . . . . . . . . . . . . . . . . . . . . . . . . . . . . .89-90
    Italian . . . . . . . . . . . . . . . . . . . . . . . . . . . . . . . . . .23, 36, 101
    Japanese . . . . . . . . . . . . . . . . . . . . . . . . . . . . . .23, 36, 89-90
    Korean . . . . . . . . . . . . . . . . . . . . . . . . . . . . . . . . . . . .89-90
    Mayan . . . . . . . . . . . . . . . . . . . . . . . . . . . . . . . . . . . . .89-90
    Norwegian . . . . . . . . . . . . . . . . . . . . . . . . . . . . . . . . . . . .101
    Polish . . . . . . . . . . . . . . . . . . . . . . . . . . . . . . . . . . . . . .23, 36
    Portuguese . . . . . . . . . . . . . . . . . . . . . . . . . . . . . . . . . . . .101
    Russia . . . . . . . . . . . . . . . . . . . . . . . . . . . . . . . . . . .23, 36, 89
    Spanish . . . . . . . . . . . . . . . . . . . . . . . . . . . . . . . . .23, 36, 101
    Swahili . . . . . . . . . . . . . . . . . . . . . . . . . . . . . . . . . . . . . . . .89
    Swedish . . . . . . . . . . . . . . . . . . . . . . . . . . . . . . . . . . . . . . .101
    Tagalog . . . . . . . . . . . . . . . . . . . . . . . . . . . . . . . . . . . . .36, 89
    Thailand . . . . . . . . . . . . . . . . . . . . . . . . . . . . . . . . . . . . . . .89
    Turkish . . . . . . . . . . . . . . . . . . . . . . . . . . . . . . . . . . . . . . . .89
    world . . . . . . . . . . . . . . . . . . . . . . . . .35-36, 89-90, 92, 100-101
Lantern Festival . . . . . . . . . . . . . . . . . . . . . . . . . . . . . . . . . . . .33
Las Posadas . . . . . . . . . . . . . . . . . . . . . . . . . . . . . . . . . . . .26, 30
Latin America . . . . . . . . . . . . . . . . . . . . . . . . . . . . . . . . . .86, 92
Law courts . . . . . . . . . . . . . . . . . . . . . . . . . . . . . . . . . . . . . . . .86
Lawrence, T.E. . . . . . . . . . . . . . . . . . . . . . . . . . . . . . . . . . . . . .16
Lebanon
    Beirut . . . . . . . . . . . . . . . . . . . . . . . . . . . . . . . . . . . . . . . . .2
    cookery . . . . . . . . . . . . . . . . . . . . . . . . . . . . . . . . . . . . . . .26
    folktales . . . . . . . . . . . . . . . . . . . . . . . . . . . . . . . . . . . . . . .41
Legendary animals . . . . . . . . . . . . . . . . . . . . . . . . . . . . . . . . . .79
Legends . . . . . . . . . . . . . . . . . . . . . . . . . . . . . . . . . . . . .36-52, 79
    See also Folktales; Mythology.
Li Chi, Chinese queen . . . . . . . . . . . . . . . . . . . . . . . . . . . .16, 51
Life tables . . . . . . . . . . . . . . . . . . . . . . . . . . . . . . . . . . . . .88, 93
Lifestyles . . . . . . . . . . . . . . . . . . . . . . . . . . . . . . . . . . . . . . . . .92
Lighthouse at Alexandria . . . . . . . . . . . . . . . . . . . . . . . . . .6, 90
Liliuokalani, Queen of Hawaii . . . . . . . . . . . . . . . . . . . . . . . .16
Lindbergh, Charles . . . . . . . . . . . . . . . . . . . . . . . . . . . . . . . . .17
Listservs . . . . . . . . . . . . . . . . . . . . . . . . . . . . . . . . . . . . .111, 113
Literacy . . . . . . . . . . . . . . . . . . . . . . . . . . . . . . . . . . . . . . .88, 93
Livestock farming
    See Farming.
Livingstone, David . . . . . . . . . . . . . . . . . . . . . . . . . . . . . . . . .14
London, England . . . . . . . . . . . . . . . . . . . . . . . . . . . . . . . . . . .55
Louis IX, King of France . . . . . . . . . . . . . . . . . . . . . . . . . . . .42
Lydia (Biblical character) . . . . . . . . . . . . . . . . . . . . . . . . . . . .68
Lyme disease . . . . . . . . . . . . . . . . . . . . . . . . . . . . . . . . . . . . . .74
    See also Disease.

# M

MIR Space Station
    See Space Stations.

*Subject Index* 141

Machines . . . . . . . . . . . . . . . . . . . . . . . . . . . . . . . . . . . . . . . . . 6-7
Magellan, Ferdinand . . . . . . . . . . . . . . . . . . . . . . . . . . . . . . . . .14
Malaysia
    folktales . . . . . . . . . . . . . . . . . . . . . . . . . . . . . . . . . . . . .43
    Mulu Caves . . . . . . . . . . . . . . . . . . . . . . . . . . . . . . . . . .71
Mali Empire (Africa) . . . . . . . . . . . . . . . . . . . . . . . . . . . . . .5, 8
Malta
    folktales . . . . . . . . . . . . . . . . . . . . . . . . . . . . . . . . . . . . .52
    games . . . . . . . . . . . . . . . . . . . . . . . . . . . . . . . . . . . . . . .29
Mandela, Nelson . . . . . . . . . . . . . . . . . . . .15, 16, 55, 61-62, 82
Mao Zedong . . . . . . . . . . . . . . . . . . . . . . . . . . .13, 17, 59, 61-62
Maori (New Zealand)
    folktales . . . . . . . . . . . . . . . . . . . . . . . . . . . .40, 41, 49, 50
    mythology . . . . . . . . . . . . . . . . . . . . . . . . . . . . . . . .46, 51
Maps . . . . . . . . . . . . . . . .52-58, 83, 86, 87, 88, 93, 96-97, 99, 101-103
Marital status . . . . . . . . . . . . . . . . . . . . . . . . . . . . . . . . . . . .88
Marriages
    arranged . . . . . . . . . . . . . . . . . . . . . . . . . . . . . . . . . . . .61
    gay . . . . . . . . . . . . . . . . . . . . . . . . . . . . . . . . . . . . . . . . .61
    traditions . . . . . . . . . . . . . . . . . . . . . . . . . . . . . . . . . . . .35
Martha (Biblical character) . . . . . . . . . . . . . . . . . . . . . . . . .68
Marx, Karl . . . . . . . . . . . . . . . . . . . . . . . . . . . . . . . . . . . .17, 82
Mary (Biblical character) . . . . . . . . . . . . . . . . . . . . . . . . . . .68
Mary Magdalene (Biblical character) . . . . . . . . . . . . . . . . .68
Mary of Nazareth (Biblical character) . . . . . . . . . . . . . . . .68
Masada . . . . . . . . . . . . . . . . . . . . . . . . . . . . . . . . . . . . . . . . . .2
Masih, Iqba . . . . . . . . . . . . . . . . . . . . . . . . . . . . . . . . . . . . . .42
Masks . . . . . . . . . . . . . . . . . . . . . . . . . . . . . . . . . . . . . . . . . .79
Mata Hari . . . . . . . . . . . . . . . . . . . . . . . . . . . . . . . . . . . . . . .16
Maya (Americas)
    culture . . . . . . . . . . . . . . . . . . . . . . . . . . . . . . . . . . . . . .93
    empire . . . . . . . . . . . . . . . . . . . . . . . . . . . . . . . . . . . . .4, 6
    language . . . . . . . . . . . . . . . . . . . . . . . . . . . . . . . . . .89-90
    mythology . . . . . . . . . . . . . . . . . . . . . . . . . . . . . .80, 81-82
Mead, Margaret . . . . . . . . . . . . . . . . . . . . . . . . . . . . . . . . . .14
Medici, Catherine de . . . . . . . . . . . . . . . . . . . . . . . . . . . . . .16
Medicine . . . . . . . . . . . . . . . . . . . . . . . . . . . . . . . . . .7, 74, 76
Medieval Europe . . . . . . . . . . . . . . . . . . . . . . . . . . . . . . . . . .8
Mediterranean . . . . . . . . . . . . . . . . . . . . . . . . . . . . . . . . . . .92
Meelad-ul-Nabal . . . . . . . . . . . . . . . . . . . . . . . . . . . . . . . . . .67
Meir, Golda . . . . . . . . . . . . . . . . . . . . . . . . . . . . . . .13, 16, 66
Melting pot . . . . . . . . . . . . . . . . . . . . . . . . . . . . . . . . . .50, 64
Menchu, Rigoberta
Mendelssohn, Fanny . . . . . . . . . . . . . . . . . . . . . . . . . . . . . .17
Mermaid tales . . . . . . . . . . . . . . . . . . . . . . . . . . . . . . .38, 47-48
Mesopotamia
    culture . . . . . . . . . . . . . . . . . . . . . . . . . . . . . . . . . . . . . .89
    mythology . . . . . . . . . . . . . . . . . . . . . . . . . . . . . . . . . . .80
    ziggurats . . . . . . . . . . . . . . . . . . . . . . . . . . . . . . . . . . . . . .6
Mexican American
    art . . . . . . . . . . . . . . . . . . . . . . . . . . . . . . . . . . . . . . .10, 79
Mexico
    Chichen Itza . . . . . . . . . . . . . . . . . . . . . . . . . . . . . . . . . . .6
    children . . . . . . . . . . . . . . . . . . . . . . . . . . . . . . . . . . .21, 23
    cookery . . . . . . . . . . . . . . . . . . . . . . . . . . . . . . . .26, 32, 34
    culture . . . . . . . . . . . . . . . . . . . . . . . . . . . . . . . . . . . . . .85
    folktales . . . . . . . . . . . . . . . . . . . . . . . .37, 39, 41, 45, 49, 81
    games . . . . . . . . . . . . . . . . . . . . . . . . . . . . . . . . . . . .28, 29
    holidays . . . . . . . . . . . . . . . . . . . . . . . . . . . . . . . . . . . . .85
    mythology . . . . . . . . . . . . . . . . . . . . . . . . . . . . . . . . . . .47
Micronesian
    folktales . . . . . . . . . . . . . . . . . . . . . . . . . . . . . . . . . . . . .31
Mid-Autumn Festival . . . . . . . . . . . . . . . . . . . . . . . . . . . . .31

Midas, King of Phrygia . . . . . . . . . . . . . . . . . . . . . . . . . . . .43
Middle East
    ancient . . . . . . . . . . . . . . . . . . . . . . . . . . . . . . . .1, 2, 6, 7
    art . . . . . . . . . . . . . . . . . . . . . . . . . . . . . . . . . . . . . . .79, 80
    cookery . . . . . . . . . . . . . . . . . . . . . . . . . . . . . . . .27, 32, 85
    culture . . . . . . . . . . . . . . . . . . . . . . . . . . . . . . . . . . . . . .85
    folktales . . . . . . . . . . . . . . . . . . . . . . . . . . . . . . . . . . . . .81
    games . . . . . . . . . . . . . . . . . . . . . . . . . . . . . . . . . . . . . . .31
    holidays . . . . . . . . . . . . . . . . . . . . . . . . . . . . . . . . . . . . .85
    mythology . . . . . . . . . . . . . . . . . . . . . . . . . . . . . . . . . . .47
    religion . . . . . . . . . . . . . . . . . . . . . . . . . . . . . . . . . . . . .69
Midrash (Hebrew scriptures) . . . . . . . . . . . . . . . . . . . . . . .66
Migrant workers . . . . . . . . . . . . . . . . . . . . . . . . . . . . . . . . .62
Migration . . . . . . . . . . . . . . . . . . . . . . . . . . . . . . . . . . . . . . .88
Milarepa, saint and poet of Tibetan Buddhism . . . . . . . . .42
Military Leaders
    Amin, Idi . . . . . . . . . . . . . . . . . . . . . . . . . . . . . . . . .13, 16
    Bonaparte, Napoleon . . . . . . . . . . . . . . . . . . . . . . . .15, 16
    Guevara, Che . . . . . . . . . . . . . . . . . . . . . . . . . . . . . . . . .14
    Cochise (Native American) . . . . . . . . . . . . . . . . . . . . .16
    Franco, Francisco . . . . . . . . . . . . . . . . . . . . . . . . . . .13, 16
    Hitler, Adolf . . . . . . . . . . . . . . . . . . . . . . . . . . . . . . .13, 16
    Ho Chi Minh . . . . . . . . . . . . . . . . . . . . . . . . . . . . . . . . .16
    Mata Hari . . . . . . . . . . . . . . . . . . . . . . . . . . . . . . . . . . .16
    Osceola (Native American) . . . . . . . . . . . . . . . . . . . . .16
    Rabin, Yitzak . . . . . . . . . . . . . . . . . . . . . . . . . . . . . . . . .16
    Shaka, King of Africa . . . . . . . . . . . . . . . . . . . . .12, 13, 16
Milosevic, Slobodan . . . . . . . . . . . . . . . . . . . . . . . . . . . . . .16
Ministries . . . . . . . . . . . . . . . . . . . . . . . . . . . . . . . . . . . .86, 89
Miriam (Biblical character) . . . . . . . . . . . . . . . . . . . . . . . . .68
Moghul India . . . . . . . . . . . . . . . . . . . . . . . . . . . . . . . . . . . . .5
Mohenjo-Daro (Indus Valley) . . . . . . . . . . . . . . . . . . . . . . .6
Moliere (Jean Baptiste Poquelin) . . . . . . . . . . . . . . . . . . . . .8
Money
    See Currency.
Monsters . . . . . . . . . . . . . . . . . . . . . . . . . . . . . . . . . . . . .44, 80
Morocco (Africa)
    children . . . . . . . . . . . . . . . . . . . . . . . . . . . . . . . . . . . . .21
    cookery . . . . . . . . . . . . . . . . . . . . . . . . . . . . . . . . . . . . .33
    folktales . . . . . . . . . . . . . . . . . . . . . . . . . . . . . . . . . .41, 50
Morrigan, goddess of war . . . . . . . . . . . . . . . . . . . . . . . . . .45
Mosaics . . . . . . . . . . . . . . . . . . . . . . . . . . . . . . . . . . . . . . . . . .1
Moscow . . . . . . . . . . . . . . . . . . . . . . . . . . . . . . . . . . . . .55, 84
Moses (Biblical character) . . . . . . . . . . . . . . . . . . . . . . . . . .66
Mother Goose . . . . . . . . . . . . . . . . . . . . . . . . . . . . . . . . .43-44
Mother Teresa . . . . . . . . . . . . . . . . . . . . . . . . . . . . . . . . . . .66
Mount Everest . . . . . . . . . . . . . . . . . . . . . . . . . . . . . . . . . . .71
Mount Fuji . . . . . . . . . . . . . . . . . . . . . . . . . . . . . . . . . . . . . .71
Mount Rushmore . . . . . . . . . . . . . . . . . . . . . . . . . . . . . . . . .22
Mountains . . . . . . . . . . . . . . . . . . . . . . . . . . . . . . . . . . . . . .53
Muhammed (Mohammed), prophet of Islam . . . . . . . .65, 66, 69, 106
Mulu Caves (Malaysia) . . . . . . . . . . . . . . . . . . . . . . . . . . . .71
Musa, Mansa, King of Mali (Africa) . . . . . . . . . . . . . . . . . .12
Museums . . . . . . . . . . . . . . . . . . . . . . . . . . . .79, 80, 81, 92, 103
Music . . . . . . . . . . . . . . . . . . . . . . . . . . . . . . . . . . . .45, 81, 92
Muslims . . . . . . . . . . . . . . . . . . . . . . . . . . . . . .65, 67, 69, 104, 106
    See also Islam.
Mussolini, Benito . . . . . . . . . . . . . . . . . . . . . . . . . . . . . . . .17
Mythology . . . . . . . . . . . . . . . . . . . . . . . . . . . . . . .36-52, 80, 81
    See also Folktales.
    Aborigines . . . . . . . . . . . . . . . . . . . . . . . . . . . . . . . .46, 81
    Africa . . . . . . . . . . . . . . . . . . . . . . . . . . . . . . .44, 46, 51, 80
    Amazon . . . . . . . . . . . . . . . . . . . . . . . . . . . . . . . . . . .81-82
    ancient world . . . . . . . . . . . . . . . . . . . . . . . . . . . . . . . .84

| | |
|---|---|
| Australia | .44, 48 |
| Aztecs | .80, 81-82 |
| Bantu | .46-47 |
| Bolivia | .47 |
| Caribbean | .48 |
| Celtic | .44 |
| Central America | .44, 48 |
| Ceylon | .46-47 |
| China | .44, 46, 47, 48, 51, 80, 81-82 |
| Congo | .46-47 |
| dictionary | .44 |
| Egypt | .44, 46-47, 48, 80, 81-82 |
| Ethiopia | .47 |
| Europe | .51 |
| Fon | .81-82 |
| Ghana | .46-47 |
| Greece | .44, 48, 51 |
| Haiti | .51, 80 |
| Hebrew | .51 |
| Hindu | .46-47, 51, 80, 81-82 |
| Incas | .51, 80 |
| India | .44, 46, 47, 48 |
| Jain | .51 |
| Japan | .44, 46, 47, 48, 80, 81-82 |
| Judaism | .80 |
| Kenya | .47 |
| Korean | .80 |
| Maori | .46, 51 |
| Maya | .80, 81-82 |
| Melanesia | .46 |
| Mesopotamia | .80 |
| Mexico | .47 |
| Middle East | .47 |
| Mongolia | .46 |
| Near East | .44 |
| Non-Western | .80 |
| North America | .44 |
| Northern Europe | .48 |
| Norway | .44, 51 |
| Oceania | .44 |
| Persia | .46, 80 |
| Polynesia | .47, 48, 80, 81-82 |
| Rome | .44, 48 |
| Russia | .47 |
| Siberia | .46-47 |
| South America | .44 |
| Southeast Asia | .44 |
| Sumeria | .46, 47, 48, 81-82 |
| West Africa | .46-47, 48 |
| Western | .80 |
| women | .46-47 |
| world | .44, 79, 81 |
| Yoruba | .81-82 |

# N

| | |
|---|---|
| Nairobi (Africa) | .20 |
| The Namib Desert (Africa) | .71 |
| Namibia (Africa) | .26 |
| Napoleon Bonaparte | |
|     *See* Bonaparte, Napoleon. | |
| National anthems | |
|     *See* Anthems. | |
| National Council for the Social Studies ten thematic strands | .vi |
| National Geography Standards | .viii, 52, 53, 57, 74, 89 |
| National Standards for History K-4 | .vii, 74, 89 |
| National Standards for United States History | .vii, 74, 89 |
| National Standards for World History | .vii, 74, 89 |
| Native American | |
|     authors | .18 |
|     culture | .93 |
|     games | .28 |
|     folktales | .39, 49 |
|     Trail of Tears | .9 |
| Native Americans | |
|     Cochise | .16 |
|     Osceola | .16 |
|     Pocahantas | .42 |
|     Sitting Bull | .9 |
| Native religions | .65 |
| Natural gas | .90-91 |
|     *See also* Energy. | |
| Natural wonders | .71 |
| Navajo | |
|     folktales | .49 |
| Near East (Asia) | |
|     ancient | .86 |
|     art | .79 |
|     folktales | .37 |
|     mythology | .44 |
| Nepal | |
|     children | .21 |
|     folktales | .40 |
| Nero | .13 |
| New Age movements (Religion) | .66 |
| New Guinea (Pacific Islands) | |
|     children | .21 |
| New Independent States | .91 |
| New Testament (Bible) | .68 |
| New Yam Festival | .31 |
| New Year's celebrations | .23, 28-29, 32, 33, 46, 67, 69 |
|     *See also* Festivals; Holidays. | |
| New Zealand | |
|     children | .21 |
|     folktales | .38, 41 |
|     games | .30 |
| News | |
|     world | .85, 94-95 |
| Nigeria (Africa) | |
|     festivals | .28-29 |
|     folktales | .43, 49 |
|     games | .30 |
|     human rights | .61-62 |
| Non-Western | |
|     mythology | .80 |
| North Africa | .90, 91 |
| North America | |
|     art | .9 |
|     cookery | .85 |
|     culture | .85 |
|     folktales | .37, 39, 43 |
|     holidays | .85 |
|     mythology | .44 |
|     spirit religions | .66 |
| Northern Europe | .19 |
| Northeastern Europe | .19 |
| Northern Africa | .19 |
| Northern Route | .53 |

Norway
- folktales ... 51
- language ... 101
- mythology ... 44, 51

Now-Ruz festivals ... 30

Nuclear
- energy ... 90-91
  - *See also* Energy.
- families ... 61

Nunez de Balboa, Vasco ... 14
Nutrition ... 99
Nzingha, Queen of Africa ... 13, 16

# O

Oceania ... 4, 19
- mythology ... 44

Odin (mythological character) ... 43
Old Testament (Bible) ... 68
Olmec (Americas) ... 6
O'Malley, Grace (legendary character) ... 50
Organic food ... 70
  *See also* Food.
Organization of American States ... 91
Orthodox Christianity ... 105
Osceola (Native American) ... 16
Ozone
- effects of ... 75
- hole ... 75
- layer ... 75

# P

Pacific
- art ... 79
- culture ... 79
- folktales ... 38
- games ... 31
- geography ... 90, 91
- music ... 81

Pacific Islands ... 19
- Easter Island ... 22
- New Guinea ... 21

Pakistan
- games ... 29
- stories ... 26

Palace of Knossos ... 6

Panama
- children ... 21

Pantanal (Brazil) ... 71
Paper ... 27

Papua New Guinea
- babies ... 18

Paris
- museums ... 81

Parliaments ... 86
Passover ... 99
Pasteur, Louis ... 9
Peking, China ... 69
Pen pal (penpal) ... 109-113
People of the Book ... 69
Peres, Shimon ... 16
Peron, Eva ... 13
Peron, Juan ... 61-62
Persia
- ancient ... 92
- games ... 31
- mythology ... 80

Persian Gulf War ... 55, 61-62
Petra (Jordan) ... 22
Petroleum ... 90-91
  *See also* Fuel.
Peru (South America)
- art ... 10
- mythology ... 46, 80

Philippines
- children ... 33
- folktales ... 49, 51

Philosophy ... 104-108
Phoebe (Biblical character) ... 68
Pinochet, Augusto ... 13, 61-62
Plains
- lifestyle ... 54
- settlement of West ... 54
- types ... 54

Plate tectonics ... 73
Pocahontas (Native American) ... 42
Pol Pot ... 9
Political Leaders
- Bismarck, Otto von ... 17
- Bolívar, Simón ... 9, 17
- Churchill, Winston ... 17
- Dulles, John Foster ... 17
- Engels, Friedrich ... 17
- Mao Zedong ... 13, 17, 59, 61-62
- Marx, Karl ... 17, 82
- Mussolini, Benito ... 17
- Selassie, Haile ... 17
- Thatcher, Margaret ... 14, 16, 17
- Victoria, Queen of England ... 14, 16, 17

Political parties ... 86
Political resources ... 83, 89
Politics ... 83-93
Pollution ... 23, 70
Polo, Marco ... 12
Polynesia
- exploration ... 8
- mythology ... 80

Pongal ... 31
The Pope ... 68
Population
- Agenda 21 of the Earth Summit ... 71, 73, 75
- analysis ... 87, 88, 93, 100-101
- crisis ... 73
- explosion ... 18, 23, 70
- growth ... 60
- sustainable development ... 71, 73, 75
- world ... 73, 102
- World Population Clock Project ... 90

Portugal
- language ... 101
- Northern Route ... 53

Postal codes ... 93, 102
Potter, Beatrix ... 12
Pottery ... 3
Poverty ... 60
Prejudice ... 59, 60, 61, 62, 63, 81
  *See also* Racism.
Princess Diana
  *See* Diana, Princess of Wales.

Princess tales . . . . . . . . . . . . . . . . . . . . . . . . . . . . . . . . . . . .38, 46
Priscilla (Biblical character) . . . . . . . . . . . . . . . . . . . . . . . . . .68
Procula (Biblical character) . . . . . . . . . . . . . . . . . . . . . . . . . .68
Project Central America . . . . . . . . . . . . . . . . . . . . . . . . . . . .83
Propaganda . . . . . . . . . . . . . . . . . . . . . . . . . . . . . . . . . . . . . . .63
Protestantism . . . . . . . . . . . . . . . . . . . . . . . . . . . . . .68, 105, 107
    customs . . . . . . . . . . . . . . . . . . . . . . . . . . . . . . . . . . . . .68
    history . . . . . . . . . . . . . . . . . . . . . . . . . . . . . . . . . . . . . .68
    holy days . . . . . . . . . . . . . . . . . . . . . . . . . . . . . . . . . . . .68
    rituals . . . . . . . . . . . . . . . . . . . . . . . . . . . . . . . . . . . . . . .68
Puerto Rico
    cookery . . . . . . . . . . . . . . . . . . . . . . . . . . . . . . . . . . . . .27
    folktales . . . . . . . . . . . . . . . . . . . . . . . . . . . . . . . . . .38, 43
Punishment . . . . . . . . . . . . . . . . . . . . . . . . . . . . . . . . . . . . . . .59
Purdah (India) . . . . . . . . . . . . . . . . . . . . . . . . . . . . . . . . . .62-63
Purim . . . . . . . . . . . . . . . . . . . . . . . . . . . . . . . . . . . . . . . . .28, 30
Pyramids . . . . . . . . . . . . . . . . . . . . . . . . . . . . . . . . . . .6, 90, 92

# Q

Qing Dynasty . . . . . . . . . . . . . . . . . . . . . . . . . . . . . . . . . . . . . .8
Qiu Jin . . . . . . . . . . . . . . . . . . . . . . . . . . . . . . . . . . . . . . . . . . .15
Queen Isabella of Spain
    *See* Isabella, Queen of Spain.

Queen Liliuokalani
    *See* Liliuokalani, Queen of Hawaii.
Queen of Sheba (Biblical character) . . . . . . . . . . . . . . . . . . .68
Queen Victoria
    *See* Victoria, Queen of England.
Qur'an (Koran, Quran) . . . . . . . . . . . . . . . . . . . . . . .65, 69, 104

# R

Rabin, Yitzak . . . . . . . . . . . . . . . . . . . . . . . . . . . . . . . . . . . . . .16
Race . . . . . . . . . . . . . . . . . . . . . . . . . . . . . . . . . . . . . . . . . .59, 90
Racism . . . . . . . . . . . . . . . . . . . . . . . . . . . . . . . . .23, 58-64, 81
    *See also* Prejudice.
Rahab (Biblical character) . . . . . . . . . . . . . . . . . . . . . . . . . . .68
Rain forest (rainforest)
    Amazon . . . . . . . . . . . . . . . . . . . . . . . . . . . . . . . . . . . . .71
    animals . . . . . . . . . . . . . . . . . . . . . . . . . . . . . . .54, 73, 76
    deforestation . . . . . . . . . . . . . . . . . . . . . . . . . . . . . . . . .73
    endangered species . . . . . . . . . . . . . . . . . . . . . . . . .73, 76
    people . . . . . . . . . . . . . . . . . . . . . . . . . . . . . . . . . . .54, 76
    plants . . . . . . . . . . . . . . . . . . . . . . . . . . . . . . . .54, 73, 76
    protection . . . . . . . . . . . . . . . . . . . . . . . . . .54, 76, 86-87, 108
Ramadan . . . . . . . . . . . . . . . . . . . .21, 26, 30, 65, 67, 69, 99, 105
Ramphele, Mamphela . . . . . . . . . . . . . . . . . . . . . . . . . . . . . .14
Rastafarianism . . . . . . . . . . . . . . . . . . . . . . . . . . . . . . . . . . .105
Reader's Theater . . . . . . . . . . . . . . . . . . . . . . . . . . . . . . .36, 79
Rebekah (Biblical character) . . . . . . . . . . . . . . . . . . . . . . . . .68
Recycling . . . . . . . . . . . . . . . . . . . . . . . . . . . . . . . . . . . . . . . .70
    *See also* Ecology.
Reformation . . . . . . . . . . . . . . . . . . . . . . . . . . . . . . . . . . . . . . .8
Religion
    ancient . . . . . . . . . . . . . . . . . . . . . . . . . . . . . . . . . . . . . .65
    Baha'i . . . . . . . . . . . . . . . . . . . . . . . . . . . . . . . . . . .66, 106
    Bahaism . . . . . . . . . . . . . . . . . . . . . . . . . . . . . . . . . . . .106
    Buddhism . . . . . . . .65, 66, 67, 68, 69, 91-92, 104, 105, 106, 107
    Catholicism . . . . . . . . . . . . . . . . . . . . . . . . . . . .66, 68, 105
    China . . . . . . . . . . . . . . . . . . . . . . . . . . . . . . . . . . . . . . .65
    Christianity . . . . . . . .28, 65, 66, 67, 69, 91-92, 105, 106, 107
    Confucianism . . . . . . . . . . . . . . . . . . . . . . . . . . .67, 105, 107
    Eastern Orthodox Christianity . . . . . . . . . . . . . .66, 68, 107
    Folk religion . . . . . . . . . . . . . . . . . . . . . . . . . . . . . . . . .107
    Hare Krishna . . . . . . . . . . . . . . . . . . . . . . . . . . . . . . . . . . . . . .66
    Hinduism . . . . . . . . . . . . . . . . . .65, 66, 67, 69, 105, 106, 107
    Islam . . . . . . . . . . . . . . . . . .65, 66, 67, 91, 104, 105, 106, 107
    Jainism . . . . . . . . . . . . . . . . . . . . . . . . . . .65, 66, 67, 105, 106
    Japan . . . . . . . . . . . . . . . . . . . . . . . . . . . . . . . . . . . . . . .65
    Judaism . . . . . . . . . . . . . . . . . . . .65, 66, 67, 69, 105, 107
    Muslims . . . . . . . . . . . . . . . . . . . . . . . . . . . . . . .65, 67, 69
    Native religions . . . . . . . . . . . . . . . . . . . . . . . . . . . . . . .65
    New Age movements . . . . . . . . . . . . . . . . . . . . . . . . . .66
    Orthodox Christianity . . . . . . . . . . . . . . . . . . . . . . . . .105
    Protestantism . . . . . . . . . . . . . . . . . . . . . . . . . .68, 105, 107
    Rastafarianism . . . . . . . . . . . . . . . . . . . . . . . . . . . . . . .105
    Roman Catholicism
        *See* Catholicism.
    Shinto . . . . . . . . . . . . . . . . . . . . . . . . . . . . . . . .67, 105, 106
    Sikhism . . . . . . . . . . . . . . . . . . . . . . . . . .65, 66, 67, 105, 106
    Spirit religions . . . . . . . . . . . . . . . . . . . . . . . . . . . . . . . .66
    Taoism (Daoism) . . . . . . . . . . . . . . . . . .9, 67, 105, 107, 108
    world religions . . . . . . . . . . . . . . . . . . .83-84, 89, 104-108
    Zen . . . . . . . . . . . . . . . . . . . . . . . . . . . . . . . . . . . .105, 108
    Zoroastrianism . . . . . . . . . . . . . . . . . . . . . . . . .44, 67, 106
Remarkable Women
    Albright, Madeleine . . . . . . . . . . . . . . . . . . . . . . . . . . . . .9
    Angelou, Maya . . . . . . . . . . . . . . . . . . . . . . . . . . . . . . .12
    Aquino, Corazon . . . . . . . . . . . . . . . . . . . . . . . . . . .15, 16
    Aung San Suu Kyi . . . . . . . . . . . . . . . . . . . . . . . . . .13, 62
    Bandaranaike, Sirimavo . . . . . . . . . . . . . . . . . . . . . . . . .15
    Bethune, Mary McLeod . . . . . . . . . . . . . . . . . . . . . . . . .17
    Bhutto, Benazir . . . . . . . . . . . . . . . . . . . . . . . . . . . .14, 16
    Blackwell, Elizabeth . . . . . . . . . . . . . . . . . . . . . . . . . . .14
    Bourke-White, Margaret . . . . . . . . . . . . . . . . . . . . . . . .12
    Carson, Rachel . . . . . . . . . . . . . . . . . . . . . . . . . . . . . . . .17
    Catherine the Great, Tsarina . . . . . . . . . . . . . .12, 13, 14, 16
    Chiyo, Uno . . . . . . . . . . . . . . . . . . . . . . . . . . . . . . . . . .12
    Cleopatra, Queen of
        Egypt . . . . . . . . . . . . . . . . . . . . . . . . . . . .13, 14, 15, 16
    de Beauvoir, Simone . . . . . . . . . . . . . . . . . . . . . . . . . . .17
    Desai, Anita . . . . . . . . . . . . . . . . . . . . . . . . . . . . . . . . . .12
    Diana, Princess of Wales . . . . . . . . . . . . . . . . . . . . . . . .17
    Dickinson, Emily . . . . . . . . . . . . . . . . . . . . . . . . . . . . . .12
    Ding Ling . . . . . . . . . . . . . . . . . . . . . . . . . . . . . . . . . . .12
    Earle, Sylvia Alice . . . . . . . . . . . . . . . . . . . . . . . . . . . . .14
    Earhart, Amelia . . . . . . . . . . . . . . . . . . . . . . . . . . . . . . . .9
    Elizabeth I, Queen of England . . . . . . . . . . . . . . . . . . .14
    En Hedu'Anna . . . . . . . . . . . . . . . . . . . . . . . . . . . . . . .82
    Frank, Anne . . . . . . . . . . . . . . . . . . . . . . . . . . . . . . . . . .12
    Gandhi, Indira . . . . . . . . . . . . . . . . . . . . . . . . .12, 13, 15, 16
    Hatshepsut . . . . . . . . . . . . . . . . . . . . . . . . . . . . . . . . . . .16
    Hortensia . . . . . . . . . . . . . . . . . . . . . . . . . . . . . . . . . . . .12
    Isabella I, Queen of Spain . . . . . . . . . . . . . . . . .13, 14, 16
    Jemison, Mae . . . . . . . . . . . . . . . . . . . . . . . . . . . . . . . . .14
    Kahlo, Frida . . . . . . . . . . . . . . . . . . . . . . . . . . . .11, 12, 13
    Keller, Helen . . . . . . . . . . . . . . . . . . . . . . . . . . . . . . . . .42
    Kingsley, Mary . . . . . . . . . . . . . . . . . . . . . . . . . . . . . . .14
    Kubler-Ross, Elisabeth . . . . . . . . . . . . . . . . . . . . . . . . . .14
    Lange, Dorothea . . . . . . . . . . . . . . . . . . . . . . . . . . . . . .12
    Liliuokalani, Queen of Hawaii . . . . . . . . . . . . . . . . . . .16
    Mead, Margaret . . . . . . . . . . . . . . . . . . . . . . . . . . . . . . .14
    Medici, Catherine de . . . . . . . . . . . . . . . . . . . . . . . . . . .16
    Meir, Golda . . . . . . . . . . . . . . . . . . . . . . . . . .12, 13, 14, 16
    Menchu, Rigoberta . . . . . . . . . . . . . . . . . . . . . . . . . . . .17
    Mother Teresa . . . . . . . . . . . . . . . . . . . . . . . . . . . . . . . .15
    Nzingha, Queen of Africa . . . . . . . . . . . . . . . . . . . .13, 16

Peron, Eva .................................................. 13
　　　Pocahontas (Native American) ............................... 42
　　　Potter, Beatrix ............................................. 12
　　　Qiu Jin ..................................................... 15
　　　Ramphele, Mamphela .......................................... 14
　　　Ringgold, Faith ............................................. 12
　　　Roosevelt, Eleanor .......................................... 17
　　　Rossi, Properzia de' ........................................ 12
　　　Rudolph, Wilma .............................................. 42
　　　Shikibu, Murasaki ....................................... 13, 15
　　　Sullivan, Anne .............................................. 42
　　　Tao-sheng, Kuan ............................................. 12
　　　Thatcher, Margaret ...................................... 14, 16
　　　Uemura, Naomi ............................................... 14
　　　Victoria, Queen of England .............................. 14, 16
　　　Wilder, Laura Ingalls ....................................... 12
Rembrandt van Rijn ................................................. 8
Renewable energy sources ..................................... 72, 90-91
　　　*See also* Energy.
Rhee, Syngman .................................................... 13
Rights
　　　children's .................................................. 61
　　　home ........................................................ 61
　　　human rights
　　　　　*See* Human Rights.
　　　right to dignity ............................................ 61
　　　right to privacy ............................................ 61
　　　women's ................................................. 60, 62-63
　　　workers ..................................................... 62
Rivers
　　　energy ...................................................... 54
　　　preservation ................................................ 54
　　　transportation .............................................. 54
Robin Hood ....................................................... 50
Rome
　　　calendar ............................................... 3, 5, 31
Roman Empire ................................................... 1, 4
Roosevelt, Eleanor ............................................... 17
Rosh Hashanah .................................................... 33
The Ross Ice Shelf ............................................... 71
Rossi, Properzia de' (sculptor) .................................. 12
Rudolph, Wilma ................................................... 42
Rulers ........................................................... 83
Rushdie, Salman ............................................... 61-62
Rushmore, Mount .................................................. 22
Russia
　　　Catherine the Great, Tsarina ........................ 12, 13, 14, 16
　　　children ........................................... 20, 21, 22, 23
　　　chronology .................................................. 91
　　　cookery ................................................. 32, 34
　　　culture ..................................................... 24
　　　Easter .................................................. 26, 29
　　　folktales ................ 36, 39, 42, 43, 44, 45, 47, 50, 81
　　　games ................................................... 29, 31
　　　holidays .................................................... 98
　　　language ............................................ 23, 36, 89-90
　　　Moscow .................................................. 55, 84
　　　mythology ................................................... 47
　　　rhymes ...................................................... 11
　　　traditions .................................................. 28
Ruth (Biblical character) ........................................ 68
Rwanda (Africa)
　　　human rights ................................................ 59

# S

S.S. Manhattan
　　　*See* Ships.
Sabbath .......................................................... 69
Safety on the job ................................................ 62
Sahara Desert ........................................... 53-54, 56, 57
Saladin .......................................................... 12
Sale of people ................................................... 62
Sarah (Biblical character) ........................................
Sari ......................................................... 23, 26
Sasani, Sadako ................................................... 16
Sati .......................................................... 62-63
Saudi Arabia
　　　Children ................................................ 21, 22
Sea
　　　dams ........................................................ 54
　　　floods ...................................................... 54
　　　lifestyle ................................................... 54
　　　resources ................................................... 54
Selassie, Haile .................................................. 17
7-5-3 Festival ................................................... 67
Seven Wonders of the World ....................... 6, 18, 22, 90, 92
　　　Hanging Gardens of Babylon ............................. 6, 90
　　　Pharos (lighthouse) of Alexandria ......................... 90
　　　Pyramids of Egypt ...................................... 6, 90
Seven Years' War .................................................. 9
Seyin-no-Hi ...................................................... 67
Shaka, King of Africa ................................... 12, 13, 16
Shakespeare, William .............................................. 8
Shapka ........................................................... 23
Shavuot
　　　*See also* Holidays, Religious.
Shikibu, Murasaki ............................................ 13, 15
Shinto ................................................ 67, 105, 106
　　　customs ..................................................... 67
　　　history ..................................................... 67
　　　holy days ................................................... 67
　　　marriage rituals ............................................ 67
Ships
　　　S.S. Manhattan .............................................. 14
Siberia
　　　folktales ................................................... 81
　　　mythology ............................................... 46-47
Siddhartha Gautama .......................................... 67, 104
　　　*See also* Buddhism.
Sikhism .......................................... 65, 66, 67, 105, 106
Singapore ...................................................... 8, 84
Singh, Guru Gobind ............................................... 12
Sitting Bull (Native American) .................................... 9
Slavery ....................................................... 62-63
Snail mail .................................................. 109, 111
Social issues ................................................. 58-64
　　　alcoholism .............................................. 58-59
　　　ethics ...................................................... 60
　　　prejudice ..................... 59, 60, 61, 62, 63, 81
　　　　　*See also* Racism.
　　　prostitution ................................................ 59
　　　shelters .................................................... 59
Social Studies Standards ................................ vii, 74, 89
Solar power ...................................................... 72
　　　*See also* Energy.
Solzhenitsyn, Alexander ....................................... 61-62
Somalia (Africa)
　　　games ....................................................... 30

Songhai (Songhay) (Africa) . . . . . . . . . . . . . . . . . . . . . . . . . . .12
South America . . . . . . . . . . . . . . . . . . . . . . . . . . . . . .19, 89, 92
    Argentina . . . . . . . . . . . . . . . . . . . . . . . . . . . . . . . . . . .24
    Brazil . . . . . . . . . . . . . . . . . . . . .10, 11, 13, 18, 20, 22, 26, 29, 30
    Bolivia . . . . . . . . . . . . . . . . . . . . . . . . . . . . . . . . . . . . .30
    children . . . . . . . . . . . . . . . . . . . . . . . . . . . . . . . . . .18, 22
    chronology . . . . . . . . . . . . . . . . . . . . . . . . . . . . . . . .91-92
    culture . . . . . . . . . . . . . . . . . . . . . . . . . . . . . . . . . . . . .85
    folktale . . . . . . . . . . . . . . . . . . . . . . . . . . . . . . . . . . . . .37
    games . . . . . . . . . . . . . . . . . . . . . . . . . . . . . . . . . . . . .31
    holidays . . . . . . . . . . . . . . . . . . . . . . . . . . . . . . . . . . . .85
    mythology . . . . . . . . . . . . . . . . . . . . . . . . . . . . . . . . . . .44
    Peru . . . . . . . . . . . . . . . . . . . . . . . . . . . . . . . . . .10, 46, 80
    spirit religions . . . . . . . . . . . . . . . . . . . . . . . . . . . . . . . . .66
South Asia . . . . . . . . . . . . . . . . . . . . . . . . . . . . . . . . . . .4, 91
Southeast Asia . . . . . . . . . . . . . . . . . . . . . . . . . . . . . . . . . .89
    folktale . . . . . . . . . . . . . . . . . . . . . . . . . . . . . . . . . . . . .42
    mythology . . . . . . . . . . . . . . . . . . . . . . . . . . . . . . . . . . .44
Southern Africa . . . . . . . . . . . . . . . . . . . . . . . . . . . . . . .18, 81
    folktale . . . . . . . . . . . . . . . . . . . . . . . . . . . . . . . . . . . . .38
Southern Asia . . . . . . . . . . . . . . . . . . . . . . . . . . . . . . . .19, 91
Space . . . . . . . . . . . . . . . . . . . . . . . . . . . . . . . . . . . . . . . .92
Space Stations
    MIR . . . . . . . . . . . . . . . . . . . . . . . . . . . . . . . . . . . . . . .22
Spain
    culture . . . . . . . . . . . . . . . . . . . . . . . . . . . . . . . . . . . . .93
    life in a castle . . . . . . . . . . . . . . . . . . . . . . . . . . . . . . . . . .5
    language . . . . . . . . . . . . . . . . . . . . . . . . . . . . .23, 36, 101
Sphinx . . . . . . . . . . . . . . . . . . . . . . . . . . . . . . . . . . . . . . . .6
Spirit religions . . . . . . . . . . . . . . . . . . . . . . . . . . . . . . . . . .66
Sports . . . . . . . . . . . . . . . . . . . . . . . . . . . . . . .25, 30, 35, 93
Spring Festival . . . . . . . . . . . . . . . . . . . . . . . . . . . . . . . . . .26
Sri Lanka
    cookery . . . . . . . . . . . . . . . . . . . . . . . . . . . . . . . . . . . .26
    folktales . . . . . . . . . . . . . . . . . . . . . . . . . . . . . . . . . . . .45
    holidays . . . . . . . . . . . . . . . . . . . . . . . . . . . . . . . . . . . .29
Stalin, Joseph . . . . . . . . . . . . . . . . . . . . . . . . . . . . . . . .13, 82
Standards
    information literacy . . . . . . . . . . . . . . . . . . . . . . . . . . . . .vii
    geography . . . . . . . . . . . . . . . . . . . .viii, 52, 53, 57, 74, 89
    social studies . . . . . . . . . . . . . . . . . . . . . . . . . . .vii, 74, 89
Statistical indicators . . . . . . . . . . . . . . . . . . . . . . . . . . . .88, 90
Storytelling . . . . . . . . . . . . . . . . . . . . . . . . . . . . . . . . . .43, 44
    See also Folktales; Mythology.
The Subcontinent
    immigration . . . . . . . . . . . . . . . . . . . . . . . . . . . . . . . . . .64
Sub-Saharan Africa . . . . . . . . . . . . . . . . . . . . . . . . . . . .90, 91
Sudan (Africa)
    children . . . . . . . . . . . . . . . . . . . . . . . . . . . . . . . . . . . .23
    folktales . . . . . . . . . . . . . . . . . . . . . . . . . . . . . . . . . . . .42
Suez Canal . . . . . . . . . . . . . . . . . . . . . . . . . . . . . . . . . . . . .9
Sugihara, Chiune . . . . . . . . . . . . . . . . . . . . . . . . . . . . . . . .15
Sukarno, Achmed . . . . . . . . . . . . . . . . . . . . . . . . . . . . . . .12
Sukkot . . . . . . . . . . . . . . . . . . . . . . . . . . . . . . . . . . . . . . .31
Suleyman the Merchant (Suleiman I) . . . . . . . . . . . . . .12, 14, 82
Sullivan, Anne . . . . . . . . . . . . . . . . . . . . . . . . . . . . . . . . . .42
Sumerians . . . . . . . . . . . . . . . . . . . . . . . . .4, 6, 46, 47, 48, 81-82
    mythology . . . . . . . . . . . . . . . . . . . . . . . .46, 47, 48, 81-82
Sumers of Urak . . . . . . . . . . . . . . . . . . . . . . . . . . . . . . . . . .2
Sundiata, African warrior . . . . . . . . . . . . . . . . . . . . . . . . . . .42
Sunnah . . . . . . . . . . . . . . . . . . . . . . . . . . . . . . . . . . .104, 107
Supernatural creatures . . . . . . . . . . . . . . . . . . . . . . . . . . . .79
Sustainable development . . . . . . . . . . . . . . . . . . . . .71, 73, 75

Sustainable farming
    See Farming.
Sutras . . . . . . . . . . . . . . . . . . . . . . . . . . . . . . . . . . . . . . .68
Sutton Hoo Boat Burial . . . . . . . . . . . . . . . . . . . . . . . . . . . . .2
Swahili . . . . . . . . . . . . . . . . . . . . . . . . . . . . . . . . . . . .89-90
Sydney, Australia . . . . . . . . . . . . . . . . . . . . . . . . . . . . . . . .20
    Opera House . . . . . . . . . . . . . . . . . . . . . . . . . . . . . . . . .22

# T

Tabitha (Biblical character) . . . . . . . . . . . . . . . . . . . . . . . . . .68
Tagalog . . . . . . . . . . . . . . . . . . . . . . . . . . . . . . . . . .36, 89-90
Tagore, Rabindranath . . . . . . . . . . . . . . . . . . . . . . . . . . .11, 17
Taiwan
    folk religion . . . . . . . . . . . . . . . . . . . . . . . . . . . . . . . . .107
Taliban (Afghanistan) . . . . . . . . . . . . . . . . . . . . . . . . . . .62-63
Tanabata (Star Festival) . . . . . . . . . . . . . . . . . . . . . . . . .28, 29
Tanzania (Africa) . . . . . . . . . . . . . . . . . . . . . . . . . . . . . . . .20
Taoism (Daoisim) . . . . . . . . . . . . . . . . . . . .9, 67, 105, 107, 108
Tao-sheng, Kuan . . . . . . . . . . . . . . . . . . . . . . . . . . . . . . . .12
Tell al-Amarna (Egypt) . . . . . . . . . . . . . . . . . . . . . . . . . . . . .6
Terra-cotta warriors (China) . . . . . . . . . . . . . . . . . . . . . . . . . .2
Tet Nguyen-Dan (Vietnamese Lunar New Year Festival) . . . . . . . . . .30
    See also Festivals; Holidays; Vietnam.
Thailand
    art . . . . . . . . . . . . . . . . . . . . . . . . . . . . . . . . . . . . . . . . .9
    Bangkok . . . . . . . . . . . . . . . . . . . . . . . . . . . . . . . . . .20, 84
    cookery . . . . . . . . . . . . . . . . . . . . . . . . . . . . . . . . . . . .32
    folktales . . . . . . . . . . . . . . . . . . . . . . . . . . . . . . . . . . . .43
    language . . . . . . . . . . . . . . . . . . . . . . . . . . . . . . . . .89-90
    rhymes . . . . . . . . . . . . . . . . . . . . . . . . . . . . . . . . . . . . .11
Thatcher, Margaret . . . . . . . . . . . . . . . . . . . . . . . . . .14, 16, 17
Tiananmen Square (China) . . . . . . . . . . . . . . . . . . . . . . .61-62
Tibetan Buddhism . . . . . . . . . . . . . . . . . . . . . . . . .66, 105, 107
    See also Buddhism.
    Dalai Lama . . . . . . . . . . . . . . . . . . . . . . . . . . . . . . . .15, 17
    Milarepa, saint and poet . . . . . . . . . . . . . . . . . . . . . . . . .42
Tigris and Euphrates River valleys . . . . . . . . . . . . . . . . . . . . .5
Time . . . . . . . . . . . . . . . . . . . . . . . . . . . . . . . . .5, 74, 93, 102
Tobago (Caribbean)
    games . . . . . . . . . . . . . . . . . . . . . . . . . . . . . . . . . . . . .30
Togo (Africa) . . . . . . . . . . . . . . . . . . . . . . . . . . . . . . . . . . .10
Tokugawa, Ieyasu . . . . . . . . . . . . . . . . . . . . . . . . . . . . .12, 13
Tokyo
    See also Japan.
Tolerance . . . . . . . . . . . . . . . . . . . . . . . . . . . . . . . . . . . . .81
Tolstoy, Leo . . . . . . . . . . . . . . . . . . . . . . . . . . . . . . . . . . . .12
Tomb of Tutankhamen . . . . . . . . . . . . . . . . . . . . . . . . . . . . .2
Toyotama (mythological character) . . . . . . . . . . . . . . . . . . . .42
Trail of Tears (Native American) . . . . . . . . . . . . . . . . . . . . . . .9
Transportation . . . . . . . . . . . . . . . . . . . . . . . . . . . . . . . . . .71
Travel warnings . . . . . . . . . . . . . . . . . . . . . . . . . . . . . . . . .90
Trees . . . . . . . . . . . . . . . . . . . . . . . . . . . . . . . . . . . . . . .108
Trickster tales . . . . . . . . . . . . . . . . . . . . . . . . . . . .41, 43, 50
Trinidad (Caribbean)
    games . . . . . . . . . . . . . . . . . . . . . . . . . . . . . . . . . . . . .30
Turkey
    cookery . . . . . . . . . . . . . . . . . . . . . . . . . . . . . . . . . . . .32
    folktales . . . . . . . . . . . . . . . . . . . . . . . . . . .38, 39, 43, 45, 49
    holidays . . . . . . . . . . . . . . . . . . . . . . . . . . . . . . . . . . . .29
    language . . . . . . . . . . . . . . . . . . . . . . . . . . . . . . . . .89-90
Tutankhamen . . . . . . . . . . . . . . . . . . . . . . . . . . . . . . . . . . .2
Tutu, Desmond . . . . . . . . . . . . . . . . . . . . . . . . . . . . .15, 59-60
Twelfth Night . . . . . . . . . . . . . . . . . . . . . . . . . . . . . . . . . .46

*Subject Index* 147

Tyrants
- Amin, Idi .................... 13, 16
- Dracula, Vlad .................... 13
- Herod .................... 13
- Hitler, Adolf .................... 13, 16
- Hussein, Saddam .................... 13, 16
- Ivan the Terrible .................... 12, 13
- Khan, Genghis .................... 12, 13, 15
- Kim Il-Sung .................... 13
- Nero .................... 13
- Peron, Eva .................... 13
- Pinochet, Augusto .................... 13
- Pol Pot .................... 9, 13
- Shaka, King of Africa .................... 12, 13, 16
- Syngman Rhee .................... 13

Tokugawa, Ieyasu .................... 12, 13

## U

Uemura, Naomi .................... 14
Uganda (Africa) .................... 11
Ukraine
- folktales .................... 47-48
- games .................... 29
- rhymes .................... 11

United Kingdom
- children .................... 20, 22

United Nations .................... 86, 90, 91
- organizations .................... 90

United States
- cookery .................... 34
- folktales .................... 37, 39, 41, 49

Universal Declaration of Human
Rights .................... 61, 104

## V

Vedas .................... 68
Vegetarianism .................... 34, 105
Vesak .................... 28
Victoria, Queen of England .................... 14, 16, 17
Victoria Falls (Africa) .................... 71
Vietnam
- children .................... 20, 22
- cookery .................... 27
- folktales .................... 40, 41
- games .................... 19
- Hanoi .................... 33
- Holidays .................... 29
- Tet Nguyen-Dan (Lunar New Year Festival) .................... 28-29
- Trung Thu Festival .................... 29

Vietnam War .................... 9, 61-62
Viking calendar .................... 3
Vishnu the Protector (Hinduism) .................... 66

## W

Warfare .................... 3, 10
Warriors' Memorial Day .................... 32
Weapons .................... 3
Weather .................... 74, 85, 87, 94, 102, 103
Web-based projects .................... 110
West Asia .................... 4, 91-92
West Indies .................... 19, 55
West Nile virus
*See* Disease. Western Africa .................... 19

mythology .................... 46-47, 48
Western Asia .................... 19
Western Hemisphere .................... 91
Western mythology .................... 80
Wilder, Laura Ingalls .................... 12
Wind power .................... 72
*See also* Energy.
Winter Solstice .................... 46
The Witch of Endor (Biblical character) .................... 68
Women
*See also* Remarkable Women.
- Africa .................... 63
- Bible .................... 68
- Communist China .................... 62-63
- condition of women .................... 63
- equal pay .................... 62-63
- equal rights .................... 62-63
- folktales .................... 51
- Hindu .................... 106
- in poetry .................... 10
- India .................... 62-63
- Islam .................... 104, 107
- Jewish .................... 82
- Russia .................... 62-63
- scientists .................... 82
- Taliban (Afghanistan) .................... 62-63
- Warriors .................... 45-46

women's rights .................... 60, 62-63
Wonders of the World .................... 71, 90, 92, 102-103
World
- cookery .................... 64, 98-99
- country resources .................... 17-25
- maps .................... 52-58, 83, 86, 87, 88, 93, 96-97, 99, 101-103
- mythology .................... 44, 79, 81
- religions .................... 83-84, 89, 104-108
- resources .................... 70, 71, 72, 74, 75, 90-91, 92

World Population Clock Project .................... 90

## X

Xuan Zang .................... 14

## Y

Yangzi Gorges (China) .................... 71
Yeltsin, Boris .................... 16
Yom Kippur .................... 31
Yoruba mythology .................... 81-82
Young, Brigham .................... 17
Yugoslavia
- Adana massacre .................... 59-60
- genocide .................... 59-60

## Z

Zambia (Africa)
- festivals .................... 29

Zen .................... 104, 105, 108
Zhang Qian .................... 14
Zhengzhou (China) .................... 6
Ziggurats .................... 6
Zimbabwe (Africa) .................... 17, 30
Zip codes .................... 93, 102
Zoroastrianism .................... 44

www.ingramcontent.com/pod-product-compliance
Lightning Source LLC
Chambersburg PA
CBHW080412300426
44113CB00015B/2487